REAL ESTATE DOUGH™

Your Recipe for Real Estate Success!

Bernice L. Ross, Ph.D.

Published in the United States of America by
RossdalePress.com
12400 Hwy 71 West Ste 350 PMB 343
Austin, TX 78738
(512) 263-2986

Cover Design: Klinginsmith & Company

First edition published October 2008

The Library of Congress Cataloging-in-Publication Data Applied For

Ross, Bernice L.
Real Estate Dough™: Your Recipe for Real Estate Success

ISBN 10: 0-9763243-6-9
ISBN 13: 978-0-9763243-6-2

Printed in the United States of America

This book contains information of a general nature. As laws may vary from state to state, readers should consult a competent professional regarding their own particular state laws. The business world is ever changing and dynamic and involves risks and uncertainties. The author and publisher cannot and do not warrant or guarantee that use of information in this book will work for you.

Dedication

To the Chief Cook and Laugh Maker

Table of Contents

Basic Ingredients

Recipes for Marketing Success

Lead Generation: Tried and True Recipes for Success

Recipes for Online Success

Knead More Buyer Dough

Listing Dough: Are You Ready to Rise to the Top?

Advanced Real Estate Dough™ Recipes

Foreword

by Bradley Inman
Founder and Publisher of *Inman News*

This is a challenging housing market and a tough environment for real estate agents:

- Home sales are down 30 percent nationwide.
- Home prices have fallen 10-60 percent, depending on the market.
- The financial markets are in disarray, making it exceedingly difficult for home buyers to obtain mortgage loans.
- The costs of everyday real estate transactions are being scrutinized.
- Real estate commission rates are under siege as agent value is questioned.
- Many agents are getting out of the business altogether as others hang on through the sub-prime tsunami.

That does not stop author and real estate coach Bernice Ross from championing success and opportunity for agents working their way through brutal real estate conditions.

In her new book, *Real Estate Dough™—Your Recipe for Real Estate Success,* Ross is a passionate defender of the industry that she contends should confront the bad news, embrace innovation, and survive and thrive in the downturn.

She does not duck the facts, writing:

> "The old models of conducting real estate are broken. The press tells us we're not serving our customers well. Commissions are too high. The Harris poll ranks real estate professionals at the bottom of the heap, below attorneys and used car salespeople. Technological innovation threatens to overwhelm us. Banks, credit unions, discount warehouses, and a host of other outsiders seek a piece of the real estate pie. We are constantly under assault, not only from outside sources, but from those within our business as well. Hundreds of thousands of untrained agents haven't learned the fundamentals of negotiation, much less how to adequately market their services. The result: poor levels of customer satisfaction coupled *with a significant decline in commission rates."*

Ross calls for a "revolutionary business model for the 21st century"—one that is based on collaboration, integrated marketing, and teamwork—departing from the "centric" and "strength over weakness" business models of the last 30 years.

The book is packed with tips, strategies, and a workbook-style approach to finding those things that work best for you, the agent or broker.

Ross always sets an upbeat mood in her books, not allowing agents to get down on themselves and coaching them to reach higher, even when the housing market is so difficult.

Most importantly, Ross is a tireless advocate for the industry, offering REALTORS® a wealth of new ideas, strategies, and arguments to find success and to defend their work and compensation.

Introduction

The doors we open and close each
day decide the lives we live.
Flora Whittemore

Our Business Is Under Siege

The old models of conducting real estate are broken. The press tells us we're not serving our customers well. Commissions are too high. The Harris poll ranks real estate professionals at the bottom of the heap, below attorneys and used car salespeople. Technological innovation threatens to overwhelm us. Banks, credit unions, discount warehouses, and a host of other outsiders seek a piece of the real estate pie. We are constantly under assault, not only from outside sources, but from those within our business as well. Hundreds of thousands of untrained agents haven't learned the fundamentals of negotiation, much less how to adequately market their services. The result: poor levels of customer satisfaction coupled with a significant decline in commission rates.

The Current Real Estate Model Is Broken

When I started in the business in 1978, the business was broker-centric. During my first listing appointment, I dutifully flipped through my company's 20-page presentation. The sellers patiently indulged my need to cover every point. Since I had no track record, I had to rely on my company's reputation instead.

In the 1980s, the business shifted to being a combination of broker-centric and agent-centric. I remember training new agents to prepare their "brag books." The beginning of the book included your resume followed by information about the company. You included sample marketing materials, a marketing plan, a service guarantee, and possibly some testimonials from past clients. You also showed your clients all the awards and designations that you had earned.

In the 1990s, the business became agent-centric. You needed a personal brochure with your picture to let people know who you are—show your kids, your spouse, and your pets. Plaster your name and picture on billboards, bus stops, grocery carts, or anywhere else where you could get recognition.

Competition for top-producing agents during the '90s became fierce. Brokers offered marketing bonuses, mink coats, European vacations, and other perks to attract top producers. Broker profits dropped as low as $125 per transaction. The battle to retain top performers meant that many brokerages were actually losing money on their best agents. Brokers were also caught in the squeeze of attempting to keep up with new technology while struggling to stay in business as alternative business models spread like wildfire.

During this time, the team concept became popular. Top producers formed their own mini-companies within the umbrella organizations such as RE/MAX and Keller Williams. Without a doubt, agents were king.

As more consumers moved online, the consumer demanded that the agents, brokers, and technology meet their needs. This was the beginning of the business becoming more client-centric. Nevertheless, despite consumer demand, a substantial proportion of agents and brokers today are still in the agent-centric model. Real estate billboards, vanity websites, and print marketing almost always display the agents' pictures. It was the "me-me-me show."

Clients, however, are now demanding that the "me-me-me" be about them. Those of us who have been training a client-centric model have argued that the customer is king. Agents and brokers should focus on what the client wants and needs. We should provide our Multiple Listing Service data, mapping, community information, mortgage advice, and a host of other services instantaneously if we have any hope of doing business with today's consumer. Furthermore, the consumer is clear about how they feel about us: "Don't call us—we'll contact you!"

To cope with the public's reluctance, we have responded with "call capture," bulk email, and other strategies in hopes of persuading them to do business with us. In fact, many practitioners today still rely on the antiquated "Hunt 'em, tell 'em, and sell 'em model." Hunt down prospects, tell them how great you are, and use manipulative tactics to get them to do business with you.

This environment is also adversarial. Brokers and agents become adversaries when they negotiate commission splits. Agents and consumers often become adversarial during the negotiation process. Agents feel that the brokers are making loads of money, when many are just scraping by. Brokers believe agents have too much power. Many consumers think that we earn too much in commission. The squeeze is on both brokers and agents, as alternative business models chip away at the more traditional business models as well as the historical commission structures. "Sixty Minutes," the *New York Times,* CNN, and numerous other media continue to grind us from the outside as well. They tell us that the alternative models are the future of real estate and that we should accept the new world order, or at least their vision of it.

Everyone is out to protect their turf—but what if it didn't have to be that way?

A Revolutionary Model for the 21st Century

Real Estate Dough™ proposes a revolutionary new model for the real estate industry. What makes this book revolutionary is the shift away from the "centric" models that have evolved over the last 30 years. In its place, the new model consists of five core components:

1. A "Collaborative" model replaces the "Centric" models of the past.

2. Questions and dialogues are at the heart of all aspects of the real estate transaction.

3. "Opposite Strengths" replaces the old "strength-weakness" model.

4. Choice management replaces time management.

5. Fragmented approaches to business such as relying exclusively on the web, by referral, or print media are replaced with an integrated approach that takes the best from each model and weaves it into a single process that generates repeatable, measurable results.

What Is the Basis for the Collaborative Real Estate Model?

The new model for conducting real estate in the 21st century is collaborative. The transactions that go the most smoothly are those where all parties work together. The agents, the brokers, the buyers, the sellers, and the other professionals who participate in the transaction function as a team with one goal in mind: close the transaction and make it a win-win for everyone involved. Becoming adversarial generally results in a win-lose situation. When someone in the transaction loses, you lose future referrals and increase the possibility of unhappy outcomes.

Steve Kantor's book, *Billion Dollar Agent—Lessons Learned*, shares the secrets of agents who have or are on track to close a billion dollars worth of real estate. Their success relies on the effectiveness of their teams, their emphasis on strong customer service, and giving back to their communities. Even if you are an individual agent, you still rely on a team of support people to conduct your business. The more smoothly and effortlessly you work together, the better your business will be. Top performers almost always rely on a collaborative approach.

How Do Questions Apply to this Model?

Questions are at the heart of this new model. Inherent in asking questions is the assumption that you will listen for an answer.

Questions also imply a dialogue. In the collaborative model, "Listening Consultations" replace the traditional listing presentation where the agent does all the talking. Prospecting shifts from being "hunt 'em, tell 'em, and sell 'em," to social networking and being of service to your community. Marketing focuses on the benefits the client will receive, not only from doing business with the agent, but with the brokerage. Rather than marketing the features of a given property, (i.e., the physical characteristics of the property), today the agent's role is to help buyers and sellers fulfill their unique dream of home ownership.

What Is the Strengths-Strengths Model?

The real estate business is built upon a "strengths-weaknesses" model. For years, professional coaches have encouraged their clients to build their business on their strengths. The flaw in this approach is that when we think of strengths, we automatically assume that there are weaknesses.

In the book *The Power of Opposite Strengths*, Jay and Tommy Thomas propose a model in which we have only strengths. The strengths exist in pairs. The two core strengths are "risking" (i.e., taking action) and "thinking."

In the Thomas Model, each of us has lead and supporting strengths that function as pairs. There are no weaknesses. Challenges occur when we become "polarized" on one of the two strengths. These pairs work in harmony, much the same way that you use your two feet. You may lead with your right foot when you walk; however, your left foot is equally important. You will reach your destination much faster when you use both feet instead of hopping toward your goal only on one foot.

As you read *Real Estate Dough*™ notice that there is no discussion of correcting your weaknesses. Instead, the collaborative model integrates traditional and innovative approaches while simultaneously focusing on the value that each person and each company brings to the transaction. Each chapter encourages you to look for the strengths that support your business and to build on those. There is no right or wrong. There is only a wonderful array of opportunities to create your business in a way that is unique to you.

Choice Management Replaces Time Management

No one can control time. What you can control are your choices. The issue then becomes how to best manage the implementation of the choices that you make. *Real Estate Dough*™ is packed with recipes for your personal and business success. As you evaluate choices that you will add or subtract from your business, pay attention to your energy level. If something seems too difficult or the thought of doing it seems daunting, continue searching until you identify those activities that make you feel excited about trying them.

The next step is the most important. Identify the top five activities from this book that will allow your expertise to shine and that you enjoy doing. Place them in priority order and then implement them one at a time. Business success results from small steps taken consistently over time.

The same approach works well for making decisions about your daily business activities. Choose the three most important activities that you must complete each day. Complete these first prior to doing anything else. This simple approach of completing your three most important activities each day and building your business around your two or three greatest strengths will generate plenty of *Real Estate Dough*™ for years to come. The key point to remember is that choice management, not time management, is the secret to real estate success.

What Are the Elements of an Integrated Business Approach for the 21st Century?

In the past, there were two primary means of building your business. The first was to use traditional marketing and prospecting. Traditional methods fell into one of two categories: passive or active. Passive approaches included taking floor time or up time (i.e., waiting for the customer to call you), placing ads in the paper or in magazines, holding open house without door knocking or sending out invitations, or waiting for sign calls from your listings. Active strategies included cold calling, warm calling, door knocking to invite neighbors to an open house, and prospecting expired and for-sale-by-owner (FSBO) listings. The difference between these two categories is that the passive approach waits for the customer to come to you. In contrast, the active approach allows you to control your lead generation. A certain percentage of contacts will convert into closed business. You simply have to hit your numbers.

One of the greatest challenges agents faced arose when our "private" Multiple Listing Service (MLS) data became public. Clients hired real estate brokers to access the MLS data. Today that data is available in hundreds of places.

Sadly, many agents mistakenly believed that their sole value was in supplying data or information to consumers. The result was a tidal wave of commission cutting. Many agents, the press, and the public at large, failed to understand the distinction between information (that which is static and can reside in a computer database) and wisdom or knowledge (the ability to solve problems based upon a combination of past experience, knowledge, and creativity). REALTORS® who were able to articulate a strong value proposition continued to earn high commissions. Those who could not turned to commission cutting to compete.

In 2005, I wrote *Waging War on Real Estate's Discounters*. This book shows you how to demonstrate your value proposition and earn more full commissions. The strategies outlined in *Waging War* are particularly effective in a seller's market, especially where there is upward pressure on prices and downward pressure on commissions. In fact, thousands of readers implemented the suggestions in that book and built businesses that are prospering today, in spite of market changes.

Real Estate Dough™ is the companion book to *Waging War* and updates the technology sections as well as illustrating what works in today's highly competitive real estate market. As the web continues to develop as a marketing medium, agents can no longer afford to limit their lead generation to only a single channel such as working by referral or traditional prospecting. The most effective way to generate leads today is to integrate the best traditional lead generation strategies with the new Web 2.0 marketing models that include blogging and social networking. Below you'll find summaries of key factors that will help you increase your real estate success.

1. **The tried and true of traditional lead generation**
   Today's consumer still responds positively to many of the tried and true techniques from the past. Among these are building referrals through being of service to your community, providing incentives such as property evaluations designed to help homeowners lower their taxes, as well as other strategies that increase the quality of the consumer's experience. Active prospecting strategies such as contacting owners of expired listings and FSBOs also continue to be effective.

   On the other hand, cold calling and vanity marketing are no longer effective Neither are the manipulative hard sales tactics from the past. Furthermore, traditional "just listed" and "just sold" postcards do little to promote your business. Because there are over 2,000,000 people who hold real estate licenses, being unique is critical. Throughout *Real Estate Dough*™, you'll find "Recipes for Success" that share the best tips from the best real estate minds in the country. These sections illustrate how to make your traditional and web marketing strategies stand out from the crowd.

2. **Smart technology that meets the public's demand for immediacy**
   If you don't have a PDA, smart phone, or some other device that lets you respond to email and text messages without being at your computer, you are lacking a fundamental tool for doing business today. The younger your clients are, the more quickly they expect you to respond. Today's website visitors want information now. Meet this demand by hiring an assistant, using smart phone technology, or working with the new "push to talk" technology. Furthermore, advances in technology now allow you to market on over 40 different websites and track responses. A new tool called "predictive marketing" motivates clients to do business with you. By helping them become better educated about market conditions they will be more realistic about price.

3. **Social networking and blogging strategies establish trust and meet consumers' demands for anonymity**
   The collaborative model of real estate is built upon trust. Today's buyers and sellers often rely on referrals to determine the agent with whom they will work. On the other hand, many are turning to blogging and social networking sites as

a way to get to know different agents in an anonymous fashion. If you're not actively participating in this new marketing venue, you are missing an excellent way to develop business today.

While the web may determine who contacts you, your face-to-face interaction will determine whether a lead will do business with you. When buyers and sellers know more than one real estate agent, they often do business with the agent with whom they most recently had face-to-face contact.

Real Estate Dough ™ has multiple recipes for real estate success. Choose the ones that work best for you and enjoy—there's a banquet waiting for you along with plenty of dough to put in the bank.

How to Use this Book

At the beginning of each chapter, you will find a list of strategies the chapter covers. To make the best use of this book, follow the guidelines below:

1. Before reading the chapter, note the items listed at the beginning of the chapter and put a check mark (√) next to the strategies you already use.

2. Some chapters contain supporting scripts. Review the scripts to determine whether they fit how you do business. Practice the scripts you select out-loud until you have mastered them. Some agents find that writing out their scripts on cards is helpful. Others record their scripts and then listen to them while driving.

3. Most chapters have an Action Plan that includes recommendations on how to implement the strategies covered in the chapter. Note the strategies that you would like to implement and record the date that you complete the action step.

4. When you begin to implement changes in your business, avoid trying to accomplish too much at one time. This can overwhelm you. Instead, experiment with one strategy at a time. Determine what works best for you and make those strategies a permanent part of your business.

5. "Recipes for Success" share innovative strategies that work in today's market. Be willing to experiment to discover what works best for you. Not only is it fun, it can also help you make lots of *Real Estate Dough*™ for many years to come.

6. For the latest updates on how to meet the challenges you face, visit our website at RealEstateCoach.com. We have a variety of resources that can help you. Our audio subscription series lets you "Listen and Learn" from the best practitioners in the business, whether they are agents, managers, owner/brokers, marketing experts, or technology specialists. ListenAndLearnRealEstate.com is available 24-7 and can be heard on your computer or downloaded to your MP3 player or iPod.

Unlock the Door to a Great Business and a Great Life

By implementing the guidelines in this book, you will be able to:

1. Generate and convert more leads from traditional, referral, and web sources.

2. Take more listings at the right price and at a full commission.

3. Convert more buyer leads into closed business.

4. Negotiate more effectively.

5. Motivate clients to use your services because of the value you provide.

6. Build a successful, sustainable business based upon your strengths.

7. Have more time to enjoy life and the ones you love.

Basic Ingredients

Chapter 1:
Don't Let the Psychic Vampires Get You Down

When you do nothing, you feel overwhelmed and powerless. But when you get involved, you feel the sense of hope and accomplishment that comes from knowing you are working to make things better.
Source Unknown

How would you describe the fifth-best real estate market ever in terms of sales? Believe it or not, that year was 2007, a year described by virtually everyone as being extraordinarily difficult. As the subprime mess spread, one of the greatest challenges agents faced was maintaining a positive attitude. In spite of the difficulties, many agents had their best years ever in 2007 and 2008. Creating the right mindset is one of the most powerful steps that you can take to keep your business strong, no matter what the market does.

Knead the Dough Secret #1
Environment is stronger than will.
(Buckminster Fuller)

How to Create a Supportive Environment

Just as the wrong environment can keep bread dough from rising, the environment you create for your business will determine whether your *Real Estate Dough*™ rises or shrinks. Even though you intend to change your thoughts and actions, if you don't address your environment, you will be unable to create sustainable change. If you listen to the negative news around you, your environment will support you to attract negative events. Psychologists call this self fulfilling prophecy (Rosenthal, 1973). What you concentrate on and what you expect to happen generally does happen.

In fact, an experiment with elementary school children demonstrated the power our thoughts have on our physical environment. Elementary school students filled two bowls of water. When they walked by the first bowl, they told the water that it was "bad." When they walked by the second bowl, they told the water how good and wonderful it was. When the water was examined under an electron microscope, the water molecules in the "bad" water were ragged and ill formed. The molecules in the "good" water formed beautiful, well defined patterns. Never underestimate the power of your environment to influence your real estate success.

Maintaining a positive mindset is one of the most important elements in creating real estate sales success. Consider each of the following statements. Can you spot what they have in common?

There's just no inventory/buyers.

I've been taking floor time and haven't had a lead in months!

I've been holding open house every Sunday, but I never get any leads.

Each statement illustrates a reactive approach to the real estate business. Being reactive means waiting for the business to come to you rather than going out and proactively generating leads from prospecting, blogging, and social networking.

Examine the next two statements. What do they have in common?

Buyers are liars—I've worked with these buyers for six months and they go to an open house and buy it!

I can't believe it. I worked my fingers to the bone on that listing. I kept telling the sellers they needed to reduce the price. And you know what they did? They let the listing expire, dropped the price, listed it with XYZ Realty, and it sold immediately.

These two statements illustrate how agents who lack strong skills can end up spending months working with clients who end up doing business with someone else. This occurs when agents fail to obtain clear agreements from their clients when they begin working together. Another issue is working with clients who drain agents of their time and energy. These people are known as psychic vampires. Sadly, they're everywhere. They complain about how bad the market and their personal situation are and then expect you to commiserate.

One of the best ways to keep a positive mindset is to avoid listening to the news or reading stories about how bad the market is. Another alternative is to listen to our Positive News for Positive REALTORS® at ListenAndLearnRealEstate.com to learn how to counteract the negativity in the press.

If your office is filled with negative people, a third alternative is to work from home. If you must interact with someone who is negative, you can stop their negative comments by asking, "Tell me one thing that went right today." Again, the best strategy is to avoid them all together.

A fourth strategy is to upgrade the people in your peer group by joining a mastermind group or some other group of highly successful people. Jack Canfield talks about how he didn't start making lots of money until he changed his peer group. According to Canfield, if you take the average income of your ten closest friends and/or colleagues, you can accurately predict what your earnings will be. Upgrade your peer group and you can upgrade your income.

Clients today are searching for positive, knowledgeable, competent, and technologically savvy agents who provide outstanding levels of customer service. How can you get there? The next chapter reviews the fundamentals you will need to have a great real estate career. In the meantime, don't let the psychic vampires get you down.

Recipes for Success
A Bad Client is like Bad Cholesterol

Ira Serkes
BerkeleyHomes.com
HandCraftedRealEstate.com
GMAC Pacific Union

Ira Serkes is one of the most innovative and technologically savvy agents in the business. He's also one of the most successful. Ira made a decision that creating a big team was not the road he wanted to take. In the interview below, Ira shares his personal recipe for real estate sales success.

Several years ago, I decided that I was tired of trying to become the best real estate agent in Berkeley with the biggest team. Instead, I decided that I wanted to be the happiest agent in Berkeley.

My background is in engineering. My wife is my partner. We work from a new custom office that we built in the back of our house adjacent to a beautiful garden. We aggressively market on the web and consistently generate a substantial number of leads. Our goal was to create a company that married high touch with high tech. We're currently marketing our company as HandCraftedRealEstate.com.

Because of all the leads that we generate, we had to make a decision about how we would handle them. One option was to begin building a team. The other option was to choose the leads that best suited our business model and refer the remaining leads to other agents. When I did the calculations on the costs of putting together a team, training them, and supervising them, it didn't make sense to me. I decided to handle our excess leads by referring them to other qualified agents in the area.

The next step was to describe our ideal client. Here's what's on our list.

1. **The clients must be nice**
   A bad client is like bad cholesterol—they block your energy and can give you a heart attack.

2. **We avoid clients who have unrealistic expectations or who are extremely demanding**
   If we feel that we can't meet a client's expectations, we refer them to another agent. There's no need to insult them. I just simply say "No," by telling them, "We simply can't meet your expectations. We're not a good match. I'm not the right agent for you. I'd be happy to introduce you to another agent who could help you."

3. **We established a list of purchase criteria that buyers must meet to work with us**
   In terms of price range, they must be purchasing in the median price range or higher. (The median is the point where half the prices are above and half the prices are below.) They must have 10 percent or more down. They cannot have a contingent sale. If they must purchase with a contingency, they are not a good fit for us.

4. **We only work in an area that is approximately five miles from our office. We refer everything else**

In order to make our referral system work, we needed a system for handling all the incoming calls. I'm a Mac user, so we use a system called PhoneValet.com that captures any audio messages on our phone system and emails them to our cell phone. This saves us a considerable amount of time. We also use the Fujitsu Scan Snap Scanner to save time in terms of scanning receipts and documents. The system converts the scan to a PDF file. This system works beautifully with the iPhone as well as Skype, the Internet Long Distance service.

We convert about 1 out of 20 of our web leads. Generally, I can process approximately 20 leads per hour. Of those we refer to other agents, our conversion rate is 26.89 percent.

The next step was to develop a strong referral network. That is something that we did over time based upon whom we had worked with in the past and who had done an outstanding job in terms of their customer service.

In terms of fees, we ask for a 37 percent referral fee. Most agents charge 20 to 25 percent. Before we make the referral, we spend the time necessary to determine that the buyer actually has the ability to purchase.

Last year we did a lot of traveling and really enjoyed ourselves. We also made $60,000 in referral fees from our network. Best of all, we didn't have all the overhead, stress, and hassle of managing a team.

Being willing to turn away clients who are not a right fit for your business is critical to your real estate success. It is fundamental to the "Law of Attraction."

Chapter 2
The Ultimate Knead the Dough Secret: The Law of Attraction

You attract who you are.
Thomas Leonard

Skills Check:
Put a checkmark (√) next to what you do now. Leave the remaining items blank. Review the action steps at the end of the chapter to determine the strategies that you will implement in your business.

___ 1. I am satisfied with the quality of the clients that I have attracted in my business.

___ 2. I refuse to work with clients who are unethical or whose standards do not reflect my core values.

___ 3. I have a detailed description of my "ideal" client.

___ 4. I regularly take time off including at least one great vacation per year.

___ 5. I take time each day to give thanks for all that is working well in my life.

___ 6. I regularly express my gratitude not only to my clients, but to those I work with as well as my friends and family.

___ 7. I spend 5 to 10 minutes per day visualizing myself achieving and enjoying the personal and business goals that I set.

___ 8. Participating in activities that contribute to others is an important part of my life.

Put Attraction into Action

When I began my formal training as a coach in 1996, my initial response to "The Law of Attraction" was: "Yeah, right—there's no way that's going to work." Since then, I have personally witnessed how thousands of agents have used attraction to create the life they want. While there have been numerous books written about attraction, the six steps outlined in this chapter provide a simple road map for implementing attraction in your life.

Attraction is the foundation upon which long-term, sustainable business is built. In fact, most agents who have 15, 20, or 30 years of consistent top production use attraction rather than relying on scripts and techniques. These highly successful individuals understand the importance of professionalism, excellent service, and building strong relationships with their clients. When I speak to groups about the principles of attraction, the top producers nod in agreement because they know that it works. They use attraction naturally. On the other hand, those agents who are struggling often respond by saying:

> *Yeah, that's great, but how can I get more listings? What scripts do I need to use?*

Agents who rely solely on scripts and techniques will always have challenges because they are focusing on the tools rather than the connection with the client.

These concepts are powerful and have the potential to completely remake your life for the better. If you are unfamiliar with the concepts, this is the starting point in creating the business and the life you want. While the relationship between attraction and business success may not be apparent when you first begin the process, this approach definitely works. Top performers use these principles to attract top-notch clientele. To make yourself more attractive to higher quality clients who are happy to pay for your premium services, start working on implementing these changes in your life today.

A Simple Six-Step Model of Attraction

The six-step model of attraction outlined below can help you to create the life and business that you want. For attraction to work, be sure to address each area. If after reading this you are still skeptical, experiment with these principles for one month and see if your business improves. Chances are you will be surprised at the results.

> **Knead the Dough Secret #2**
> Your clients mirror who you are.

1. **You attract who you are**
   If our personal lives are in chaos, we will attract clients whose lives are in chaos. If we are stressed out, we will attract clients who are also stressed out. While it may be painful, take a realistic look at whom you have attracted in your

business. Are your clients completely loyal or do they end up dumping you for some inexplicable reason? Do your transactions go smoothly or are you always having one disastrous transaction after another? Do you attract truthful clients or people who misrepresent the truth? The concept of attraction explains why this occurs.

a. First, the people we attract mirror what is occurring elsewhere in our lives. If you attract disloyal people, have you failed to keep your word or do what you promised to do? If your transactions are always filled with problems, are you lacking integrity somewhere else in your life? The first step in cleaning up a personal challenge is recognizing that it exists.

b. The next step is to start taking better care of you. Be honest: how long has it been since you have taken off a full weekend? How many times have you had dinner with those you love in the past month? I used to work 12 to 14 hours per day until my coach nagged me long enough that I started taking time off to do some fun things for me. The result: my productivity increased by 50 percent. By taking time off to unwind, I actually accomplished more. The biggest surprise, however, was how all those difficult people in my life magically disappeared. Remember, a frazzled, stressed-out agent is not who most sellers or buyers want negotiating on their behalf. In contrast, caring for yourself makes you more attractive to both potential sellers and buyers.

c. Adrenaline decreases attraction. Adrenaline is a substance that your body releases when it is under stress. It increases heart rate and prepares for "fight or flight." Consuming caffeine, rushing too much, or becoming upset or angry increases adrenaline levels. To minimize the amount of adrenaline that you experience, allow more time than you had planned to complete tasks. When you are with clients, leave your troubles in your car. (A good strategy is to write them down and lock them in your trunk. They'll still be there when you return. Writing them down, however, gets the upset energy out of your system.) Avoid caffeine, sugary foods and drinks, as well as limiting your alcohol intake. Get plenty of sleep and take time off from work each week. These activities will make you calm while also helping you to attract higher quality clients.

Even when you are functioning at high levels of attraction, you can still attract dishonest or chaotic people into your life. The key is being able to recognize when someone does not fit your style of doing business. For example, how many times have you had that little voice inside tell you "don't take this listing" or "don't work with this buyer" and by not listening, you ended up with a disaster on your hands? Being able to say "No" is an important key to increasing your attraction and your production. Consequently, when that little voice inside says, "No"—listen to it!

Knead the Dough Secret #3
When you need to increase your business, take a vacation!

2. **Create space**
   Experienced agents know the moment they plan a vacation, business immediately picks up. In scientific terms, nature abhors a vacuum. When you create space in your business, more business usually shows up. On the other hand, if your schedule is already packed 24/7, your production will remain capped at its current level because there is no room for new business to come into your life.

   This next suggestion may seem a little odd, but virtually everyone who follows it increases their business. To make more room for new business, clean your closet, clean your desk, clean your garage, file those stacks of papers, fire those buyers who are wasting your time, and refer that listing you have had for 12 months to another agent. It makes no difference where you start. Begin by eliminating whatever is easiest that is taking up unnecessary space.

   The next point is extremely important. Creating the space for more business does not mean to stop working. Instead, it means getting rid of sellers who won't sell, buyers who won't buy, and people who waste your time and give you nothing back. It also means learning how to utilize the best technology tools currently available. Technology can dramatically cut down on the time, effort, and costs involved in operating a successful real estate business. Better yet, it gives you a huge competitive edge against those agents who lag behind in this area.

3. **Have clarity about what you want to attract**
   What does it mean to have clarity about what you want to attract? An agent who had created a phenomenal income in just six months had this reply when I asked him how he did it:

   > *The first thing I did was to sit down and write a list of characteristics of my ideal client. It was 15 pages long, right down to the type of belt and tie he wore.*

   When I asked if his ideal client had shown up yet, his response was:

   > *No, but a lot of his brothers and sisters sure have.*

If you do not have a detailed list describing your ideal client, now is a great time to begin one. The more specific you are, the easier it will be to say "Yes" when the right sellers and buyers show up and "No" to those who are a poor fit because they are difficult, unreasonable, or dishonest. In fact, saying "No" to over-priced listings, to unethical sellers, or to sellers who are unwilling to pay a full commission actually increases the quality of clients you will attract. Again, the principle of attraction says, "like attracts like." In other words, when you have high standards and high ethics, you attract people who are like you. When you lower your personal standards because you are desperate for money or for business, you often attract difficult clients.

4. Visualize what you want to create

Esther and Jerry Hicks, authors of *The Law of Attraction* as well as major contributors to the movie *The Secret,* discuss the importance of visualizing what you want to create. For example, have you ever seen someone pin up a picture of a car that they wanted and before long, they were driving it? This illustrates the importance having clarity about what you want to attract and visualizing yourself as if it has already happened.

In terms of your real estate business, if you want to work with better quality clients, take time at least once or twice per day to imagine yourself working with that type of client. What type of clothes are you wearing? What kind of car are you driving? What types of properties are you showing? The more detailed you can be about what you want to attract the more likely it will be to come to pass.

5. Give back

There's an old adage that says, "When you give to a giver, what do they do? They give back!" If you constantly take from others without giving back, you will find that your business will require four to five times as much effort to make it grow. Agents who do not honor the principle of giving back have to prospect constantly for new business since they seldom receive referrals from past clients. Generating a new lead from cold prospecting takes five times more effort than generating a new lead from a past client. Take a hard look at your business. Do you give back in some way to both past and present clients? For example, do you hold client appreciation events, update past clients on their home's value annually, or provide some other service that your clients find useful? Are you contributing to your community? Remember, if you want people to contribute to your business, you need to contribute to others.

6. The attitude is gratitude

This final component of attraction can be summed up in a simple question:

How can I ask for more when I don't appreciate what I already have?

How many times have you expressed your gratitude to buyers or sellers for doing business with you before the transaction is closed? Have you ever told your office manager you appreciate the fact that he or she is there to help you? What about the people at the mortgage or title company?

Unfortunately, many people in our business focus on what they lack rather than all the things they do have. For example, many agents believe top producers receive more than their fair share of leads from management. Whether or not this is true, when agents focus on the unfair distribution of referrals, they are not taking responsibility for actively building their own business. When they complain, they reduce their attractiveness to potential clients. This results in less income. This pattern can result in a dangerous downward spiral that can cause the agent to leave the business. In contrast, showing gratitude for what you have is an excellent way to be more attractive.

To increase your level of attraction, take time to tell others how much you appreciate them. Along the same lines, take a few moments each day to record five things in your life that are really great—whether it's something as simple as your health, a roof over your head, clean water, or food. You can keep track in a journal, in your appointment book, or in your contact manager. A great way to start your day is to do this before you begin work. Remember, if you want more business or more of anything in your life, you need to appreciate and be grateful for what you already have.

The next time you encounter someone who seems greedy, recognize that this person lacks abundance. Their response to you may be to try to bring you to their level (like attracts like) or they may envy what you have and decide not to do business with you. In other cases, they will be attracted to you because they sense you will attract a higher quality buyer for their property because of who you are.

When you create an abundance mindset, you may lose some friends who don't share your approach. Some may try to pull you back to their level. Others will want to join you on your journey. Remember, environment is stronger than will. Choose the people you spend time with carefully. Your choice can literally make or break your career.

Chapter 2
Action Plan

Identify the action steps that you would like to take and rewrite items that may not fit. Circle the number of each strategy that you plan to implement in your business and then record the date you complete the item in the space provided. Make one or two changes at a time. Making too many changes at once can be overwhelming. Integrate the changes one at a time prior to making other changes. Keep in mind that your goal is to find an activity that is both motivating and sustainable over time.

Action Steps:

___ 1. I will go through my client list and delete anyone whose ethics or values are not in alignment with my personal standards.

___ 2. I will make an ideal client list that is at least two full pages long in order to have clarity about the type of clients I would like to attract.

___ 3. I will change my business plan to include two full weeks of vacation each year as well as at least one day off each week.

___ 4. I will take at least five minutes per day to express my thanks for all that is working well in my life.

___ 5. I will make a point of regularly expressing my gratitude not only to my clients, but to those I work with as well as my friends and family.

___ 6. I will take at least 5 to 10 minutes per day to visualize myself achieving and enjoying the goals that I set for myself.

___ 7. I will regularly take part in activities that make a contribution to my family, friends, and/or community.

Attraction is the foundation upon which *Real Estate Dough*™ is built. Master these concepts and your life will flow effortlessly. If you want to achieve stratospheric success, couple the principles of attraction with the "Five Laws of Stratospheric Success" in the next Recipes for Success.

Recipes for Success
The Five Laws of Stratospheric Success
Bob Burg and John David Mann
TheGoGiver.com

I've worked with the Law of Attraction since 1996. If you apply them, the results are nothing less than miraculous. Nevertheless, I was still experiencing some blocks in my business. Maybe I didn't have enough clarity about what I wanted to attract. Perhaps I needed to be more generous in my giving. I then read Bob Burg's and John David Mann's book The Go-Giver *In a beautifully told parable, they not only illustrate how attraction works, they also show how to remove the blocks that are holding you back. The jacket of* The Go Giver *begins with a quotation:*

> Most people just laugh when they hear that the secret to success is giving. Then again, most people are nowhere near as successful as they wish they were…Giving is the secret to success.

In the interview below, Bob Burg shares his recipe for "Stratospheric Success."

You can't always get what you want, but you do get what you expect. In other words, what you focus on is what you get. Go looking for the best in people and you'll be amazed at how much talent, ingenuity, empathy, and good will you'll find. On the other hand, if you go looking for trouble, that's what you will find. If you want to catapult your business to stratospheric success, follow the five laws below.

The Law of Value

Your true worth is determined by how much more you give in value than you take in payment.

Many people confuse value with price. Price refers to the cost of purchase. In contrast, value includes both the cost plus a wide variety of other factors. For example, if your accountant charges you $500 for preparing your tax return and saves you $2,000, your accountant made a profit and still gave you more in value than what you paid. He or she saved you the time required to prepare the return, the tedium of checking the tax laws, plus knowing that you have an advocate should you face an audit.

When REALTORS® list a house, they normally sell it for more money than the sellers would on their own. In addition, they save the sellers the time and effort required to market the property. Their expertise also helps the seller to navigate through the complex web of disclosures, negotiations, and other closing requirements.

A key point to recognize is that, "All things being equal, people will do business with and refer business to those people they know, like, and trust."

The Law of Compensation

Your income is determined by how many people you serve and how well you serve them.

People often ask why teachers are not compensated as well as actors, athletes, and CEOs. The Law of Compensation says that your compensation is directly proportional to how many lives you touch. It's not just your value, it's a question of impact. There are no limitations on what you can earn because there are always more people that you can find to serve. The value you provide is your potential for earning. The number of people you serve determines how well you will be compensated. Look for ways to serve others, whether it's your family, your friends, your clients, or people you don't even know.

The Law of Influence

Your influence is determined by how abundantly you place other people's interests first.

When people think of a network, they normally think of their customers or clients. There's a much more important type of network—a network of people who know you, like you, and trust you. They are people who are invested in seeing you succeed, even if they never buy anything from you. Putting it a little differently, they are your own army of "personal walking ambassadors." The way to create this type of network is to stop keeping score. Instead, focus on creating "win-win" situations. In other words, look out for the other guy and keep your focus on the other person's win. When you place the interests of others first, your needs will always be taken care of.

If you have ever wondered what makes people truly attractive, what makes them "magnetic," it's because they love to give. Givers attract.

The Law of Authenticity

The most valuable gift you have to offer is yourself.

No matter what you think you are selling, the most valuable thing that you have to give to people is yourself. Do you want great people skills? Then be a person! It's worth ten thousand times more than all the closing techniques that ever have been or will be invented.

The Law of Receptivity

The key to effective giving is to stay open to receiving.

One of John's clients said that Laws 1-4 were like smooth, polished wood. Law 5, on the other hand, gave him splinters. Many people give without expectation. There's nothing wrong with having an emotional expectation that the universe will reward you. The point is, you must give without emotional attachment. When you lack attachment, you are more open to receiving with abundance.

Recently, I noticed that my bookkeeper had a very nice pen. It wasn't expensive. She offered to give it to me and I said, "No. I'll just go out and buy one." She offered again and I declined again. She then looked at me and said, "Take the pen and say thank you."

The key to giving is being open to receiving. All the giving in the world won't bring success, won't create the results you want, unless you also make yourself willing and able to receive in like measure. Because if you don't let yourself receive, you're refusing the gifts of others and you shut down the flow.

For me, this last law was a huge "aha." Giving works in tandem with receiving. If you want to achieve a level of personal satisfaction and success unlike anything that you have experienced ever before, the six principles of attraction and the five laws above hold the secret to your personal "stratospheric success."

Chapter 3
The Collaborative Real Estate Experience

Great teamwork is the only way we create the
breakthroughs that define our careers.
Pat Riley

Skills Check:
Put a checkmark (√) next to what you do now. Leave the remaining items blank. Review the action steps at the end of this chapter to determine the strategies you will implement in your business.

___ 1. I establish strong personal connections with my clients.

___ 2. I am genuinely interested in my clients and enjoy hearing about what they love to do.

___ 3. I present a strong, professional image.

___ 4. I have an in-depth knowledge of the inventory in my market area.

___ 5. I have a strong grasp of market statistics in my area including how many months of inventory are on the market, what the average days on market is, as well as how this affects the buyers and sellers that I serve.

___ 6. I take time to take care of me.

___ 7. Providing all my clients with premium service is a top priority in my business.

Knead the Dough Secret #4
A sustainable real estate business is collaborative, not broker-centric, agent-centric, or client-centric.

The Collaborative Symphony

Companies like Nordstrom and Starbucks epitomize outstanding customer service. Bernd Schmitt's book, *Customer Experience Management,* proposes that these two companies are doing more than just providing excellent customer service. What differentiates Nordstrom and Starbucks from other retailers, is the customer's complete experience from initial point of contact to well after the close of the sale. For example, at Starbuck's, the atmosphere is warm and inviting. It's the ideal spot to do business away from the office. You can send email, surf the web, or just sink into the comfortable seats and enjoy your favorite brew. Contrast this experience with grabbing a cup of coffee from a convenience store. The convenience store provides utility, but little in the way of service.

Customer service is no longer enough. Today's salespeople must address the customer's complete experience, not just the services they provide to consumers.

As mentioned in the Introduction, the "Centric" real estate models are no longer viable in today's market. The challenge with being broker-centric, agent-centric, or client-centric is that the experience centers on one particular entity. Other important aspects of the experience are minimized.

A good way to think about the collaborative model is to imagine a symphony. Every musician/agent works together to create the final outcome. Each has his or her own music. Some will play parts of the symphony solo while others will play only with the rest of the orchestra.

In the collaborative model, the agent is the conductor. You coordinate the various elements of the transaction for your client. The other agent does the same for his or her client. The clients play a buyer-seller duet. Your broker provides the advertising, the stage, and a host of other supporting elements. Ultimately, the success of the symphony (or in this case, the real estate transaction) is contingent upon how well each of you plays your individual part as well as how well you work together.

A transaction where there is a high level of collaboration creates trust. Each person plays their part, does what he or she commits to do in a timely manner, and if there is a problem, works to solve the situation as amicably as possible.

It may be tempting to argue that the negotiation process pits the buyer and seller side against each other and that commissions pit the brokers and agents against the sellers, and possibly each other. Nevertheless, the concept of conducting "win-win" negotiations has taken hold in many companies. Instead of being adversaries, agents and brokers using this strategy approach the transaction as a partnership. Collaboration is at the heart of this new model.

Collaboration Begins with Connection

You may be wondering how you can possibly change the firm you work for or the other people in your environment. The only person you can change is you. To attract collaborative people in your life, you must be collaborative. You must also have a clear concept of which clients are not a good fit for you and be willing to refer them to someone else. By taking these steps, the quality of the business you attract will increase. Instead of changing others, you will start to attract a higher quality client.

More than anything, clients want their agent to listen to and be responsive to their needs. Ask questions about what matters to them. Explore how they live their lives. Most importantly, avoid inserting yourself into their decision making process.

Personal connection is the foundation upon which both collaboration and a great customer experience is built. Having a pleasant, professional demeanor is an excellent place to begin, but more is needed. To build strong connection, you must be genuinely curious and caring about your clients. Establishing connection consists of three basic steps: curiosity, communication, and commonality.

Step 1: Curiosity

Are you curious about the people you meet? Do you inquire about what recreational activities they enjoy? What hobbies they have? How about where they like to spend their free time? What is their favorite type of food? Avoid very personal questions until you develop rapport. When working with sellers, ask about what they have enjoyed about living in their property. Have them tell you about features in their home you might not normally notice as you walk through the property. Ask them questions about the neighborhood. Do your best to learn what matters to them and what gives their lives meaning.

Step 2: Communication

Communication implies a two-way conversation. Some people are reluctant to talk about themselves. A great way to persuade this type of individual to open up is to share an interesting story about a local haunted house, a celebrity property, or something unusual that happened during a showing. Another great source is the tabloids. Nobody admits to reading them, yet everybody sees them at the grocery store. Avoid controversial topics such as politics or religion.

Knead the Dough Secret #5

Commonality is the basis for building trust and connection.

Step 3: Commonality

The moment you say, "I've done that" or "I have eaten there," your shared experience or commonality forms the basis for building connection. People prefer to work with others who share similarities. You can observe this any time you have a party where new people meet. People will group themselves with those who share similar interests. The cooks and the sports enthusiasts always seem to find each other.

To make yourself more attractive to more people, stay up with movies, current events, and sports. Take time to read major best sellers or business books. Know who has the best ethnic food in town as well as the best kept secret about where to shop. In most cases, a little bit of knowledge goes a long ways in building connection. When you connect based upon commonality, you can literally see the other person's face light up as their energy also increases. Most people are eager to share their passion. At that point, all you have to do is ask "how" and "what" questions and be a good listener. Listening strengthens the connection.

Once you establish a connection, creating trust is the next step. Trust occurs when you walk your talk and keep your commitments. If you fail to do so, the connection lessens and trust disappears. When trust is strong, your clients are loyal, they recommend you to their friends, and your business grows.

When past clients have trust and confidence in you, they are unlikely to do business with a stranger they just met face-to-face or on the Internet. The most common error agents make is taking these precious personal relationships for granted. According to the *2007 NAR Profile of Home Buyers and Sellers*, 81 percent of all sellers surveyed said that they would use their real estate agent again. Only 23 percent of the sellers surveyed said they actually used the same agent. Agents often assume these wonderful people will remember to call them. Nothing could be further from the truth. Most people do what is expedient. Remember, 73 percent of all sellers do business with the first REALTOR® they contact. Unless you have a strategy to prospect your database regularly, these precious leads may go to the agent who knocks on the sellers' door the morning they decide to list.

Remember, "You get what you give." When you give connection, you get connection. Connection ultimately forms the basis for all great business and personal relationships. When you make the connection, you are no longer perceived as that "pesky real estate salesperson." Instead, you become "our real estate salesperson."

Knead the Dough Secret #6

You never have a second chance to make a good first impression.

Knowledgeable and Professional

According to the *2007 NAR Profile of Home Buyers and Sellers,* your level of professional competence is the most highly ranked quality that clients want. The challenge that you face is that people make these judgments in a matter of seconds. In order to make sure that you personally convey the highest possible level of competence, use the following guidelines.

1. **Master the inventory**

   One common trait all top producers share is excellent product knowledge. Clients want to know that you can accurately price their property, aggressively market it, and successfully close the transaction once the property is under contract. For the areas where you work, you should be able to name the best-priced listings, how much it costs to purchase a typical three or four bedroom home, as well as what types of properties are available in various price ranges. If you don't know the inventory well enough to do this right now, then start spending part of each day building your knowledge.

2. **Numbers give you credibility**
   What is the average market time in your area? How many months of inventory are on the market? How do these numbers affect your client's ability to buy or sell a home? Having a mastery of market statistics is one of the best ways to enhance your professional credibility as well as your personal sense of confidence.

3. **Dress for success**
   People make judgments based upon appearance. As a rule of thumb, dress the way your clientele dresses when they are at work. Understated classics are generally better for business, especially since they never go out of style. Save your trendy clothing and jewelry for after work.

4. **What you say and how you say it**
   Watch your rate of speech. If you talk fast, slow down, and speak clearly. Fast speech can make you appear like the stereotypical fast-talking salesperson. Avoid using slang, foul language, or chewing gum while at work. Never criticize anyone, especially your competitors. Religion and politics are also taboo. Finally, if you have a heavy accent or if you want to improve how you speak, consider taking a diction class or joining Toastmasters.

Presenting a high quality image with high quality supporting business materials enhances the probability you will convert your leads into signed business. When you don't value yourself, you increase the probability clients will work with someone else.

Chapter 3
Action Plan

Preparation is a key step in marketing and prospecting. An easy place to begin is by improving your professional image. Consider implementing each of the suggestions below or rewrite them so they fit the action that you would like to take. Circle the number of each strategy that you plan to implement in your business. Remember, trying to implement too much at one time can overwhelm you. If you select more than one item, place the items in priority order and work on implementing one item at a time. Record the date that you complete each item on the line provided. Then move on to subsequent chapters.

Action Steps:

___ 1. I will build stronger connections with clients by listening more carefully.

___ 2. I am genuinely interested in my clients and enjoy hearing about what they love to do.

___ 3. For the next 30 days, I will spend at least 15 minutes per day upgrading my knowledge of the inventory.

___ 4. I have a strong grasp of market statistics in my area including how many months of inventory are on the market, what the average days on market is, as well as how this affects the buyers and sellers that I serve.

___ 5. I will make providing my clients the best possible service a top priority in my business.

___ 6. I will focus on speaking more clearly.

___ 7. I will make improving my customers' experience a top priority in my business.

___ 8. I will take time to take care of me.

Asking powerful questions is one of the best ways to build trust and connection. Chapter 4 shows you how to integrate this powerful technique into your business.

Chapter 4
Question Your Way to Real Estate Success

The important thing is not to stop questioning.
Albert Einstein

Skills Check:
Put a checkmark (√) next to what you do now. Leave the remaining items blank. Review the action steps at the end of the chapter to determine the strategies that you will implement in your business.

___ 1. When I work with buyers and sellers, I listen more than I talk.

___ 2. When I work with sellers, I don't present information. Instead, I ask questions and write down the answers that the sellers give me.

___ 3. I regularly practice the principle of "shut up and sell."

___ 4. I normally handle objections by responding with a question.

___ 5. When I work with clients, I ask "what" and "how" questions and avoid asking "who," "when" "where," and "why" questions.

___ 6. Whenever I feel frustrated with a client's decision not to purchase or to take additional time to make a decision, I always try to remember, "It's not my house, it's not my mortgage, and it's not my decision."

Knead the Dough Secret #7
Ask "how" and "what" questions; never ask, "Why?"

Are You Asking the Right Questions?

A fundamental way to build rapport is to ask questions. The correct question can unlock a treasure trove of useful information and motivate your client to take action. Asking the wrong question shuts off discussion, lessens rapport, and undermines your connection. Being able to ask powerful questions will help you obtain more listings, establish trust and rapport more quickly, and allow your clients to feel that you truly listen to them.

The typical buyer's agent asks buyers what price range they are looking in, where they want to live, and how many bedrooms and baths they want. This is where the questions stop. In contrast, a complete "Buyer's Interview" would include 15 to 20 questions including facts about the buyer's lifestyle, what's important to buyers about their present property, what they dislike about their present property, where they spend their time at home, and what types of activities they enjoy. Each of these questions uncovers important pieces of information that will reduce the time it takes you to locate the correct property for the buyer. These questions also build the buyer's sense of connection with you. Finally, if you write down the buyers' responses and read them back to them, you have demonstrated that you have really heard the buyers' concerns.

The same thing is also true for sellers. Most listing agents talk about the services they provide, how great their company is (the "We're number one at something" conversation), and how the price they're proposing is the correct listing price. Few agents take the time to ask the seller what matters about their home. In fact, two of the most commonly heard complaints about agents are that they don't listen and they don't follow up. Asking the right questions and addressing your clients' concerns, results in more effective communication and more closed business.

The Four Shifts Required to Ask Powerful Questions

Shift 1: Shut Up and Sell

Have you ever been in a negotiation where things were going well until the other agent made a remark that made the seller angry? If so, you know how devastating the wrong comment can be. Silence is one of the most powerful tools in your real estate tool box. Another way of saying this is, "shut up and sell." This means never interrupting your clients, especially when you disagree. It also means that when you write or present an offer, you give the principals the facts and then allow the clients to make their own decision. Remember, no matter how good your ideas are your job is to hear the client first. Share your opinions only when they are asked for; if the client doesn't ask your opinion, then remember—shut up and sell!

Shift 2: When you do open your mouth, only do so to ask a question

Have you ever shown a property where the listing agent pointed to a feature that your buyer hated? Sometimes a single comment can cost you the sale.

A better approach is to ask questions. For example, when the buyer says, "This has a beautiful view," respond with a question. "It is a beautiful view, isn't it?" If the buyer objects to a specific feature, avoid telling the buyer how to fix the problem. Ask a question instead. Specifically, if the buyer says, "I hate these dark wood cabinets," respond by asking, "Would you paint them a lighter color or have them replaced?" This question not only asks for the buyers' feedback, it has them respond as if they are the owners of the property.

Shift 3: Ask open-ended questions rather than closed-ended questions

A common challenge many agents face is asking closed-ended questions rather than open-ended questions. A closed ended question has a single word answer. "Where," "when," and "who" normally result in one word answers. For example, an agent might ask, "Where do you plan on moving?" or "When do you plan on moving."

In contrast, an open-ended question requires a much more detailed response. A better question would be, "What is it about those areas that you find attractive?" Open ended questions provide answers that are more complete. They will also help you uncover the reasons the buyer will accept some properties and reject others.

Avoid asking "why," because "why" puts the other person on the defensive. In a subtle way, it makes the other person wrong. For example, if you ask another agent, "Why did you write such a low offer," you're making both the agent and their clients wrong for how they handled the negotiation. This puts the other agent on the defensive and makes it harder to bring the parties together. A better question would be, "What was your buyer's rationale in offering this price?" This gives the other agent an opportunity to explain their buyer's position without becoming defensive. Whenever possible, ask "how" and "what" questions and avoid, "who," "where," "when," and "why."

Shift 4: It's not your house and it's not your decision

Most agents want what's best for their clients. It's tempting for agents to become attached to their clients' decisions or to try to persuade their clients that the agent's position is the correct one. Agents who concentrate on forcing their clients to agree with their position are no longer collaborative; they are agent-centric.

To avoid this trap, remember, "It's not your house, it's not your mortgage, and it's not your decision." Focus on being a conduit of information. Your role is to be a trusted resource that provides buyers and sellers with the best information possible so that they can make the best decision possible. Using powerful questions uncovers the principal's motivation, strengthens your connection, increases the likelihood of closing the transaction, and generates future referrals.

Chapter 4
Action Plan

Identify the action steps that you would like to take and rewrite items that may not fit. Circle the number of each strategy that you plan to implement in your business and then record the date you complete the item in the space provided. Make one or two changes at a time. Making too many changes at once can be overwhelming. Integrate the changes one at a time prior to making other changes. Keep in mind that your goal is to find an activity that is both motivating and sustainable over time.

Action Steps:

___ 1. When I work with buyers and sellers in the future, I will listen more than I talk.

___ 2. When I work with sellers in the future, I will focus on asking questions.

___ 3. When I interview buyer and sellers, I will take notes on what they say.

___ 4. I will regularly practice the principle of "shut up and sell."

___ 5. In the future, I will focus on asking "what" and "how" questions and avoid asking "who," "when," "where," and "why" questions.

___ 6. I will handle objections by responding with a question.

___ 7. Whenever I feel frustrated with a client's decision not to purchase or to take additional time to make a decision, I will remember, "It's not my house, it's not my mortgage, and it's not my decision."

Asking powerful questions strengthens communication and ultimately helps you to close more business. Another equally important component for real estate success is mastering market statistics.

Chapter 5
Reading the Tea Leaves

Change is the law of life. And those who look only to the past or present are certain to miss the future.
John F. Kennedy

Skills Check:
Put a checkmark (√) next to what you do now. Leave the remaining items blank. Review the action steps at the end of the chapter to determine the strategies that you will implement in your business.

___ 1. I know how many months of inventory are currently on the market in each of my service areas.

___ 2. I can show sellers whether we are in a seller's market, transitional market, or buyer's market based upon how much inventory is on the market.

___ 3. Even if I don't work the luxury market or the first-time buyer market, I still track market statistics in those areas to see how they may influence the portion of the market where I do work.

___ 4. I track new housing activity in my area and know whether builders are offering incentives that may indicate a market shift.

___ 5. I track market statistics such as days on the market, foreclosure rates, and second home sales.

Knead the Dough Secret #8
You don't need a crystal ball to predict whether prices will be going up or down—just track how many months of inventory are available at different price points in your market area.

Statistics or Crystal Ball?

Is it possible to predict what the real estate market in your area will be like six months from now? Do you need a fortune teller to read the tea leaves to know for sure? Clearly, no one can predict precisely what the market will do. Nevertheless, there are strategies to help you spot trends long before any of your competitors. Spotting these trends early allows you to adjust your business plan before your competitors even notice the change. Instead of scrambling to catch up with market adjustments, anticipating market changes provides you with a huge competitive advantage.

The real estate market is cyclical. An important point to remember about market adjustments is that there are three phases. A strong seller's market will be followed by a transitional market where there are approximately the same number of buyers and sellers. The transitional market may then shift to a buyer's market or it could, in rare cases, return to a seller's market. The typical cycle runs from too much inventory to too little inventory.

How Can I Tell If I'm in an Up, Down, or Flat Market?

The number of months of inventory on the market is the best predictor of whether market values are increasing, stable, or decreasing. As a rule of thumb, if there are six or less months of inventory on the market, you are in a seller's market with too little inventory and upward pressure on prices. If there are seven or eight months of inventory on the market, you are in a flat or transitional market with stable prices. If there are nine or more months of inventory on the market, you are in a buyer's market with downward pressure on prices. There are three key reasons you should know these statistics.

1. Knowledge of market statistics will allow you to have a more realistic discussion with your clients about pricing as well as the amount of time it will take their property to sell.

2. You can often have a buyer's market, a transitional market, and a seller's market all in the same area. Consequently, it's important to track the numbers in specific neighborhoods. If you are experiencing a mixed market, concentrating your efforts in the areas experiencing a seller's market (i.e., a high demand with low amounts of inventory) will help you to conduct more sales.

3. Tracking market statistics allows you to spot opportunities to do more business. For example, if you notice that the amount of inventory is decreasing, it's smart to obtain as many listings as possible to meet growing demand. On the other hand, if the inventory is increasing, this would be an excellent time to do more work with buyers.

It's also important to realize that you may have a seller's market in some price ranges and a buyer's market in other price ranges, especially if the market is in transition. In most areas, the luxury and move-up markets are the first to experience slowdown. What was odd about the 2007 slow down was that the move-up market was the least affected until the credit crunch hit in mid-2007. The real pain was in the first-time buyer market. Consequently, it's important to consider what is going on in all market segments, not just within your personal market niche. A slow down in one aspect of your market can signal slow downs in other price ranges.

Knead the Dough Secret #9
Markets are always cyclical—they always get worse and they always get better.

Builders: Your Early Warning System

How can you recognize whether a storm is brewing in your market? Builders are your early warning system. For example, when the market in Denver started to languish back in 2005, D. R. Horton, a major national builder, began slashing prices to move their inventory. Horton also began offering a host of upgrades to attract buyers. This was followed by interest rate buy downs and even more incentives to attract buyers.

Major builders actively monitor where the market is heading. While their forecasts may not always accurately predict a storm, cuts in production usually indicate a slowdown. A key point to keep in mind is that all real estate is local. Even at the height of the subprime mess, Happyrenews.com reported that more than 2,500 cities were experiencing price appreciation.

Consequently, watching builder activity in your area will give you a good idea of what the market will do. If housing starts are increasing and new homes sell quickly, prices will increase. If this is the case, builders offer virtually no incentives. In some cases, there may be lotteries because the demand is so high. In contrast, as a market begins to soften, builders will begin to offer incentives to attract buyers. Since agents generally control which properties a buyer sees, builders may offer strong incentives for agents as well. In this environment, commissions normally increase.

What Are Some of the Other Warning Signs?

Many metropolitan areas have few tracts of new construction. If you work in a market where new construction is minimal, you can still spot changes in the market by tracking any of the following.

1. **Multiple offers**
   The hallmark of a seller's market is multiple offers, often over asking price. If you have been in a market where multiple offers were common, be especially wary when the multiple offers decline or disappear entirely. This is an early warning

sign that the market is slowing down. As multiple offers disappear, properties no longer sell over asking price. Consequently, if properties on average are selling at 100 percent of ask price and they drop to 98 or 99 percent of ask price, you are already in the midst of a market decline.

2. **Increased days on market**
   One of the easiest ways to spot a market shift is to use the Multiple Listing Service to track days on the market. If you are not tracking this statistic, it's important to look at it at least monthly, no matter what your market is doing. When there are big changes in this statistic, it's time to analyze whether a change in strategy is necessary. For example, if days on the market decrease, then there will be less inventory. This can result in a seller's market with upward pressure on prices. When the days on the market increase, the market could be shifting into a flat or transitional market. If this continues over a long period of time, the market could shift to a buyer's market. When the days on the market are unchanged, market conditions are stable. This means that if your present strategies are working, there's no urgent need to shift strategies.

3. **Increased commissions**
   When there are too many sellers and not enough buyers, builders generally take the lead in paying increased commissions. The trend may begin with builders offering mortgage buy-downs, free up-grades, televisions, and other benefits. When sales slow, builders raise commission rates they pay to agents. When owners of resale listings become desperate, agents advise their sellers to match these incentives. Instead of a competition to see who can undercut commissions the most, the exact opposite happens. The competition becomes about who can offer the best incentives to motivate agents and buyers to see their listings.

4. **Flipping disappears**
   Flipping (buying a property, fixing it up, and selling it for a profit in a short period of time) comes to a grinding halt in a buyer's market. Normally, flipping rates hit their maximum just before the market peaks. The rates begin to slow when people try to sell their investment property and are unable to make any money from the sale. Their projected profits dwindle away as their property sits on the market month after month. If you see an increase in vacant, remodeled properties sitting on the market and not selling, this is almost always a sign of a market slow down. This situation may parallel what happened in the dot-com bust. When the little guys start speculating, they're normally the ones who are

hurt. As one economist put it, "When the guy who cuts my hair and the woman who does my nails start advising me on how to invest in real estate, I know it's time to get out of the market."

5. Foreclosure rates increase

When people are unable to sell their homes in a heated market, this often means the market has peaked. For example, the foreclosure rate in California began to rise in March of 2005. The market was still exceptionally strong, but this was one of the earliest concrete signs that a slowdown was beginning. Six months later in September of 2005, the red hot sellers market in both San Francisco and Southern California started to slow. As Malcolm Kaufman declared in his San Francisco "Pulse of the Market Newsletter," "The soufflé has arrived." While properties were still selling quickly, the double digit appreciation, multiple offers, and one- and two-day market times virtually disappeared.

An additional reason to be particularly sensitive to foreclosure rates is due to the huge numbers of homeowners who have purchased their property with 100 percent financing and/or exceptionally low Adjustable Rate Mortgages (ARMs). Other owners have refinanced their properties in order to buy cars or pay off credit card debt. When these owners have no equity and are unable to pay an adjustable rate mortgage rate increase or cannot sell, many simply decide to give the keys back to the lender. Since lenders want to minimize how long they have any REO property (Real Estate Owned by a bank, usually through foreclosure), they will cut the price to whatever is necessary to sell. This tends to be a vicious circle. As foreclosure rates increase, prices decrease. Each time prices decline, the number of people who are unable to sell increases as does the number of foreclosures.

6. Second home sales slow

Another warning signal is a slowdown in the second home market. If your market area contains a large number of second homes or investment properties, you may experience a slowdown sooner than agents who work in areas where most people own primary residences. When people with second homes become over-extended, they are often more willing to drop their price so that they can avoid losing their primary residence. If there is a glut of investment property that is sitting vacant, investors are often willing to sell at a loss rather than continue to hold a non-performing asset.

Sunshine on the Horizon

While it's important to watch for signs of a weakening or flattening market, it's equally important to know the signs of an improving market. Here are some of the most important hallmarks of an improving market.

1. **Months of inventory declines**
   Just as an increase in inventory can signal a declining market, a decrease signals that the market is improving. You may also observe this as a decline in the number of days on the market. Tracking either of these statistics will help you to more accurately predict what the market will do.

2. **Foreclosure rates decline**
   The 2007 downturn was unusual for a number of reasons. First, the credit crunch caused by the collapse of the subprime mortgage market made it virtually impossible for even highly qualified buyers to obtain financing. Due to interest rate declines plus foreclosure workout programs, the foreclosure rates are finally beginning to decline in some areas.

3. **Multiple offers on prime properties**
   When the market slows down, multiple offers generally disappear. When the market starts to come back, you will see multiple offers appearing on the best properties in all price ranges.

4. **Increased web traffic to real estate and home builder sites**
   Long before people buy a new home, they will spend a substantial amount of time online previewing properties. You can track traffic on various websites using a tool like the one provided by Amazon at Alexa.com. Simply enter the company names that you want to track and you can see what the overall market is doing in terms of web visitors.

5. **Builders no longer offer incentives and have waiting lists for their new product**
   Tracking what builders are doing is an excellent way to predict both slow downs and market improvements. When builders offer fewer incentives or no incentives at all, it's a pretty safe bet that their market is doing well. An additional sign is having waiting lists. The longer the list, the less likely builders are to provide additional incentives to improve their rate of sale.

Chapter 5
Action Plan

Don't be blind-sided by market shifts. Track market statistics including days on the market, foreclosure rates, and builder incentives. This approach gives you a competitive advantage against other agents who are merely reacting to the market rather than proactively evaluating and responding to market changes.

Identify the action steps that you would like to take and rewrite items that may not fit. Circle the number of each strategy that you plan to implement in your business and then record the date you complete the item in the space provided. Make one or two changes at a time. Making too many changes at once can be overwhelming. Integrate the changes one at a time prior to making other changes. Remember, you're searching for activities that are both motivating and sustainable over time.

Action Steps:

___ 1. In the future, I will track new housing activity in order to determine whether builders are offering incentives that may indicate a market shift.

___ 2. I have started tracking market statistics such as days on the market, months of inventory available, foreclosure rates, and second home sales. I know how to clearly explain these numbers to my sellers.

___ 3. Using the months of inventory on the market, I have mastered how to explain whether my market area is experiencing a buyer's market, a transitional market, or a seller's market.

___ 4. I will track website traffic for the builders as well as the real estate companies in my area to anticipate market trends.

___ 5. I will track both the luxury market and the areas where I work to spot market shifts.

___ 6. I track new housing activity in my area and know whether builders are offering incentives, which may indicate a market shift.

You may have excellent product and market knowledge, however, the way that you deliver the information determines whether clients will work with you. Chapter 6 shows you how what you say and how you say it is critical to your real estate sales success.

Chapter 6
What Do I Say and How Do I Say It?

The most important trip you may take in
life is meeting people half way.
Henry Boyle

Skills Check:
Put a checkmark (√) next to what you do now. Leave the remaining items blank. Review the action steps at the end of the chapter to determine the strategies that you will implement in your business.

___ 1. When I work with my clients, I focus on using "you" language rather than "I" language.

___ 2. I know what "charge neutral" is and use it regularly when I negotiate.

___ 3. When I work with my clients, I understand how to use mirroring and matching techniques to make the client feel comfortable with me.

___ 4. I always turn the decision making process back over to my clients.

___ 5. I avoid using the words "try," "should," "but," "hope," and other words that weaken my communication.

Knead the Dough Secret #10
The secret to successful negotiation is to question, question, question.

Which Works Better—"I" Language, "You" Language or "We" Language?

One of the most important changes that you can make when working with clients is to switch from using the word "I" and start using the word "you." When you use the word "I," the focus is on you rather than on your client. Instead, make the conversation about the client's wants and needs. For example,

I would like to drop some information off on loan rates. What time can I come by?

I just finished doing a comparable market analysis on your property. Based upon the numbers, I think your property should be listed at $349,000.

OR

You might find some additional information on various loan programs to be very useful. When would be a good time to drop it by?

The numbers on the comparable market analysis suggest your property is worth approximately $349,000. Where would you like to position your property in the marketplace?

Also avoid using the word, "we." When agents say, "When we list your property" or "When we get an offer," then when something goes wrong, "we" are responsible and "we" have to pay for it.

Knead the Dough Secret #11
Charge neutral is the most effective negotiation tool in your negotiation toolbox.

What Is Charge Neutral?

Have you ever wondered how some television interviewers persuade people to reveal personal things about themselves? In most cases, they use a strategy called "charge neutral." Charge neutral refers to speaking in a calm soothing voice, much as you would if you were speaking to a friend who is facing a difficult time.

Charge neutral also refers to keeping your body still. If you watch the most effective interviewers on television, you will note that they usually keep their bodies perfectly still when they conduct an interview. This is the ideal way to position yourself when you work with clients. If you are a high energy person, you may find it difficult to be calm. Nevertheless, short, quick, or nervous movements are nonverbal cues that can heighten an already tense negotiation situation.

What Is Mirroring and Matching?

Mirroring and matching is a Neurolinguistic Programming (NLP) technique. The approach is simple. If your client crosses her arms, you cross your arms. If your client leans forward, you lean forward. If she places her finger on the tip of her chin, you do the same thing. This can be a powerful tool to make your negotiations go more smoothly, provided that you use it appropriately.

The best way to mirror and match is to always add at least one additional move between each mirror and match. For example, if your client goes from crossed arms to placing her finger on the tip of her chin, your motion would be to uncross your arms, jot something down with your pen, and then mirror her position. You could also cough, brush your hair away from your face, and then mirror her position. Avoid doing this frequently since sophisticated negotiators often recognize the technique.

How Can I Use Mirroring and Matching with Deal Breakers?

Mirroring and matching also works well with deal breakers. For example, suppose that you are working with a client whose father is the deal breaker. If the father has a good relationship with his child, all you need to do is mirror your client's body language, not the father's body language. This approach sends a powerful nonverbal signal that you are in synchrony with his child.

If the deal breaker gives you attitude, respond by using charge neutral. Explain that your job is to locate the property and to handle the transaction details. It's your client's responsibility to make the decision, not yours. On the other hand, if your client and the deal breaker have a poor relationship, don't use the technique. It will only make the situation more difficult.

When used properly, mirroring and matching builds rapport and makes negotiating easier. Avoid using this technique to manipulate your clients. Instead, focus on doing the best possible job on their behalf.

Why Is Charge Neutral Preferable to Using Mirroring and Matching?

Many people are familiar with mirroring and matching, especially if they have ever been in sales or negotiate for a living. If you mirror and match, you may get away with it. If your clients spot it however, there's a high probability you will lose them.

Given a choice between using charge neutral vs. mirroring and matching, charge neutral is normally the better choice. There is no manipulation and there is no need to worry about your clients discovering the technique you are using.

Remember, mirroring and matching can be a manipulation and no one likes being manipulated. In contrast, charge neutral simply lets your words speak without emotion and without distracting body movements. This allows your client to concentrate on what is being said as well as improving the communication.

> **Knead the Dough Secret #12**
> It's not your house, it's not your mortgage, and it's not your decision. ALWAYS allow your clients to make their own choices.

What Is the Most Important Phrase in Negotiation?

On January 22, 2008, the *New York Times* reported that a seller had filed a suit against a real estate agent for "deliberately misleading her about the value of the house" that she bought at the peak of the market in 2005. If this plaintiff wins this lawsuit, expect to see more lawsuits from disgruntled buyers.

How can you avoid this type of litigation? The answer is a simple question that turns the decision making process over to the client:

It's your choice, what would you like to do?

Rather than putting yourself in the role of the decision maker, the collaborative model casts your role as the provider of information. You are the resource who helps the seller or buyer make the best possible decision. Using this strategy is simple: outline what the client's options are, ask if there are any options that you have missed, and then end with, "It's your choice, what would you like to do?"

Although it may sound odd, avoid advising your clients what to do. Instead, when your clients ask for advice, outline the options and then turn the choice back to the clients. For example, if your buyers ask how much they should offer in a multiple offer situation, outline three options:

1. The buyers can make an offer as they would normally when there are no other offers.

2. If the buyers really want the house, they can offer close to asking price.

3. If the situation is very competitive or the buyer is desperate for the property, then the buyer can offer full price or over asking.

After outlining the options, you would conclude by saying, "It's your choice, what would you like to do?" Listen to their response and act accordingly.

If you are struggling to remain quiet, ask yourself whether what you want to say supports your clients in their process or is it your personal need to be heard? In most cases, it is best to keep your opinions to yourself. Again, if you must say something, ask a question to clarify what you are hearing from your clients.

A corollary to the question above is to ask, "Is that a strategy that works for you?" This phrase works especially well when the client is feeling reluctant or if the client is in the process of interviewing agents.

For example, if you are competing against other agents for a listing, outline your marketing plan and then ask, "Do you believe that I can get your house sold?" If the seller says, "We're interviewing other agents," respond by saying,

> *Great! Please compare our premium marketing plan with those provided by the other agents and then decide which agent can help you obtain the highest possible price for your property in the shortest amount of time. Is that a strategy that works for you?*

What makes this approach powerful is that you have set the expectation that the other agents will bring their marketing plans to their meeting with the sellers. When they show up without a marketing plan, the sellers will most probably hire you. More importantly, you have allowed your client be the decision maker.

What Is the White Knight Syndrome?

A major mistake many inexperienced negotiators make is acting as if they were one of the principals. A classic example is the agent who says, "I'm not going to let my sellers take a price that low!" This is known as the "White Knight Syndrome."

When it comes to your personal negotiating style, the way to combat the White Knight Syndrome is to always turn the decision back to your clients. Again, to briefly review the process:

1. Outline the choices that the client has.

2. Ask your client if there are any other options that you have missed.

3. Once you have identified the options, ask which option your client prefers.

This is a very simple, but powerful approach. By allowing your clients to make the decision, they will no longer feel that they're being closed or manipulated. That's why the question, "It's your choice, what would you like to do?" is so powerful when you are negotiating.

When the other agent in the transaction is being a White Knight, you can handle the situation by doing the following:

1. Explain to the other agent that your buyer/seller has requested that both agents say nothing until the buyer/seller has voiced a response. This goes back to the old sales axiom that the first one who speaks loses. If possible, have this conversation prior to meeting with any of the principals in the transaction.

2. If the White Knight won't shut up, turn to the sellers/buyers and say, "Mr. and Mrs. Client, this is your decision. What would you like to do?"

Be direct although avoid being rude. By asking a question, you avoid being confrontational.

Knead the Dough Secret #13
If you can't say something nice about your client, the other agent, or anyone else involved in the transaction, don't say anything.

How Can My Language Undermine My Negotiation Success?

Negotiation can be a frustrating process. The old adage that says, "If you can't say something nice, don't say anything" is wise advice. Although this seems obvious, it's common practice for agents to call people who make low offers "low-ballers," "bottom feeders," "chiselers," or some other unflattering name. It's also common for agents to refer to sellers as being "greedy" or "stupid" when the sellers insist on overpricing their property. Making these types of remarks about your client or another agent's client only reflects badly on you. It also sets up a difficult negotiation situation, because once you place a negative label on client, you then have to overcome the negative label as well.

Remember, clients come and go; the agents you work with may be around for many years to come. Whenever possible, do your best to say something positive about everyone with whom you come in contact.

What Words Undermine the Negotiation Process?

1. **How does "try" create misunderstandings?**
   The word "try" implies failure. For example, when you say, "I'll try to call you tomorrow," the client hears, "I'll call you tomorrow." What you meant to say is that you may call tomorrow, but you also might not call. If you don't call, you failed and the client is angry. When you negotiate, say exactly what you intend to do. Never reference what you will "try" to do. If your clients use the word

"try," ask for clarification. For example, when a client says, "I'll try to get back to you sometime soon." Counter with, "Does that mean I will hear from you tomorrow?" If the answer is "No," then pursue the question one step further, "How about the day after tomorrow? Will I hear from you by then?"

2. **What does "can't" really mean?**
Many people use the word "can't" as a catch-all word with multiple meanings. Specifically, "can't" may mean, "I am physically unable to do that," "I don't know how to do that," or "I don't want to do that." In most cases, the physical explanation almost never applies. Thus, when a client says, "I can't see myself selling for such a low price," respond by saying, "Is it that you can't afford to (doesn't know how to) or that you really don't want to?" The key is to avoid arguing about the situation. Instead, ask a powerful question that moves you closer to your next sale.

3. **How does "but" negate what I say?**
"But" is one of the most commonly used words in the English language, especially if two people disagree. In many cases, "but" precedes an objection. "We really like this house, but it's too close to the school." "We know the market is slowing down, but we still want to list the property at a higher price." People use "but" to give the impression that there is agreement, when in truth, they disagree. The challenge with using "but," is that it negates everything that comes before it. When you are negotiating, listen for "but" to identify what your clients dislike and to be better prepared to overcome their objections.

    In terms of your own language, substitute the word "and" for the word "but." Using "and" makes the negotiation go more smoothly. For example, when you say, "We appreciate your offer, but we have to make a counteroffer," you are negating the statement that says that you appreciate the offer. Using "and" changes the situation: "We appreciate your offer and we would like to make a counteroffer." Avoid using "but" and thereby negating a positive with a negative.

4. **What makes "hope" and "if" weak?**
"Hope" and "if" are weak words. Instead of saying, "I hope that we can find the perfect home for you," be positive by saying, "I know we can find the perfect home for you." Instead of saying, "If we get an offer," say, "When we receive an offer." Clients prefer to work with agents who are positive, no matter how dreadful the market is. If you hear yourself using "hope" or "if," drop the wishy-washy approach and make a bold statement—you know you can do it!

5. What is the most important word to avoid in negotiation?

One of the most frequently used words in our language is "should." In fact, our society "shoulds" us to death. We should lose weight, we should prospect everyday, we should spend more time with our loved ones, etc.

Do your best to eliminate the word "should" from your vocabulary. When people use "should," they are usually attempting to manipulate you or the situation. Many of us also use "should" to make ourselves feel guilty about what we are not doing.

To improve your negotiation skills and to reduce the stress in your life, go on a "should" diet for one week. You will be surprised at what you discover about yourself as well as those around you.

Chapter 6
Action Plan

Improve your negotiation skills by following the suggestions below or rewrite them so they fit the actions that you would like to take. Circle the number of each strategy that you plan to implement in your business and then record the date you complete the item in the space provided. If you select more than one item, place the items in priority order and work on implementing one item at a time. Once you complete the items you have selected, move on to the next chapter.

Action Steps:

___ 1. I will use "you" language in negotiations rather than "I" language.

___ 2. I understand "charge neutral" and will use it regularly when I am negotiating.

___ 3. I know how to "mirror and match" my clients and will use this approach only to support my clients, not to manipulate them.

___ 4. When possible, I will use charge neutral rather than mirroring and matching during negotiations.

___ 5. I will make a point of letting my clients make their own decisions by saying, "It's your choice, what would you like to do?"

___ 6. I will avoid being a "White Knight" who has to control my client's decision-making process.

___ 7. I will avoid using the words "try," "should," "but," "hope," and other words that weaken my ability to negotiate.

The language you use to describe your market can have a powerful influence on your real estate success, as illustrated in this next Recipe for Success from Jerry Rossi.

Recipes for Success
It's Not a Bad Market—
It's a Different Market

Jerry Rossi
RossiSpeaks.com

Jerry Rossi, the author of Dog Eat Dog and Vice Versa *and* Just Stop It!, *is a leading speaker on the real estate circuit. In addition to being a master practitioner of Neurolinguistic Programming (NLP), he is also an extraordinary cook. In this interview, Rossi shares his Recipe for Success in today's challenging markets.*

Agents are constantly asked, "How's the market?" The typical response is that the market is "bad" or that the market is "unbelievable." Neither approach helps the agent or their clients. Instead, a better response is, "It's not a bad market—it's a different market."

The challenge for most of us is that we have an automatic set of responses that we respond with, often without thinking. I call these personal defaults. They can be positive or negative. When we default with "it's a bad market," then that's what we will experience. If this is how you respond when someone asks you this question, then it's time to stop it!

Changing your defaults can be challenging. When you shift from using the word "bad" to using the word "different," you'll find that those around you will respond differently. Instead of saying how few buyers there are or that prices are decreasing, explain that today we are experiencing listings and sales in a different way.

One of the most dangerous ways that independent contractors sabotage their life and their success is by hanging out at the office. I work with top producers from all over the country and very few of them spend much time at the office. They do show up for meetings and are constantly learning. The reason that many of them avoid the office is that agents who aren't doing well often complain about the market or their lack of business. If you allow yourself to stay in this environment, it will sabotage your success.

Resetting your personal defaults can be a fun process. When your business slows down, identify two things that you can do in a different way. Attempting to change one thing is extraordinarily difficult, if not impossible. On the other hand, changing two things is still a struggle, but is actually less difficult.

For example, go to the office at a different time of day or take a different route. Stop watching television and spend that time doing volunteer work for a charity. In fact, one of my coaching clients was spending $300 per month in search engine optimization. It wasn't yielding any significant results in his business. He decided to take that money and to donate it to the feed the hungry for six months. Each Saturday, he and his daughter volunteered by handing out food at the food bank. His daughter enjoyed this special time they spent together every weekend. At the end of six months, his business had increased by 15 percent.

When you start to say something that is negative, whether it's about the market or anything else, stop it! Instead, focus on how it's different. That's the best way to create a powerful new set of positive defaults.

Chapter 7
Negotiating with Style

We cannot change our past. We cannot change the fact that people act in a certain way. We cannot change the inevitable. The only thing we can do it play on the string we have, and this is our attitude.
Charles R. Swindoll

Skills Check:
Put a checkmark (√) next to what you do now. Leave the remaining items blank. Review the action steps at the end of the chapter to determine the strategies that you will implement in your business.

___ 1. I know my personal behavioral style from taking the DISC assessment.

___ 2. I know how to vary my negotiation style so it fits my client's behavioral style.

___ 3. I know whether I am visual, auditory, or kinesthetic.

___ 4. I know how to recognize whether my clients are visual, auditory, or kinesthetic and how to adjust my language and pace to match their style.

___ 5. I pay close attention to body language when I work with clients and know how to interpret what their body language means.

Knead the Dough Secret #14
Being able to recognize your client's behavioral style will greatly enhance your negotiation skills.

How Does Behavioral Style Affect the Negotiation Process?

Does your listing prospect want a personal connection or just the hard data? Does your relocation client need time to bond or is it better to show your client everything on the market? Is your new buyer easy-going or a stick of dynamite ready to explode?

Great negotiators seem to intuitively understand what is needed when they are negotiating. If you haven't learned how to evaluate the subtle signals that your clients send, negotiating will be much more difficult.

The first step is to understand their behavioral style. Adapting your behavior to their style can be challenging, but the rewards you will receive in terms of more effective negotiations will be substantial.

One of the most widely used assessments in the world is Target Training International's version of the DISC assessment. This simple 15 minute test generates over 25 pages of information about how people behave in various sales situations. Their research with over one million people worldwide has demonstrated the following:

1. People tend to buy from salespeople who have behavioral styles similar to their own.

2. Salespeople tend to sell to customers who have a behavioral style similar to their own.

3. Salespeople who are aware of their own behavioral style and learn to blend with their customer's style are able to increase their sales.

To take full advantage of this chapter, it would be wise to take the DISC first (visit RealEstateCoach.com and click on the assessments tab). This way you can tell what your personal behavioral style is. It will also help you to identify your clients' styles more easily.

DISC—the Basics

1. "D" or Dominance

People who score high on the "D" factor on the DISC usually have a high ego factor. They hate wasting time. An excellent example is Donald Trump. Trump feels no compunction when he fires someone. To him, it's just business. People who score high on this factor are not interested in testimonials, bonding over lunch, or being bothered with details. They are very interested in getting the deal done as efficiently and painlessly as possible. They tend to be hard driving and bottom line focused. They often make snap decisions and can lose their tempers easily. Nevertheless, their anger usually dissipates quickly. They normally don't hold grudges and may not even remember what set them off in the first place.

In terms of the real estate business, most top producers score high on the dominance factor on the DISC. In fact, many top achievers, CEOs, and other successful business people score high on this factor as well.

When you work with someone who has a high "D" factor, stay focused on the facts. Be especially sensitive about wasting their time. Allow them be in charge, but don't let them run over you. Show them only the properties most suited to their needs. Don't be hurt if they don't want to socialize with you. Instead, keep your focus on helping them achieve their bottom line.

2. "I" or Influencing

People who score high on the "I" factor tend to be friendly, out-going people who would rather talk and socialize than do detail work. Take time over lunch to really get to know your client, including her accomplishments as well as her dreams. Focus on the high points of each property including how much fun she'll have entertaining. Don't waste her time with details—she's simply not interested.

People who score high on the "I" factor generally prefer new, innovative, and showy products. They love being on the cutting edge. The more gadgets and high tech toys a property has, the better they like it. The challenge you will face is that they may talk about purchasing and be quite excited about it; they're just not very good at following up on the details that will make it happen.

Many successful salespeople score high on the "I" factor as do people who are more emotionally sensitive. The most successful real estate salespeople score high on both the "D" and "I" factors. These people tend to have a high drive coupled with a high need to be liked by others. The two factors together result in strong sales.

To generate referrals from your clients who are people-people, staying in regular contact is critical. Remember, this type of client loves to connect. If they like you, they'll tell all their friends how great you are.

3. "S" or Steadiness

People who score high on the "S" factor tend to hide their emotions and can be suspicious. They may want to be your friend, but will be slow to trust you. Security and low risk are important. The property they purchase must be located in a good neighborhood with good schools. Thorough inspections and a home warranty are must-haves since the buyer "doesn't want any surprises" after the transaction closes.

In terms of career, these individuals typically choose a job with a high amount of security rather than risking their security for more pay. People who score high on the "S" factor make up a substantial proportion of the population. They generally prefer traditional products. They also exhibit high brand loyalty.

Agents who score high on the "S" factor often succeed best with repeatable systems. While it may take them longer to succeed than those with high scores on the "D" or "I" factors, their systems approach can yield long-term, sustainable results.

If you have clients who appear to have a strong "S" style, don't rush them. Take time to get to know them and make sure they are protected with a home warranty, security system, and that their property is a "safe" investment. If you do a great job for this type of client, they will be a constant source of referrals because of their trust and their brand loyalty.

4. "C" or Compliance

People who score high on the "C" factor tend to respect the rules and go by the book. These people pay a lot of attention to detail and are often quiet. They typically prefer what is proven. They tend to be traditional in their approach to life. Career wise, people who score high on this factor often work in accounting, engineering, and computer science where paying attention to details is important. These clients will carefully read and evaluate every last detail of the transaction. If you quote closing costs, they will expect them to be accurate to the penny.

In terms of working with them, get right to the point with the most detailed data available. Avoid using a hard sell or an emotional approach. Be sure to explain what happens in the counteroffer process as well as emphasizing the potential losses caused by delaying action.

To get referrals from clients who are detailed oriented, you must be meticulous about detail, punctuality, and allowing the facts do the talking rather than your emotions. Give them time to carefully evaluate their decisions and avoid pressuring them. Constantly feed them data. They will appreciate your attention to detail.

Agents who score high on the "C" or Compliance factor often thrive in an assistant or administrative position due to their excellent attention to detail. This is especially true if their scores on the "D" and the "I" factors are lower than the 50th percentile.

Understanding behavioral styles will help you match your negotiation process to what works best for the client. In addition, a person's primary sensory modality (visual, auditory, or kinesthetic), refers to how their brain best processes information. You can improve your negotiation abilities even more by learning how to identify whether your clients are visual, auditory, or kinesthetic.

Are Your Clients Visual, Auditory, or Kinesthetic?

Have you ever wondered why you and a particular client didn't connect? Do certain client types drive you crazy, but you just don't know why? The answer may be in recognizing whether you (and your clients) are visual (V), auditory (A), or kinesthetic (K). Psychologists have demonstrated we use all three styles or modalities (sight, hearing, and touch) when we process information, but usually one modality is dominant.

For those who are visual, how things look is most important. You can recognize a visual by their quick rate of speech and their attention to being color coordinated. A visual will disregard comfort to look good. They frequently use the words, "look" and "see." Most visuals like views and an open, airy floor plan.

In contrast, an auditory individual is concerned about how things sound. You can recognize someone who is auditory by how they use their voice—they often sound like a radio disc jockey or have a dramatic speaking style. They frequently use the word "sound" and often want a home with a great music system or a place where they can enjoy peace and quiet.

Kinesthetics place great emphasis on how things feel as opposed to how they look or sound. Their speech patterns are slow and deliberate. Comfort is paramount. They are more likely to choose a home that has small, more intimate feeling space. Someone who is visual will tolerate uncomfortable shoes provided they look good. A kinesthetic person would never make a purchase unless it feels comfortable.

How Can I Recognize My Client's Style?

By recognizing your clients' primary sensory modality, you can speak to them in a way that will improve both your connection and your sales. Below you will find the key words that will allow you to identify your clients' preferred modality as well as the best way to speak to them based upon their preference.

People who are visual are most likely to use the phrases "I see" or "light and bright" as well as the words "look" and "picture." They normally prefer a house with a view or one that looks out at something pleasant such as a beautiful garden or patio. They often make the following types of comments when viewing a property:

I really liked the way the property looks from the street.

I can just picture how our grand piano would look in this room.

I could spend hours looking at this wonderful view.

I love this light and bright entry with the cathedral ceilings.

Auditory individuals will use phrases such as, "I hear," "tell me about," or "this sounds good." They normally prefer a quiet location or one that has the sounds of water, birds, or other pleasant background noises.

I hear the market is improving.

Please tell me about any new listings in my price range.

I love the sound of the waves crashing on shore.

Those wind chimes make such a pretty sound.

Those who are kinesthetic will often uses phrases such as "I feel," "warm and cozy," "comfortable," or "homey." When they describe what they want, they will often use the word "feel" in their description. For example, "we want a house that has a traditional/contemporary feel."

I feel the market is improving.

Please let us know about any new listings that you feel might be right for us.

Something about this property just doesn't feel right to me.

What a warm and inviting study.

What Is the Best Way to Communicate with Each Style?

Visual clients prefer face-to-face communications rather than the phone. They also normally prefer what is written to what is spoken. In general, the more pictures that you can show them, the better. Furthermore, don't count on someone who is visual remembering what you tell them. Put it in writing.

When you speak to a visual person, use phrases such as:

How does that look to you?

Let's take a careful look at each item.

Let's see what the numbers look like.

Auditory clients generally prefer verbal communication, preferably by telephone. Don't expect them to carefully read written documentation. Give them frequent verbal updates about what is happening in their transaction. Document everything in writing.

When you speak to someone who is auditory, use phrases like the ones listed below:

I heard about a wonderful new listing.

Does that sound okay to you?

What do you say about meeting Friday at 11:00?

How does that interest rate sound to you?

Kinesthetic clients are guided by their feelings. While kinesthetic individuals often reference how they feel, they may not be able to articulate what feels right or wrong about a given property. When working with kinesthetic clients, don't pressure them to rush their decision. They use their feelings rather than their heads. They also tend to be detail-oriented. Be patient and let them proceed at their own rate. This is the best way to build trust and rapport.

When you speak to someone who is kinesthetic, use phrases such as:

I believe that now is a good time to make an offer. How do you feel?

I have a hunch that we might be able to obtain this house for a really good price.

This sophisticated security system certainly makes one feel safer.

This kitchen feels so warm and homey.

What Do I Say When My Clients Have Different Styles?

It's very common to have clients whose styles differ from one another. If this is the case, vary your approach as you speak to each client. For example, if Bill is visual and Mary is kinesthetic, you could say, "Bill, I can see this is the right house for you, and Mary, I have a hunch that you feel that way too."

How Can I Identify My Own Style?

Have a friend ask you to spell a long word and tell your friend to look carefully at your face as you spell the word, paying special attention to your eyes. If you "look up" when you spell the word, you're visual. If your eyes stay still or move from side-to-side at ear level, you're auditory. If you look down, you're kinesthetic.

Body Language: What They're Really Saying

While it's easy to recognize when a negotiation is proceeding well, most agents are poor at interpreting why a negotiation goes awry. Effective negotiators recognize when they need to slow down or speed up the negotiation process. They know how to relieve the client's anxiety and what to say to calm difficult situations. Rather than relying on verbal cues, however, the primary way they gauge what is happening is by watching their client's body language.

If you focus exclusively on closing the client, you may overlook the nonverbal messages that your clients are constantly sending. For the most part, these are unconscious and hence, unmonitored. In fact, what the clients say may be exactly opposite of what their body language is saying. When there is a contradiction, body language trumps the spoken word. The reason for this is that words carry about 10 percent of our communication. The bulk of our communication comes from our tone of voice, our pace, as well as how and where we position our bodies. To increase your communication with your clients, follow the steps below.

1. **Which way do they lean?**
   A primary reason for doing face-to-face negotiation is to read the clients' body language. You can also recognize the types of objections they will make based upon whether the client is leaning forward or leaning back. When your clients lean toward you, they are agreeing with you emotionally. This is the time to highlight the emotional benefits of owning the property. When they lean back, give them logical data. Careful listening will also tell you whether your clients are making an emotional buy or if they are buying for a logical reason such as reducing their taxes. People who buy based upon logic will make emotional objections. They become scared, they find fault with some part of the property that is not perfect, or they may become angry over something that is inconsequential. On the other hand, when buyers purchase based upon emotion, they normally have logical objections. Has the market bottomed yet? Are interest rates going to drop more? Can I really afford this much house? If your clients make an emotional objection, counter with logical data such as interest rates, convenience, space needs, etc. If your clients make a logical objection, counter with the emotional benefits of owning the property.

2. **The Eyes Have It**
   Watching your client's eye movements can reveal a tremendous amount of information about what is happening during the negotiation. To determine whether your clients are accessing a memory or perhaps telling you a lie, watch their eyes. Begin by asking your clients to describe something about their current residence that you can verify. Watch whether their eyes go right or left. The side they use to recall something about their home is the side they use when they are recalling memory. When their eyes go in the opposite direction, there's a high probability that they are being "creative" or not telling the truth.

Your eyes hold other clues as well. When a person nods and their eyes become wider, your message is being well received. If they glare and/or narrow their eyes, it's time to change tactics. If they raise one eyebrow, they don't believe you.

3. **Watch Their Toes**
   Another simple way to tell whether your client is with you or withdrawing from you is to look at where they position their feet, especially if their legs are crossed. If the toe of the leg that is crossed is pointing towards you, the person is with you emotionally. If the toe is pointing away, especially if it's pointing at the door, they may be ready to run from you. In fact, the first time I heard about this approach, I watched the final episode of "The Bachelor." The Bachelor was seated between the two finalists. When it came time to hand out the final rose, this approach correctly predicted his choice. While he was sitting between the two women, his toe pointed to the woman he eventually selected.

4. **Nervous Nellies**
   Negotiations can be stressful for all involved. If your clients are leaning from side-to-side, they are probably bored, opposed to, or disagreeing with what you are saying. Laughing at an inopportune moment, fidgeting, playing with one's hair, tapping a pencil or pen, or wringing hands all indicate tension. So does a red flush, bulging veins, or a tense posture.

5. **Hostility Watch**
   Besides the eyes, here are some other important signals that indicate your client may be feeling hostile. First, if they place their hand in front of their mouth or nose, they may be lying to you. Crossed arms, hands on the hips, hands behind the neck, tapping fingers on the table, or a hands-down handshake indicate resistance or superiority. Clients who lean forward with both the legs and arms crossed, are in a protective stance. Finger pointing or abruptly adjusting their clothing also indicates hostility.

While it may take a little time to master these various ways to more thoroughly understand what your clients are experiencing, it will help you tremendously in terms of communicating more effectively. Regardless of what your clients are doing, be there to support them with the information they need. Also, never forget, it's their house and it's their decision.

Chapter 7
Action Plan

Identify the action steps that you would like to take and rewrite items that may not fit. Circle the number of each strategy that you plan to implement in your business and then record the date you complete the item in the space provided. Make one or two changes at a time. Making too many changes at once can be overwhelming. Integrate the changes one at a time prior to making other changes. Keep in mind that your goal is to find an activity that is both motivating and sustainable over time.

Action Steps:

___ 1. I will take the DISC to determine my personal behavioral style.

___ 2. I will adjust my negotiation style to address my clients' behavioral style.

___ 3. I know my personal preferred sensory modality. Write "V" for Visual, "A" for Auditory, or "K" for Kinesthetic in the space provided: _______

___ 4. When I work with someone who is visual, I will use the words "see" and "look." I will focus on finding properties that have a view or that have visually attractive spaces.

___ 5. When I work with a visual, I confirm verbal discussions in writing.

___ 6. When I work with someone who is auditory, I will use the words "hear" and "sound."

___7. When I work with someone who is auditory, I will verbally review the written contracts to make sure they completely understand all aspects of what they sign.

___8. When I work with someone who is kinesthetic, I will speak more slowly and not rush them.

___9. When I work with someone who kinesthetic, I will make sure that they feel comfortable with all aspects of the transaction.

___10. I pay attention to body language when I work with others and can now communicate more effectively.

Paying attention to behavioral style, sensory modalities, and body language are three important ways to improve your communication and negotiation skills. The next issue to address is how to market your business.

Recipes for Marketing Success

Chapter 8
Make More Dough with a Marketable Real Estate Brand

The road to success is always under construction.
Lily Tomlin

Skills Check:
Put a checkmark (√) next to what you do now. Leave the remaining items blank. Review the action steps at the end of the chapter to determine the strategies that you will implement in your business.

___ 1. My personal brand uses the words "real estate," "homes," "properties," or some other term that indicates I am in the real estate business.

___ 2. I have created a brand that describes who I serve, what I do, and where I do it.

___ 3. My personal brand references the geographical areas where I work or the specific market segments I serve such as estates, new homes, or relocation.

___ 4. I am the recognized expert in at least one market niche.

___ 5. I will change my business cards, advertising, and website so it reflects my new brand and the niches I serve.

___ 6. I have added at least one new niche to my business in the last year.

Knead the Dough Secret #15
People are lousy at remembering names, but they remember functions well. An effective brand describes what you do, who you do it with, and where you do it.

Smart Branding: The Road to Riches

To succeed in today's hypercompetitive environment, you must be able to stand out from the competition. The first step in successful marketing and prospecting is to create an effective brand. An effective brand for any business does each of the following:

1. It is memorable.
2. It immediately brings to mind the product that is being sold.
3. It identifies a specific target market.

Some excellent examples are the "Uncola," the "Ultimate Driving Machine" and the "Breakfast of Champions." Each of these products is easy to identify because their branding meets the three criteria above.

Are You Using the Least Memorable Brand in the Business?

The least effective way to brand your business is to use your name. The reason is that we are constantly bombarded with thousands of names each day—names of people we meet, names in the news, plus hundreds of product and place names.

Memory research demonstrates that "interference" is the primary reason we have trouble remembering names. For example, you can easily recall what you had for dinner last night. This information is stored in your long term memory. In contrast, people normally don't remember what they had for dinner a year ago today. The reason is due to interference—you have had 365 dinners since then. The same thing happens with people's names. We are exposed to so many names each day that the new names interfere with our ability to recall names from the past and vice versa. This is the primary reason it's a poor idea to brand your business with your name. Furthermore, even if the customer remembers your name, they forget 90 percent of what they learned within 24 hours.

For example, if you introduced yourself as "Terry Agent from the John Smith Company," will your listener know what you do or where you do it? Have you told the listener anything that will cause this person to remember you six months from now when they will actually need your services?

If you ever have wondered why your networking activities or other face-to-face interactions do not generate the results you want, branding with your name may be part of the challenge. Here is a list of additional challenges related to branding with your name:

1. If your broker's brand uses a person's name, the client now has two sets of names to recall.

2. Your name does not reference the real estate industry, the specific area you serve, or the niche in which you specialize. There is no way for potential clients to know whether you can assist them in the area where they are looking.

3. Your name is normally not as recognizable as your broker's branding. If you work for a major brokerage, your company spends millions of dollars marketing the company brand. As a result, potential clients are more likely to recall the name of your brokerage rather than your name.

4. Your business is much more difficult to sell or transfer if you use your name in your branding. Furthermore, using your name does not allow you to effectively add other people to your team. For example, the new person on your team could say, "I'm Jim Johnson with the Sally Agent team," but that duplicates the exact problem you're seeking to avoid. By repeating two sets of names, you increase interference and reduce memory.

5. There's nothing memorable about most names. In most cases, the person may remember what you look like and they may even remember the company you work for, but the odds are they won't remember your name. In contrast, the best brands are easy to remember.

6. If you have established your name as an effective brand, keep using it. If you want to add team members or sell your business in the future, however, incorporate the suggestions below. Co-market using your existing brand plus the brand that you will ultimately sell.

What Is the Most Effective Way to Brand My Business?

Assume that you work Scottsdale, Arizona, and your niche is working with golf course properties. In this case, you would introduce yourself as, "Your name from ScottsdaleGolfHomes.com." This branding is more effective for the following reasons.

1. First, is there any question about what business you are in, where you conduct your business, or what your niche is? Unless someone doesn't know where Scottsdale is, it's pretty clear about what you do, where you do it, as well as the location of your target market.

2. While most people are poor at remembering names, remembering what someone does is much easier. To demonstrate this point, the next time you meet someone new, see how well you remember the person one week later. In virtually every case, you will forget the name before you forget the type of work they do.

3. Branding by function also helps you obtain better search engine results. For example, while potential clients may forget your name, they will probably remember that they met someone who helps people buy golf properties in Scottsdale. If they search "Scottsdale golf homes for sale," your name and website should come up. Since most buyers now begin their search on the web, you have greatly increased the probability that your leads will find you even if they don't remember your name.

4. Your personal brand may actually be more effective than your broker's branding because it addresses a specific niche and a specific location. In contrast, your broker's brand lacks this specificity.

5. When a lead comes through your broker's branding, the probability of the lead actually getting to you is poor. In contrast, when it comes through your own branding, the contact will normally reach you. Moreover, if you decide to change companies and have your own phone numbers and website, you can continue marketing just as you have in the past with absolutely no break in the continuity of your marketing efforts. Better yet, if your broker changes their brand due to a merger or a buyout, simply change the logo on your marketing materials and continue doing exactly what you were doing before the change.

6. Using branding that identifies a specific niche also allows you to effectively add new people to your team. Thus, if you add Jim as your buyer's agent, he becomes Jim of the Scottsdale Golf Homes team. The leads that Jim generates will come back to you. More importantly, if Jim leaves the team, he can't take the brand with him. Any leads he developed will still continue to flow to your brand.

Four Simple Steps to Create an Effective Brand

To create a more effective brand for your business, use the next steps. Immediately after this section, you will find a list of niches that you can explore for your business.

1. The first step is to determine what you do and where you do it. In other words, your brand must reference words that show that you're in the real estate business. Some examples are, "real estate," "homes," "estates," "condos," "relocation," or "probate." Identify at least two or three words or phrases that show your business is real estate.

2. Reference the geographical location and/or the market segments that you serve. For example, if you work in a specific geographical area, you may want to select a brand such as BostonCondos.com. You can also brand with the city's name and the type of properties you represent: for example, Atlanta Historical Homes or Chicago Lake Homes.

3. Since people often search based upon zip code, use your zip code in your marketing (e.g., 45462GolfHomes.com or GolfHomes45462.com).

4. The best branding strategy is to combine your geographical location with the specific market segments you serve. Each of the following examples references a specific niche as well as a specific geographical location. Dallas Probate Sales; Scottsdale First Time Buyers; Jonestown Foreclosure Properties; Lake Hills Horse Properties; Westwood Estate Properties; Fort Bragg Military Relocation Services. Make a list of two or three market segments that you serve that you could use to niche your business.

Knead the Dough Secret #16
Big companies will not compete for small chunks of the market.

Get Rich in a Niche

In Marketing Warfare (1986), Reis and Trout argue that the most effective way to compete against large companies is to own a specific market niche. This is especially true on the web. The term "sliver marketing" refers to becoming the go-to expert for a very narrow part of the market.

Many agents already serve a specific geographical niche. There are numerous other niches. The challenge is selecting a niche and then sticking with it. Saying "No," to business outside of your niche can be difficult. Nevertheless, most agents report that their business actually increased when they decided to focus on one or two specific niches rather than trying to serve a wide variety of clients and areas. Your niche should make you feel happy and energized—if it doesn't, you haven't found the right fit.

1. **Activity-based niches**
   Work with people who participate in the same activities you love such as golf, skiing, gardening, or biking. When you prospect by doing activities that you enjoy, it's easier and the results are more sustainable.

2. **Niches based on past careers**
   Create a niche representing people who still work in your former career. For example, if you were a teacher, market to other teachers. If you've been a stay at home mom, consider making stay at home moms your niche. In each case, market yourself based upon the fact that you were "once one of them" and understand their specific needs.

3. **Home-based businesses**
   Due to the run-up in gas prices, an increasing number of both public and private sector employees are telecommuting rather than driving to work every day. To serve this niche, become an expert on the best properties to convert to home offices. Be a resource for reliable contractors, space design specialists, as well as the best places to obtain office equipment. Create your own personal affiliate program that includes other professionals such as attorneys, accountants, and technology specialists.

4. **Baby Boomers**
   Baby Boomers still dominate the listing inventory. Currently, many Boomers are down-sizing from their big family homes. The peak time for Boomers to purchase second homes is between the ages of 50 and 60. The largest part of the Baby Boom generation was born between 1956 and 1964. This means that the second home market should continue to be strong for a number of years to come.

5. **AARP**
   If you are over 50, become the real estate expert for your local AARP Chapter. Working with Grandpa and Grandma may also lead to business with their children and grandchildren.

6. **Couples in transition**
   Couples who are getting married need a variety of services. To specialize in this niche, prospect for affiliates who provide wedding services. If you have nerves of steel, you could also work divorces. Either of these niches will put you in contact with local businesses including decorators, furniture stores, movers, attorneys, etc.

7. **Military**
   People in the military have special needs. Career military people tend to move approximately every three years. For many military families, a bi-weekly mortgage matches their pay schedule as well as assisting them in building equity more quickly since they make the equivalent of an extra payment each year.

8. **Specialized transactions**
   Specialized transactions include foreclosures, HUD, bankruptcy, and trust properties. These niches require special training.

9. **Niches based upon your current lifestyle**
   If you're single, become an expert in properties attractive to singles. If you have young children, develop a niche serving the special needs of young families. If you enjoy riding horses, specialize in equestrian properties.

10. **Religion, politics, and charity**
    The Principles of Attraction say that we attract who we are. Normally it's wise to avoid discussing religion and politics. Nevertheless, people who share our belief systems are more likely to do business with us. The key is to avoid being a secret agent. Let your personal contacts know that you are in the real estate business. An excellent, unobtrusive way to do this is to wear your name badge at meetings. If you're at a ballgame or other casual function, wear a polo shirt, a baseball cap, or sweatshirt with your company logo on it.

11. **Immigrants and minorities**
    Up to 60 percent of first time home buyers today are immigrants, minorities, or foreign nationals. For those who speak English as a second language, many prefer to do business with someone who speaks their native language. On the other hand, some elect to work with an agent who does not speak their language to avoid the spread of gossip about them in their community. If you are fluent in another language, advertise in that language and translate the key pages of your website as well.

12. **Investments**
    Anne Randolph, Founder of *LORE Magazine* and co-author of the *Real Trends Report,* shared her research regarding the investor market at the Luxury Conclave in 2008. Randolph's data indicated that there would be up to 1.65 million sales to second home owners and real estate investors in 2008. Investors don't flip houses; they purchase them and hold them for the long term. In fact, there's an

interesting trend emerging with Gen X and Gen Y buyers. Many are purchasing their first home as an investment property while they continue to rent. This is very different from the previous generations whose primary goal was to buy an owner-occupied, single family residence.

13. "Green" houses

A "green" house is energy efficient and environmentally friendly. Become an expert on money-saving appliances, insulation, heating, and other green solutions. Become active in your local environmental groups as a way to obtain exposure for your services. You could also start a blog and/or social network to discuss environmental issues in your local community.

Putting Your Branding to Work

Once you have your branding, use it on the following marketing materials:

1. Your business card
2. Email signature line or email business cards
3. Your personal page on your company website
4. Your personal website
5. Personal brochure and other marketing material
6. Print advertising
7. Mailers
8. Web marketing including your email newsletter
9. Your blog
10. Any posts that you make on social networking sites such as ActiveRain, Facebook, LinkedIn, RealTown, or Twitter

Be sure to test out your new brand before spending money on new marketing materials. To do this, ask your family, friends, and acquaintances about what you have selected. Specifically, is the brand easy for them to remember? Does your branding make what you do and where you do it more clear to them? If "No," keep working on it until you have created something that works well for you AND for the people you meet. Your goal is to create memorable marketing materials that identify you as being in the real estate business.

Chapter 8
Action Plan

If you plan to spend money on marketing, be smart and create a strong brand. Proper branding and marketing of your business can net you thousands of extra dollars each year.

Begin by identifying the action steps that you would like to take. Rewrite items that may not fit. Remember to circle the number of each strategy that you plan to implement in your business and then record the date you complete the item in the space provided. If you select more than one item, place the items in priority order and work on implementing one item at a time. Your goal is to find an activity that is sustainable over time and that you will feel motivated to do on a regular basis. Once you complete the items you have selected, move on to the next chapter.

Action Steps:

___ 1. I will design a personal brand using the words "real estate," "homes," "properties" or some other term that indicates that I am in the real estate business.

___ 2. I have created a brand that describes who I serve, what I do, and where I do it.

___ 3. In the future, I will use a brand that uses a function rather than my name.

___ 4. My personal brand will reference the geographical areas where I work or the specific market segments I serve such as estates, new homes, or relocation.

___ 5. Rather than trying to serve all aspects of the market, I will create at least one niche in which I specialize.

___ 6. I will change my business cards, advertising, and website so it reflects my new brand.

___ 7. I will add at least one new niche to my business in the next 90 days.

Having a niche is an important way you can differentiate yourself as being uniquely different from other agents. Butch Grimes shares his "You-nique" approach in the next Recipe for Success.

Recipes for Success
"Be You-Nique"
Butch Grimes
WeTalkRealEstate.com

If you want innovative ideas about how to market your listings as well as your business, Butch Grimes is the man to see. Butch has a variety of ways to make his services stand out from competitors. In addition to having his own radio show and launching an Internet radio station, Butch also trains REALTORS® on podcasting and video blogging (vlogging). His approach to working with clients illustrates how you can put fun back into your business while simultaneously generating a considerable number of closed sales. Below, Butch shares several of his Recipes for Success.

To me, real estate is about being "You-nique." In other words, the way to build your business is based upon discovering and using the talents, interests, and abilities that make you different from every other agent in the business. Here are some of the ways that I have fun and make my business "you-nique."

1. **Celebrity of the day**
   When one of my clients is ready to close escrow, I send a limo to take them to escrow to sign their final documents. It's always fun to pick them up at work since it creates considerable buzz among their co-workers. What I really enjoy is seeing the surprised look on their faces. I picked up an elementary school teacher at work one time. Her students couldn't stop talking about the limo. In fact, my clients generally talk about the experience for weeks to come.
   The limo has signage on it that says, "I bought my home through Team Equity today." I have another sign on the back of the car that says, "Chauffeured by Team Equity." In addition, we display signs that promote the lender, the title company, and the escrow company. It's good PR for all of us. I also use the limo at election time to pick up our clients who are unable to drive and take them to the polls. We make this service available to other agents as well. It's a great way to help members of our community who have difficulty getting to the polls.

2. **Open "house" for the kids**
   When my clients close escrow, I let them use my inflatable "jumper house" where the kids can jump and play. The house creates quite a stir in the neighborhood. I always make sure that it is prominently placed on the street so that people can see my logo and contact information. It's great fun for everyone and helps me to market to people at the party as well as those who live in the neighborhood.

To keep the cost down on my inflatable house, I searched for someone who repaired inflatable balloons and inflatable structures. The man I found did it for much less than going through a supplier.

3. **An open house that stands out from all others**
The inflatable house was such a hit that I got to thinking about what would be a fun way to do open house. I came up with an idea that definitely makes our open houses stand out from all others. I had the same man who built my inflatable house create a 30 foot tall inflatable open house sign. Sometimes there are problems when it's windy, but the sign is a great attention getter and generates plenty of open house visitors.

I also wanted to make my open house directional signs stand out. I had a life size photograph taken and then took it to our sign maker. He created a sign that attaches to my regular open house signs. The sign looks as if I'm physically standing in back of the open house directional sign. People driving past my signs always do a double take to see if it's really me.

My "You-Nique" approach to marketing works. I'm always looking for creative and fun ways to build my business. If agents really want to get more business and have more fun, being "You-Nique" is the way to do it.

Chapter 9
Lizard Marketing 101

The reptilian always wins.
Clotaire Rapaille

Skills Check:
Put a checkmark (√) next to what you do now. Leave the remaining items blank. Review the action steps at the end of the chapter to determine the strategies that you will implement in your business.

___ 1. I understand the difference between features and benefits. When I work with my clients, I always seek to uncover the emotional benefits that are motivating them to purchase.

___ 2. My advertising does more than just describing the property; it illustrates what it is like to live there.

___ 3. I understand that marketing is about creating the opportunity to build relationships.

___ 4. When I market my listings, I make a point of appealing to all five senses including taste and smell.

___ 5. I have a strategy for effectively handling angry clients.

Knead the Dough Secret #17
You're not in the real estate business; you are in the business of selling the dream of American home ownership.

Market Benefits, not Features

If someone were to ask you what business you are in, how would you reply? Most agents and brokers would say that "I'm in the real estate business." In truth, you're not selling real estate. Instead, you're selling the dream of American home ownership.

According to Laurence Yun (2007), the Chief Economist from NAR, only five percent of the people in Mexico own their homes. Less than one percent owns their own home in China. In the United States, close to 70 percent of all residents own their own homes. America is a place where dreams of homeownership come true.

When you sell a property, you're not just selling the sticks and the bricks. The physical characteristics of a property such as lot size, bedroom-bath count, floor plan, yard size, and other amenities are examples of features. People never purchase a property based upon features. They purchase because of the emotional benefits they perceive to be attached to those features.

One of the classic scripts in real estate suggests the following approach when a potential lead calls your office and asks whether a particular property has a large backyard:

Is having a large back yard important to you?

This question uncovers whether having a large backyard is a feature that the lead perceives as a benefit. By asking the question first rather than supplying an answer, the agent has an opportunity to explore whether the potential client views the large back yard as a benefit or detriment.

Real estate advertising typically concentrates on features rather than benefits. Consider these two examples describing the same luxury estate:

One-of-a-kind trophy estate located on a beautiful promontory in Aspen. Elegant detail, high ceilings, exquisite moldings, extraordinary inlaid marbles, 3 living rooms, sweeping views, home theater, fully equipped gym, located adjacent to ski lifts. This is a fabulous opportunity to acquire the finest.

In this ad, the focus is on the features of the property. A key point to note is how many adjectives appear in the ad above. Now compare the following ad for the same property:

Enter your personal world of glamour and style at La Montana, a breathtaking new 7 bedroom and 10 bath masterpiece just steps from the lifts in Aspen. Lavishly entertain your guests in the Baronial Public Rooms with 24-foot hand-carved ceilings or adjacent to the sparkling indoor pool overlooking jetliner views of the valley below. After a great day on the slopes, enjoy your state-of-the-art home theater, work out in your fully equipped gym, or unwind in the sauna or steam room. Peace, relaxation, luxury—when you are at home at La Montana, you know that you have truly arrived.

What differences do you observe between the first and the second ad? One important difference is that the second ad gives the reader the sense of moving in to the property. Also, there are far fewer adjectives in the second ad. Jeff Turner of RealEstateShows.com described the challenge with using adjectives:

If you describe a property as having a "really, really, really, lovely pool," then all that the reader or listener remembers is "pool." The way to avoid this is to use verbs rather than adjectives.

The second ad has fewer adjectives and many more verbs. When you write your ads, do your best to break away from the features approach that relies primarily upon nouns and adjectives. Instead, your goal is to paint a picture of what it would be like to live in a specific property.

Another point to note is that Americans are usually under considerable stress. Thus, it's smart to emphasize the lifestyle features that promote relaxation such as a home theater, pool, or luxurious master suite.

Even when a listing has serious problems, there is usually something positive about the property, whether it's the property's fix-up potential, lot size, or nearby schools.

Marketing Secrets from the World's Leading Marketing Guru

Clotaire Rapaille is a French psychiatrist who serves as a marketing consultant to many Fortune 100 companies. His client list includes companies such as Boeing, Folgers, Hummer, plus he serves as a consultant in the U.S. Presidential campaigns. His consulting fee, according to an interview with "Sixty Minutes," is $200,000 per day. His book, *The Culture Code* (2007), explores what motivates people from the U.S. and from Europe to make luxury buying decisions.

In his earlier work, Rapaille outlines many of the principles that he uses with his consulting clients. *The Culture Code* expands on his key points as they apply to various cultures. The next four secrets are based upon Dr. Rapaille's work.

Knead the Dough Secret #18

People don't buy products and services, they buy relationships.

The collaborative model of real estate requires that you work together with your clients, other agents, as well as a host of service providers. The number of transactions that you close is contingent upon how strong your relationship is with each of these individuals.

Most top producers devote a substantial part of their marketing to keeping in contact with past customers. Research from NAR (2007) shows that regardless of how good your relationship is with a particular client, many hire the real estate agent that they have spoken with most recently. To market effectively, you must continue to maintain relationships with past clients as well as constantly generating new business.

Knead the Dough Secret #19
Unlocking the client's buying code results in a sale.

Rapaille argues that each of us has buying triggers. He calls these triggers "codes." In real estate, codes can include the memory of grandmother's fireplace that made you feel warm and cozy. It could be the smell of fresh cinnamon rolls baking. Regardless of what the trigger or code is, when buyers encounter a house that is "on code" for them, there is a high probability that they will purchase it.

According to Rapaille, these codes are both personal and cultural. For example, in the U.S., functional utility is important. We like big garages, big refrigerators, and big stoves. These features are attractive to Americans, but are irrelevant to people from other places in the world. Italians prefer what is beautifully crafted with the best materials. The French prefer something that shows wealth, is useless, and conveys a sense of luxury; hence the $500 Hermes scarves. Neither the Italians nor the French would consider a big refrigerator to be luxurious.

The key buying code for American buyers is "dream." When it comes to real estate, we talk about buying our first home as a "dream come true" or building our "dream home." As mentioned earlier, you're not just selling the sticks and bricks. Based upon Rapaille's work, what you're really selling are the benefits of American home ownership.

Knead the Dough Secret #20
Purchases are based on the reptilian brain rather than the cortex. Primal emotions rule buying decisions—not logic.

According to Rapaille, codes are triggered in the brainstem or the so-called "reptilian brain." The reptilian brain governs eating, sleeping, drinking, and virtually all basic physiological functions. When Rapaille's subjects were asked about what matters to them in the purchase of a particular product, they gave answers that originated in the cortex (i.e., the higher level thinking parts of the brain). When they make a purchase, however, their purchase is governed by codes stored in the reptilian brain. These operate unconsciously. Thus, a buyer may tell us that they want a white traditional house with a white picket fence and buy a redwood contemporary with a red brick wall. The point is that unconscious codes govern buying decisions.

Rapaille has developed a sophisticated technique for uncovering buying codes for various products. His approach is far beyond what agents could do to find out what really motivates their buyers and sellers. One of the key points he makes, however, is the importance of multisensory marketing.

Most real estate marketing is visual. We take pictures and rely on words to describe our listings. Video adds sound, but it still is predominantly visual. In contrast, Rapaille reports that one of the strongest codes or buying triggers is scent. When we market our listings, it's smart to appeal to all five senses, not just to the visual. This means having something ready for visitors to drink (water, juice, coffee, hot chocolate, tea) as well as something to eat. (Chocolates are a great choice due to their ability to raise endorphin levels.)

Since the most often ignored sense in real estate marketing is scent, it's especially important to maximize scent triggers. Cinnamon rolls are one of the most common scents that can tap a positive buying response. Candles and potpourri are other alternatives. If the property has any type of unpleasant smells, be aggressive about eliminating them.

The reason this approach is so important is that our five senses are regulated by the reptilian brain. By using a multisensory approach, you tap into the reptilian brain. As Rapaille puts it, "The reptilian always wins." In other words, we may say what we want from our logical brains, but what we purchase will be based upon the codes stored in our reptilian brain.

Knead the Dough Secret #21

In American culture, "fixing it" increases credibility.

One of the most important aspects of Rapaille's work is distinguishing how Americans differ from other cultures. For example, the Germans and Swiss place tremendous importance on being on time and doing things right the first time. It comes as no surprise that BMW is the only car company to offer a bumper to bumper 50,000 mile warranty. The Japanese also place high value on perfection. The tag line for Lexus is "the relentless pursuit of perfection."

According to Rapaille, both of these approaches are "off code" for the United States. In contrast to Europeans, Americans view perfection as "death." We are not particularly concerned about getting it right the first time. Instead, our functional/utilitarian approach places high value on "fixing it" when things go wrong. Americans forgive fairly easily, provided that the person who made the mistake is willing to take responsibility and make restitution.

In terms of real estate, it's important to note these cultural differences. People from European and Asian cultures often expect their transactions to flow smoothly.

Inform them of the types of challenges they may face in the transaction including delays and mistakes. While this will do little to change their expectations, at least they will know what to expect ahead of time.

Americans understand when things go wrong. According to Rapaille's research, Americans form a higher opinion of you when something goes wrong and you fix it. Thus, the smart approach is to own the mistake and then ask, "What can I do to fix it?" Below you'll find some additional strategies for handling upset clients.

What Is the Best Way to Handle an Angry Client?

No matter how good your connection is with your seller or buyer, there are times when your principals or other people in the transaction may become very angry. The ten steps outlined below will help you cope with virtually any angry client.

1. When your clients become angry, take immediate steps to defuse the situation by first letting go of any need you may have to be right or to win.

2. When a client is yelling, do a "pattern interrupt." This technique comes from Neurolinguistic Programming (NLP). The strategy is to stop the angry behavior as quickly as possible. A pattern interrupt may be asking a seller who is upset about a low offer to get a glass of water for you. When the seller shifts his body position, it can also change his mood. If your client is yelling, an excellent way to create a pattern interrupt is to ask the person to pause for a moment while you obtain a pen and paper to take notes on exactly what the person says.

3. In order to limit your risk, carefully note what any angry client has to say. After doing the pattern interrupt, ask the angry individual to repeat what he or she just said so you can write it down. Then carefully review what you have written down in order to determine whether you have missed anything. Having the individual review what they have already covered usually reduces some of the anger.

4. Next, ask the client to pause. Read back what your client stated in a calm, unemotional tone of voice. This defuses the situation by removing the emotion from what the client says and creates a calming effect.

5. Ask the individual if you wrote down their concerns correctly. Then ask if there is anything else. Stay with the anger until the person has said everything they needed to say. Continue to repeat back what they say in charge neutral.

6. If the anger is directed at you, respond with:

   It was never my intention to make you angry. What can I do to correct the problem?

   Notice there is no acceptance or blame, only an effort on the part of the agent to take steps to correct something that has gone wrong.

7. If the individual is still extremely angry with you, offer to arrange a meeting with your broker/owner/manager.

8. If the anger is directed at someone else, avoid criticizing the other party. Instead, say:

   That's terrible. How can I be of assistance in solving this problem?

9. If you made a mistake don't give excuses or say, "I'm sorry." "I'm sorry" requires an explanation. Use this response instead:

   Forgive me—I made a mistake. What can I do to rectify the situation?

   This puts the power in the hands of the other individual without excuses or rationalizations. It also shows your willingness to take responsibility for your actions.

10. When your client is unjustifiably angry, avoid arguing or trying to prove your point. If you cannot honestly say, "I understand your point of view," at least write down their concerns. Read back what you have written to make sure you captured your client's concerns correctly. In most cases, clients calm down once someone takes the time to listen to them.

Multisensory Staging

Many agents are offering staging services as part of their prelisting package. This is an excellent way to distinguish your services. If you're experiencing a market where there is too much inventory, persuading your sellers to put their property into the best possible condition will help them achieve a higher price in a shorter time.

Knead the Dough Secret #22
Do more than visually stage your properties—tap all five senses.

Most real estate professionals are good at marketing visually. They post virtual tours on their websites, create brochures with multiple pictures, and, in most cases, present the property in the best possible fashion. This is a solid approach since approximately 40 percent of the population is visual. Nevertheless, the other four senses have a powerful influence on the buying decision. To achieve the best results in staging your listings, follow the tips below.

1. **Visual buying**
   In most cases, visual buyers prefer houses that are light and bright. Open floor plans with high ceilings are also desirable. To best serve your visual buyers, make sure that the house is as bright and attractive as possible. Also, have the sellers clear out as much clutter as possible. This is one time when less is more.

2. **Auditory buying**
   Approximately 40 percent of the population is auditory. These people process information most easily when they hear it. Sounds are extremely important to them. When another agent contacts you about showing one of your listings, find out what type of music the buyers enjoy and have it playing when the buyers view the property. If the buyers value peace and quiet, do whatever is necessary to minimize any noise within the property. If there is background noise that you can't eliminate, you may want to consider installing a small fountain. Your goal is to create an auditory background that the buyers will perceive favorably.

3. **Kinesthetic buying**
   For those who are kinesthetic, touch and other physical sensations are the most important. It's critical that your listings are always at a comfortable temperature, no matter what time of year it is. Kinesthetic individuals love to curl up in front of a warm fireplace. In terms of staging, it's usually great to have a fire in the fireplace provided it's not too hot outside. Also, pillows are extremely important in conveying a relaxed atmosphere. Place extra pillows and throws on the sofas, beds, and any other relaxation areas.

4. **Taste buying**
   Frank McKinney (2006), who builds the most luxurious spec homes in the country, defines the "three C's of luxury marketing as being champagne, caviar, and

chocolate." McKinney's niche is building houses with price tags of $30 million and up. While very few agents may elect to serve champagne and caviar at their listings, using taste can be a strong motivator in making a favorable impression. For example, on a hot day, have a variety of cold drinks available for your open house visitors. Chocolate is a good idea as is hot chocolate on a cold day. The only caveat is to be sure that your buyers do not walk around the house eating and leaving a trail of crumbs that stain the carpets.

5. **Aroma buying**
   An often neglected and yet powerful motivator for purchasing is scent. Aromas are one of the quickest ways to tap into the reptilian brain. Use this powerful motivator by baking cinnamon rolls or chocolate chip cookies. (Put the oven on 150 degrees so that you get the aroma, but not a complete baking. One agent who was baking cookies started talking to an open house visitor and forgot the cookies and the oven caught on fire!) Other pleasant aromas include vanilla, freshly ground coffee, fresh bread, and fresh flowers. Be especially diligent in removing any offensive smells.

Chapter 9
Action Plan

Rapaille's approach works. When you market your listings, do your best to create a multisensory experience for the buyers who visit your listings. When you write your marketing materials, focus on using verbs rather than adjectives. Create a sense of what it's like to live in the property rather than just rattling off the bedroom-bath count.

As in previous chapters, identify the action steps that you would like to take. Rewrite items that may not fit. Remember to circle the number of each strategy that you plan to implement in your business and then record the date you complete the item in the space provided. If you select more than one item, place the items in priority order and work on implementing one item at a time. Remember, your goal is to find an activity that is sustainable over time and that you will feel motivated to do on a regular basis. Once you complete the items you have selected, move on to the next chapter.

Action Steps:

___ 1. When I work with my clients, I will focus on discovering the emotional benefits they are seeking when they buy or sell a property.

___ 2. From now on, I plan to focus on what it's like to live in the listings I represent by using fewer adjectives and more verbs in my advertising.

___ 3. I understand that people buy relationships and dreams, not sticks and bricks.

___ 4. When I market properties in the future, I will focus on appealing to all five senses including taste and smell.

___ 5. When a client, agent, or someone else becomes angry with me, I will listen to what they say and write it down. I will then ask "What can I do to fix this situation?"

Marketing is an important component in real estate sales success. If you want to create an effective marketing campaign, follow the suggestions outlined by Jennifer Cummings in the next Recipes for Success.

Recipes for Success
Seven Steps to Create an Effective Marketing Campaign
Jennifer Cummings
JenniferCummings.com

Jennifer Cummings is a brilliant real estate marketing coach. She helped Christina Martinez, America's top-producing real estate agent, increase her commission earnings from $4 million to $7 million in only seven months. Jennifer's story is amazing. She didn't learn to read until she was a teenager and went on to graduate at the top of her college class in economics. In her two upcoming books, Potato Chip Marketing *and* Maid to Millionaire, *Jennifer reveals the secrets of having a rich business and a rich life. Below, she shares her tried and true Recipe for Marketing Success.*

Most real estate agents have advertising campaigns, but very few have effective marketing campaigns. Advertising and marketing are different. "Advertising" creates attention and promotes an image or brand. "Marketing," in contrast, compels someone to buy. Marketing is the number one way to build your business. An effective marketing campaign has seven steps.

1. **Practice "Potato Chip Marketing"**
   Another term for "potato chip marketing" is "give-to-get marketing." Imagine that you are on a reality show. To win $100,000, you must persuade 20 squirrels to eat out of your hand. Your only tool is a bag of potato chips. You are taken to a park and must stay within 100 feet of a park bench. How would attract the squirrels? You certainly wouldn't run out and say, "Here squirrels, come get these potato chips!" That would scare them off. Instead, you would lay out a sequential trail of potato chips to attract them to where you were sitting. They will come to you only when they feel it is safe and that they can trust you.

   Today's clients seek relationship and trust. They want to "try before they buy." Potato chip marketing is about uncovering their needs, building trusting relationships, and providing service before expecting people to do business with you.

2. **Target market**
   When you ask most agents who their clients are, their response is, "Anyone who wants to buy or sell a home." In contrast, effective marketing campaigns target

a specific group. Your message must match your audience. For example, if you were marketing a luxury penthouse, your message would be quite different from the message for a first time buyer.

The next step is to decide what medium you will use. Will it be a postcard, print ad, or a web marketing piece? You must also decide the purpose of your piece as well as the message you want to send. Will you offer a special report or a checklist of pitfalls to avoid? To obtain the information, do they leave a message on your 800 number or can they download the item from your website?

3. **Research your target market's wants and needs**
To generate leads, you must know what makes your target market tick. Search for commonalities. Make it about them. This means doing your research before you begin your marketing campaign. For example, are members of your target market concerned about schools, down payment, or neighborhood safety? As you go through this process, keep in mind that you're not in the real estate business; you are in the problem solving business. The better you are at solving problems and at providing value, the better your business will be.

4. **Develop a hook**
A "hook" is a headline or hot button. Because we're constantly bombarded with advertising, it's important to cut through the clutter. You only have one or two seconds to grab their attention. The Reticular Activating System (RAS) is the brain's screening mechanism for what receives attention. While your subconscious can process up to a billion bits of information, you can only consciously pay attention to about 15 bits. A great hook cuts through the clutter and captures their attention. Some examples are, "Save up to $100,000 on Your Next Mortgage!" and "Avoid The Seven Most Expensive Mistakes Sellers Make."

5. **Keep them reading**
If the piece is about you, readers will toss it. Instead, engage them in "coffee talk." This means to write the way that you speak. Aim for the seventh grade level. "Coffee talk" copy is salesmanship in print. It's about your customers and speaks to them in an easy, conversational tone.

6. **Layout to stand out**
"Legibility" refers to the "quality of print that can be easily read." "Readability" refers to the "quality of language that makes it easy to understand." Use short paragraphs, bullet points, headlines, and sub headlines to keep the eye engaged.

7. **You must have a call to action**
   What differentiates advertising from marketing is a call to action. Prospects are begging to be lead! Remember, they want to try before they buy. On the other hand, they don't want to talk to you. Make it safe for them to contact you by creating a free hotline where they can order a special report or a checklist that will help them with their sale or purchase. You can also make the same offer online.

Ultimately, service is at the heart of attraction. We are paid according to the value we give. Get excited about creating value for your clients and being the resource to solve their problems. When you approach your business with a give-to-get mindset, you'll never want for business.

Lead Generation: Tried and True Recipes for Success

Chapter 10
Take the Best and Forget the Rest

There are things that we never want to let go of, people we never want to leave behind. But keep in mind that letting go isn't the end of the world, it's the beginning of NEW life.
Source Unknown

Skills Check:
Put a checkmark (√) next to what you do now. Leave the remaining items blank. Review the action steps at the end of the chapter to determine the strategies that you will implement in your business.

___ 1. I have evaluated my business to uncover my strongest profit centers and am working on expanding them.

___ 2. When farming or some other real estate activity doesn't produce a profit for me, I stop doing it and experiment by doing something else.

___ 3. I have an 800 Call Capture system that I use on listing appointments to demonstrate how it converts more leads.

___ 4. I use my 800 Call Capture system to help convert expired and For-Sale-by-Owner Listings.

___ 5. My business card is easy to read and has no more than two phone numbers on it—my office phone and one line that I always answer.

___ 6. I always keep my brochure boxes well stocked.

___ 7. I prospect my referral database and past client list by providing them with items of value such as discount cards, energy saving light bulbs, or ways for their home to be more energy efficient.

___ 8. If the market is declining, I give people in my sphere, referral database, or farm area information on how to get their property taxes lowered.

___ 9. My mailing materials stand out from the crowd because they are unusual and/or highly creative.

___10. I regularly update past clients on changes in their property value.

What Is the Best Way to Generate Leads?

The answer to this question is surprisingly simple. The best way to generate leads is to find an activity that you love to do that puts you in front of buyers and sellers. This doesn't necessarily have to be a real estate related activity. Thousands of agents have built businesses by being active in their children's schools, participating in networking activities, or even playing golf two days a week. The critical factor is to uncover which real estate lead generation activities are sustainable for you.

An excellent place to begin is by looking at your last 12 months in the business and examining which activities generated the most transactions for your business. While most people recommend becoming a listing agent, if you made more money by working with buyers, consider focusing on building a buyer based business. If you obtained more business from doing open houses, hold more open houses.

As part of this process, it's also smart to examine what did not work. Are you farming with no results? Are you knocking on doors and not getting any leads? If so, drop the activities that don't generate income. Again, a key point in becoming a successful agent is to focus on your strengths, not on what you don't do well. Furthermore, because something works for someone else, doesn't mean that it will work for you. Be willing to experiment, find what invigorates you, and track what is profitable. Focus on what you do well and dump or delegate the rest.

The Best of the Tried and True

What really works today? The web has revolutionized how we do business. Even so, many of the old stand-bys are just as effective today as they have been for the last twenty years. Subsequent chapters deal with open houses, referrals, expired listings, and For-Sale-by-Owners (FSBOs). Here are some additional "tried and true" ways to build your business.

Knead the Dough Secret #23
Don't just talk about your call
capture system—demonstrate it.

1. **Call Capture (IVR or Interactive Voice Recognition Systems)**
No matter what type of market you're in, this tried and true approach really works. Call capture systems typically give you an 800 number plus 1,000 extensions. You assign different extensions to your sign, brochures, print ads, and web ads. This allows you to track which ads work as well as where you obtain the most leads. People are more likely to call to hear a pre-recorded message than they are to call you.

This is a powerful tool for converting more listings. Simply leave a message on your system before your listing appointment. Explain to your sellers how most offices fail to obtain the phone number from up to 90 percent of the people who call their office. Then ask, "Would you like to see how I capture up to 95 percent of the calls on my listings?" Next, have them call your pre-recorded message. As the sellers listen, turn on your cell phone. Within seconds after they hang up, your phone will ring. Hand it to them and ask, "Do you recognize this number?" If they ask how you got their unlisted phone number, reply by saying, "Because I paid for the call, I'm entitled to your contact information." This approach also avoids problems with the "Do Not Call List" because you can document that the caller contacted you first.

When owners of expired listings or FSBOs lack access to call capture, you have a powerful way to help them understand why their property did not sell. It's also a great way to convince them to list with you.

Call capture systems have additional advantages. A Proquest Technology study of 25,000 buyers who called an agent's call capture system, found that 33 percent had listed or sold a piece of real estate in the last 60 days. Call capture also increases the response to your print advertising. According to NAR (2007), 73 percent of the buyers and sellers do business with the first agent they contact. Call capture can make you that first agent.

2. **Make your business cards stand out**
Most agents put their picture on their business cards, as well as a website address, an email address, and several phone numbers. The result is that many clients have trouble reading the small print. Use large print for your contact information and save your customers' time by having all calls forwarded to a single number. To distinguish your card from those of competitors, place a picture of one your listings on the back of your card. (Be sure to check with your brokerage about any requirements they may have about trademarks and company logos.) One agent placed a picture of the changing of the leaves in the Rocky Mountains. Much to his surprise, not only did his business increase, this picture attracted buyers with 750+ credit scores.

3. **Keep your brochure boxes well stocked**
   Steve Kantor (BestAgentBusiness.com) surveyed over 1,000 homeowners about the types of agent marketing pieces they liked and disliked. They liked brochure boxes, especially if the back of the brochure had information about other listings. On the other hand, they resented having to call the agent to find out the price or other key features. They also said most agents did a poor job of keeping their boxes stocked.

4. **Magnets**
   A substantial majority of people who responded to Kantor's study said that they enjoyed receiving magnets from agents, especially if it had important information such as emergency service phone numbers or the local high school's sports schedule.

Knead the Dough Secret #24
Be unique and use give-to-get marketing to stand out from the crowd of other agents.

5. **Give-to-get marketing**
   Items to consider include discount cards, energy saving light bulbs, coupons, and lifestyle tips. The more closely tailored the item is to the community and people's interests, the more likely they are to appreciate it. One caveat: several people indicated that they did not enjoy having a flag placed in their front yard or a pumpkin delivered to their doorstep.

6. **An Equity Check or an Annual Report**
   Erica West of Fountain Hills, Arizona, uses what she calls an "equity check-up." You have your car checked at least twice year, you see your dentist and your doctor for regular check-ups, isn't it a good idea to have the equity in your home checked? You can make this offer in both your print and your web advertising.

   An Annual Report is a CMA with pictures and property information for all sales in your area. This is an excellent item to send once or twice a year. One of the best times to do it is around tax time. It can be an especially useful tool in helping owners to lower their property taxes.

   For example, if the area where you are working has experienced a price decline, provide a letter to the recipients of your Annual Report that explains how to obtain a reduction in their property taxes. Be sure to include the appropriate contact information for the department that sets property evaluations. A letter from you explaining how much homes have declined in value would also be useful. You can also use online evaluation tools from Realtor.com, Zillow.com, and MoveUp.com if they support a lower price.

7. **Highly targeted, creative mailing pieces**
   Frances Flynn Thorsen had tremendous success with two highly creative mailing pieces. One of her listings was a charming house in a commercial area, perfect for an attorney's office. She prepared a marketing piece that looked as if it was a lawsuit. The attorney to whom it was addressed was the defendant. The attorneys who opened it loved it. She had an amazing response from the piece and sold the property quickly. She used a similar approach with doctors, except this time the mailing piece looked as if it was a sample from a pharmaceutical company.

8. **Updates from your agent**
   In Steve Kantor's study (described in the next Recipe for Success) an overwhelming majority of respondents said how much they enjoyed the fact that the agent who listed or sold their home kept them updated on sales information for their neighborhood. They also appreciated receiving useful information such as how to save money on their utility bills or how to winterize their homes.

Chapter 10
Action Plan

Obtaining an 800 Call Capture system can be an excellent way to expand your business. Because most offices still rely on agents to answer telephone inquiries, 90 percent of their telephone leads are lost. In contrast, your system will capture up to 95 percent of the phone inquiries on your ads, signs, and website. Other tried and true methods are as effective today as they were years ago.

As in previous chapters, identify the action steps that you would like to take. Rewrite items that may not fit. Remember to circle the number of each strategy that you plan to implement in your business and then record the date you complete the item in the space provided. If you select more than one item, place the items in priority order and work on implementing one item at a time. Remember, your goal is to find an activity that is sustainable over time and that you will feel motivated to do on a regular basis. Once you complete the items you have selected, move on to the next chapter.

Action Steps:

___ 1. I have identified my two strongest profit centers and am working on expanding them.

___ 2. I have eliminated at least one unprofitable real estate activity from my business and am experimenting with something new to take its place.

___ 3. I have set up an 800 Call Capture system for my business and have used it on at least one listing appointment.

___ 4. I can explain how my 800 Call Capture system helps owners of expired and For-Sale-by-Owner listings get their properties sold faster.

___ 5. My business card is easy to read and has no more than two phone numbers on it—my office phone and one line that I always answer.

___ 6. I always keep my brochure boxes well stocked.

___ 7. I regularly market using a give-to-get strategy that provides my clients with items of value before expecting them to do business with me.

___ 8. In the future, I will help people in my sphere, farm area, or referral data base to obtain property tax reductions if their property has declined in value.

___9. I have altered my mailing materials so that they stand out from the materials sent by other agents.

__10. I have updated my past clients with the most recent changes in their property value.

Steve Kantor's research reveals the best of the "tried and true." In the next Recipe for Success, he shares additional tips that still work as well as strategies that are no longer effective with today's consumers.

Recipes for Success
Who Do They Think They Are—Movie Stars?

Steve Kantor
BestAgentBusiness.com

When Steve Kantor sold his Client Relationship Management Company, he turned his attention to real estate. His sister was an agent and Steve became interested in discovering what characteristics billion (not million) dollar producers had in common. His book, Billion Dollar Agent—Lessons Learned, *is a series of revealing interviews about what makes America's top performing agents tick.*

In late 2007, Steve began researching the type of mailing materials people were receiving from agents. Steve's company, BestAgentBusiness.com, provides virtual assistants to the real estate industry. His goal was to uncover what works and what doesn't work.

What you're about to read will probably surprise you. It may make you angry. The point to remember, however, is that we must adapt and communicate with our clients in the way they would like us to communicate with them. Based upon Best Agent Business' research, here are the strategies to avoid as well as additional tips to stand out from the crowd.

1. **Cold calling: put it on ice**

   All but one person who responded to the question about cold calls had the same response:

   > *I HATE getting phone calls from agents. It made me less inclined to want to use that agent. Letters telling me they'd love to work with us also just went in the trash.*
   >
   > *Phone calls are largely ineffective as I consider them an interruption. I generally do not have time to discuss any sort of real estate over the phone.*
   >
   > *The phone calls are a waste of time, because to me, if I were interested in selling I would contact them.*
   >
   > *The phone calls are not effective because he never offers to do anything; no suggestions on how he could help, just "I am a real estate agent, and I am alive."*

2. **The biggest money waster: postcards with your picture on them**
Research from SHR, one of the major brand management firms in the country, shows that when you send a postcard with your picture on it to someone's home, you are essentially an uninvited guest. The result: you and your postcard go in the trash. The comments below illustrate how poorly this type of marketing material is received. In terms of postcards with pictures:

   They are totally useless. Photographs of agents are especially irrelevant to their purpose.

   I'm also really turned off by cards and brochures that feature your spouse, kids, church affiliations, etc.

   Why do agents always have to include their picture—who do they think they are? Movie stars?

   Offers for free home evaluations? I just toss those too.

3. **Door knocking: dead as a doornail?**
Like telephone calls, many people view door knocking by agents as an intrusion. Also, some voiced concerns about the safety issues of opening their door to someone they don't know. Here is a typical comment.

   The door knockers are annoying, I don't like having my home ID'd (identified) as not being at home.

4. **Pay attention to your marketing materials**
Many renters commented on the fact that agents had not taken the time to determine if they were owners. Target marketing works well, provided that you send materials to people who are members of that target. One way to do this is through a "list" company. For a fee, usually less than 25 cents per name, they will provide you with an updated list of current mailing addresses.

5. **What they liked**
Additional popular items include business cards that doubled as discount cards as well as coupons. Many large companies provide free coupons that you can print out or send electronically to your clients. Clients also like unusual closing gifts, such as an engraved door knocker. They also enjoy information on how to make your house more green, plus small tokens of appreciation such as energy saving light bulbs.

Chapter 11
Open Up to Open House!

A house is home when it shelters the body
and comforts the soul.
Phillip Moffitt

Skills Check:
Put a checkmark (√) next to what you do now. Leave the remaining items blank. Review the action steps at the end of the chapter to determine the strategies that you will implement in your business.

___ 1. I door knock to invite neighbors and residents of move-up areas to my open houses.

___ 2. When I door knock, I give each person a written invitation to the open house as well as a property brochure.

___ 3. I always have several good buys to share with open house visitors that are not being held open.

___ 4. I am able to obtain accurate contact information from most open house visitors.

___ 5. I hold "Invite-a-friend" open houses and/or private open houses for the neighbors.

The Truth about Open House

While the probability of selling the house you are holding open is only 2 percent, a well-planned and executed open house allows you to prospect for listings, locate buyers, and gather names for your prospecting database.

Knead the Dough Secret #25
Waiting for the phone to ring or for a client to walk into an open house is no longer a viable way to build your real estate business.

The Two Million Dollar Open House Prospecting Script

When it comes to traditional marketing and prospecting, waiting for the business to come to you meant that someone else determined how many leads you generated. The best traditional marketing approaches are proactive rather than reactive. In other words, you actively search for leads (proactive) rather than waiting for leads to come to you (reactive). If you still hold traditional open house, here's a tried and true Recipe for Success.

You will need a printed invitation and a color property brochure. The goal is to deliver the invitations to at least 20 neighbors prior to the open house. Research shows that the best time to deliver these is on Saturday morning from 9:00 to noon.

A number of years ago a woman who was in our new agent training decided to go prospecting for her open house in Bel Air (adjacent to Beverly Hills). The terrain is quite hilly. Nevertheless, she put on her high heels and her business suit and began door knocking. When someone answered the door at one of the houses, she couldn't remember the script. What she did say was, "We're having an open house—we're serving refreshments—can you please come?" The result: she obtained a $2,000,000 listing. Here's the script:

The Two Million Dollar Open House Script

Strategy: Invite neighbors and residents of move-up areas to your open house using a written invitation and a property brochure. Make sure that you have your business card attached to the brochure for the property. Attaching an invitation to the brochure is also a definite plus.

Agent: *Good morning, my name is ________ from ABC Realty. Mr. and Mrs. Jones have asked me to personally invite you to their open house at 123 Main Street on Sunday from 1:00-4:00 PM. We'll be serving refreshments—will you be able to attend?*

Listen to their response. If "Yes,"

Agent: *I look forward to seeing you on Sunday.*

If the prospect says, "No,"

Agent: *Do you know anyone who would like to move into your area?*

No matter what their response is, thank them for their time.

This simple script is one of the most effective ways to prospect for new listings. Imagine that you knock on a homeowner's door who has just decided to move to a new location. Regardless of how many postcards they have received from other agents they know, most people list with the person they have seen face-to-face most recently. The next issue to address is how to obtain good contact information.

Knead the Dough Secret #26
Hold traditional open house during the week around the time that school ends each day. Make sure that your open house is en route to the school. Have plenty of water, coffee, and some chocolate for parents who drop by.

How to Generate More Traditional Open House Leads

Strategy 1: Greet your visitors and have them sign the guest register
A simple approach is to say, "Good afternoon. I'm Bernice Ross of ABC Real Estate and your name is?" If the visitor appears to be American, extend your hand. Please note that people from the Middle East and Asia find touching hands with a stranger to be inappropriate.

Strategy 2: Obtain a valid name and phone number
One of the easiest ways to obtain a valid phone number is to have a drawing for movie tickets, a gift basket, or gift coupon. Some visitors may not want to sign the guest register. Gently remind them that the sellers have requested that all visitors to their home sign the register. If the visitors still refuse to sign ask, "If you were holding your house open, wouldn't you want the names of people who were in your home?"

Strategy 3: Ask questions
For example, "What attracted you to stop by this open house?" If they live in the neighborhood, ask about what they like about the local area. If the open house visitors are considering buying, ask about other properties they have seen.

Strategy 4: Be prepared with your Switch List
A "switch" is a well priced listing that is not open. Your Switch List can include foreclosures, probates, as well as properties priced 20 to 40 percent less than the property you are holding open. Be sure to have additional properties with different bedroom-bath counts. You can motivate the buyer to work with you by saying,

To the best of my knowledge, none of these properties is open today. However, if you're interested in seeing any of these properties, I would be happy to set up an appointment to view them.

This is an effective approach provided that your area has open house traffic. Many agents have been reporting a decline in traditional open house traffic. It may result from the slowing market or the large number of properties available on the web. Fortunately, there are three new approaches that you can use to generate open house traffic that will far exceed this more traditional approach.

Invite-a-Friend Open House

Would you like 25 or more personal introductions to your seller's friends and acquaintances in a single day? If so, an "Invite-a-Friend Open House" is an excellent way to generate new business as well as to aggressively market the seller's listing. You will cater the open house, handle the invitations, and host the gathering. To host an Invite-a-Friend open, have your sellers put together a guest list of the people they would like to invite. You can hold this on a Saturday afternoon or in the evening. Each invitee is asked to invite other friends who may be interested in purchasing the seller's property. The steps are outlined below:

1. Discuss the Invite-a-Friend Open House as part of your Premium Marketing Plan during your listing appointment.

2. Have the sellers identify their guest list and set the open house date 14 to 21 days in the future.

3. Send printed invitations to each invitee with an RSVP. Be sure to ask them to "Invite a friend" who would be interested in seeing the house. You can also send an email invitation with an email RSVP as well.

4. Contact each invitee 48 hours prior to the open house to confirm their attendance and that they have directions. To simplify this task, consider using a voice to text system such as Jott.com that allows you to record a message and then send it out to multiple users as a text, email, or MP3 file (i.e., audio recording).

5. Have a top-notch caterer handle the event so that you are available to meet people. Wear your name badge and have cards handy. Do not attempt to market your services. You want people to get to know you and form a personal connection. This is the foundation for doing business in the future. You should be prepared to discuss business when asked.

6. After the event, personally thank each person for attending. The next step is to make an offer of service. For example, "As you know, properties in some areas have declined in value. In certain cases, this can result in a reduction in property taxes. Would you be interested in receiving an update on your home's value to see if you qualify to save money now?"

7. When the sale closes, send a picture to all guests of the sellers in front of their new home. If possible, include their testimonial on your behalf as well.

Neighborhood Open House

This follows similar guidelines to the Invite-a-Friend Open House, except this time you invite the neighbors. Here are the key differences:

1. The seller should not be present for a Neighborhood open house. This may discourage people from attending. Explain to your seller that the neighbors will come snooping anyway; why not capitalize on their curiosity and see whether they know someone who would be interested in purchasing?

2. Use printed invitations, preferably that you deliver by door knocking. You can mail them or email them, but this is not as effective. On the invitation, encourage recipients to invite anyone they know who may be interested in the property.

3. Prepare a stack of updated Comparable Market Analyses for the area. Use a nice picture from the local area as the cover sheet. If prices have gone down in your area, provide your visitors with the forms and information necessary to apply for a reduction in their property taxes.

4. Serve a variety of refreshments.

5. You may want to conduct a drawing for a gift basket or movie tickets as a way to get good contact information from your attendees.

6. Be sure to follow up by telephone, in writing, or electronically to see whether your open house visitors know someone who may be interested in purchasing as well as to say thank you for their attendance.

Social Networking Open House

If you have been wondering what happened to attendance at open houses in your area, the way that you are marketing your open house might be to blame. If you are relying on directional signs and the newspaper to market your open houses, you are missing a huge percentage of potential buyers.

In 2007, NAR reported that the median age of real estate agents was 51 while the median age for first time buyers was 32. Depending on the market in your area, you can still use traditional techniques to market to people born before 1964. On the other hand, if you rely exclusively on newspapers, you will miss reaching Gen X and Gen Y, since they don't read the paper.

Frances Flynn Thorsen describes the steps that she uses to hold open houses through social networking sites such as Point2Agent, ActiveRain, Realtor.com, or LinkedIn. Other sites include MySpace, Facebook, Zillow, and Craigslist.

The process is simple. Post information about properties currently listed in specific zip codes or neighborhoods. If you take a listing, post pictures as well as a video to maximize the number of people who will see the listing. Invite neighbors to comment about the area.

In terms of holding open house, include the dates and times that the house will be open. Also include information about the cost of purchasing, where to find the best loans, as well as other pertinent information that will be useful to buyers.

When Fran did her open house, she had an amazing response from this approach. All the visitors had seen the house online, liked the video and photos, and opted to see the house in person.

CAVEAT: When promoting a social networking open house, avoid promoting yourself or your business. Stay focused on what the consumer wants. You will lose most potential buyers if they see a blatant commercial for you. Instead, invite them over for refreshments at your open house to see if this home is the right one for them or for someone they know.

The Caravan Bus

In those areas where there is too much inventory on the market, some agents are renting a bus and taking buyers out to look at the best buys in different areas. This approach creates an auction atmosphere and can motivate buyers to take action.

A slightly different approach is to schedule a progressive open house where each property is open for 15 to 20 minutes. A great strategy is to serve appetizers at the first few houses and dessert at the last house. The benefit is that you can hold multiple opens the same day and you're not wasting your time waiting for someone to show up. You can do this for the general public or for brokers.

Chapter 11
Action Plan

Open house is one of the best ways to build your business, provided that you actively prospect for leads prior to the open house. Sadly, most agents place their signs out and hope that the open house will generate leads. This technique can generate leads, but it's not as effective as proactively searching for potential buyers for your listings.

Identify the action steps that you would like to take and rewrite items that may not fit. Circle the number of each strategy that you plan to implement in your business and then record the date you complete the item in the space provided.

Remember, making too many changes at once can be overwhelming. Instead, make one or two changes at a time. Integrate these changes before making any other changes. Keep in mind that your goal is to find an activity that is both motivating and sustainable over time.

Action Steps:

___ 1. I will door knock to invite neighbors and residents of move-up areas to my open houses.

___ 2. When I door knock, I will give each person a written invitation to the open house as well as a property brochure.

___ 3. I will use the $2 million Open House Prospecting Script when I door knock.

___ 4. I will use Invite-a-Friend Open House to build my referral database.

___ 5. I will hold private neighborhood open houses.

___ 6. I will promote my open houses by posting pictures, videos, and other important data on social networking sites.

___ 7. I will hold progressive open houses.

Are you interested in learning more about multi-sensory marketing? If so, the next Recipe for Success reveals the power of chocolate.

Recipes for Success
Mmmm—Chocolate

Wanda Bolint, a former trainer at Jon Douglas Company in Southern California, pioneered a number of effective ways to use a multisensory approach to market her services. Wanda often baked cookies in different shapes (a heart for Valentine's Day or a Christmas tree at the holidays), placed them on a Popsicle stick, wrapped them in cellophane, and tied them with a pretty bow or ribbon. She always attached her business card as well. This approach made her marketing materials stand out from people who were just handing out cards or sending out postcards.

Wanda also created "Showcase Open House." In a Showcase Open House, several agents hold one house open. The Showcase house was always notable in some respect as well as having excellent curb appeal.

A lender would attend to qualify clients and a title representative would explain the title process. The agents jointly marketed the Showcase Open.

At the Showcase Open, they had plenty of refreshments plus fun activities for the kids. If a client wasn't interested in the Showcase Property, the agents would rotate and take the visitors to see the other company listings that were not being held open.

This strategy also employs multisensory marketing. People are curious and will often show up at a house if there is free food. (This is especially true of the brokerage community.) When you appeal to all five senses, especially smell and taste, you greatly increase the probability of tapping the reptilian anchors for purchasing.

The most innovative way that Wanda used the multisensory approach was in confronting transaction problems. Wanda was proactive in preparing her clients for challenges long before they actually happened. Once she placed a property under contract, she would personally deliver a box of four chocolates to each of her clients. She would then tell them to take the first chocolate out of the box and to enjoy it.

> *This is to remind you how sweet it will be the day that your transaction closes and you move into your new home. About 95 percent of the time, our transactions encounter problems that may cause them not to close. It's important for you to know that about 90 percent of the time we actually close these transactions. So when there's a problem, I'm going to call you and tell you to take out the box of chocolates and enjoy one. That's the reminder to remember how sweet the day you move into your new house will be. Then we'll talk about how we're going to solve the challenge that we're facing so that we can make sure that you can enjoy the last piece of chocolate in your new home.*

Anchoring moving with the sweetness of chocolate and the good feelings associated with the day that the clients signed the contract taps into the reptilian anchors that will motivate the client to stay in the transaction. Chocolate is almost universally perceived as a reward. Furthermore, chocolate releases beta endorphins, the brain's response to pleasant stimuli. Thus, to minimize the negative reaction to problems in your transactions, consider using taste as an anchor to what is sweet and pleasing. Establishing this relationship before a problem occurs will help you resolve it more quickly. Keep in mind what Rapaille says, "The reptilian always wins."

Chapter 12
Whip up a Bowl of Referral Dough

Pretend that every single person you meet has a sign around his or her neck that says, "Make me feel important." Not only will you succeed in sales, you will succeed in life.
Mary Kay Ash

Skills Check:
Put a checkmark (√) next to what you do now. Leave the remaining items blank. Review the action steps at the end of the chapter to determine the strategies you will implement in your business.

___ 1. I have a referral database that has at least 100 people in it.

___ 2. I use a real estate database management program such as Top Producer, Sharper Agent, or Wise Agent to manage my referral database.

___ 3. I use "give-to-get" marketing when building my referral base.

___ 4. I enjoy connecting people in my referral database with each other, especially when they share a mutual interest or can help each other build their business.

___ 5. When someone refers me business, I always thank them immediately with a phone call, a handwritten thank you note, and a token of appreciation.

Knead the Dough Secret #27
Expecting people to send you referrals before providing them with service is like asking your car to run without any gas.

Wanted: A New Referral Strategy for the 21st Century

Building a strong referral network can be one of the quickest ways to build a sustainable business. The issue is how to do it. For the last 20 years, postcards and letters coupled with an "item of value" such as a coupon, informative newsletter, or some other token of appreciation, worked well for thousands of agents.

While the traditional way of doing business still works with older clients, these strategies are generally not effective for Gen X and Gen Y. The next generation of buyers and sellers communicates by texting and social networking. They want to get to know you online before they will contact you about doing business with them. Furthermore, Gen X and Gen Y often view handwritten notes, postcards, and letters as being antiquated leftovers from the 20th century. An "Oh-by-the-way" snail mail letter or postcard to this group is a waste of money. In addition to these challenges, there are other issues with the traditional referral model as well.

Challenges with the Traditional Referral Model

Using the referral model does not let you control your lead generation. There are five specific issues:

1. The person making the referral must remember to ask the lead if they would like the name of someone who can help them buy or sell a piece of real estate.

2. The lead must not be working with another agent.

3. The lead must have enough trust in the person making the referral that they will be willing to talk to you.

4. The lead must have no challenges with you possibly saying something about their behavior or their financial condition to the person who made the referral.

5. The lead must feel comfortable enough with you to hire you.

The person's willingness to make a referral is also an issue. There are eight reasons people may not refer you business:

1. They forget. Being face-to-face or interacting regularly with them online counteracts this.

2. They are reluctant to make a recommendation on someone else's behalf.

3. They don't want to become involved in someone else's business.

4. The referral is a difficult person.

5. They are afraid if they make a referral and something goes wrong, it will cost them a relationship.

6. The person has referred someone to you in the past and you did not live up to their expectations.

7. You didn't keep the person who gave you the referral up to date on their referral's progress.

8. The person you referred expressed disappointment about the level of service you provided.

Furthermore, the referral model is passive rather than active. "Passive" means that you are waiting for someone else to come to you to do business. In contrast, active prospecting such as calling on expired listings or calling on For Sale by Owners yields a consistent number of leads over time. The number of leads you generate is totally under your control. The more people you talk to, the more leads you generate.

Based upon these challenges, should you forget about the referral model? Absolutely not! The new model for the 21st century incorporates the best of the old with Attraction and the Five Laws of Stratospheric Success.

The Best of the Old

To work by referral, you must have a referral network. To begin building your referral database, you will need a real estate database or CRM (Client Relationship Management) system. The most widely used systems in the real estate business include Top Producer, Sharper Agent, Wise Agent, and Agent 2000.

To begin building your personal referral database, identify as many people as possible in each of the following categories.

1. Whom do I know from my old job? This includes former employers, former employees, trade or professional associates, former customers, and even former competitors.

2. Whom do I know because I went to a certain school, high school, or college? This includes schoolmates, high school classmates, college classmates, fraternity/sorority friends, or your local alumni club.

3. Whom do I know because I have a particular hobby or enjoy a particular sport such as golf, reading circles, genealogy, investment clubs, skiing, music, photography, etc.?

4. Whom do I know from doing charity or public service work?

5. Whom do I know because of my religious/spiritual involvement?

6. Whom do know because I own my home? This includes former or present neighbors, the service people with whom you do business such as a gardener, painter, pest control, etc.

7. Whom do I know because of my daily experience? Over the course of the day, each of us comes in contact with a host of service providers such as salespeople, mechanics, doctors, dentists, etc.

8. Whom do I know through my family? For example, people who work with your spouse, family members, teachers, other parents, sports coaches, dance or music instructors.

Once you finish this list, most people have about 100 to 150 names. To reach the goal of identifying 250 to 300 people, the next step is to go to the Yellow Pages and look at the different services listed. Ask yourself, whom do you know that provides these services? You can also use the same approach with the white pages to determine the people you know whose names start with a particular letter.

Here is the most important step. Before you contact any of these people, ask yourself, "What can I do for them?" This could be providing an Annual Report with information about current prices in their neighborhood, a report on how to winterize their home, or some other item of value. Unlike the old school approach that says, "Oh by the way, if you know of anyone who is thinking about buying or selling a home, I'm never too busy for your referral," this approach uses give-to-get marketing.

Bob Burg, in his book *Endless Referrals* (2006), provides a great example. Imagine that you're attending a Chamber of Commerce meeting where they are conducting a standard business card exchange. Stand by the food and drinks and notice which individuals talk to the most people. These are usually the influencers in the room.

They will eventually come to where you are standing. When they do so, smile, introduce yourself, and ask for their card. Do NOT offer your card unless asked for it.

Ask them to tell you about themselves and their business, how they got into the business, as well as how their services are different from those provided by their competitors. If they mention a real estate opportunity, don't attempt to close on your services. Make the conversation entirely about them. The odds are you'll be the one person they remember.

Burg's next question is the most important. "How would I recognize when someone is a good client for your services?" Burg's philosophy is that you earn the right to receive referrals when you have established trust and have demonstrated a willingness to help others build their business with your referrals.

To use this approach when you are at a networking event, introduce two people that you have met. When you introduce them, share what each of them does. Then excuse yourself and let them have their own conversation. Guess who will be at the center of it—that nice person, "you," who introduced them to each other.

If you are in a social situation with non-business people, inquire about their children, their hobbies, or recreational activities. If you have a strong referral network, connecting people in your network who share similar interests is a wonderful way to expand your business.

If you are holding a client appreciation event or are making a special offer to your referral database, invite the new people that you meet to participate as well. Your approach will make you stand out from competitors because you gave first.

Gen X and Gen Y want to get to know you online. Your "give-to-get" strategy can include sharing resources, engaging in conversations, and providing service. Avoid pitching your services. Young people want to know about you. Then they will decide whether they want to do business with you.

By the way, there's one important point to note here. The people you serve may not be the ones who send you business. The referral may come from someone who had nothing to do with these people. According to the Laws of Attraction and the Five Laws of Stratospheric Success, it's the act of giving that triggers the referral. Where it comes from is unimportant.

Once you have added someone to your database, stay in contact. Continue to provide service. If they send you a referral, thank them immediately with a token of your appreciation. Thank them again when the transaction closes. Remember, the greatest gift you can give is yourself.

When you call people and tell them you are working on building your business by referral, your focus is on you. In contrast, Burg's approach succeeds because it's based upon providing service and building a connection based upon trust and giving back. According to Burg, this is the secret of "endless referrals."

Chapter 12
Action Plan

If you're using the traditional approach to gaining referrals, don't stop what you're doing if it's working. Instead, consider adding some of the tips from this chapter to your business. If you're like most agents, you'll be pleasantly surprised at how much easier this process is.

As in previous chapters, identify the action steps that you would like to take. Rewrite items that may not fit. Circle the number of each strategy that you plan to implement in your business and then record the date you complete the item in the space provided. If you select more than one item, place the items in priority order and work on implementing one item at a time. Once you complete the items you have selected, move on to the next chapter.

Action Steps:

___ 1. I have a referral database that has at least 100 people in it.

___ 2. I have completed the "Whom Do I Know" exercise from this chapter.

___ 3 I have implemented a real estate database management program such as Top Producer, Sharper Agent, or WiseAgent.com to manage my referral database.

___ 4. I have experimented with "give-to-get" marketing when building my referral base.

___ 5. I enjoy connecting people in my referral database with each other, especially when they share a mutual interest or can help each other build their business.

___ 6. When someone refers me business, I always thank them immediately with a phone call, a handwritten thank you note, and a token of appreciation.

___ 7. I will actively stay in contact with my referral database so I can continue connecting them with each other and providing them with service.

Technology is an important element in real estate success. It is not a substitute, however, for personal connection, as Jeff Turner illustrates in the next Recipe for Success.

Recipes for Online Success

Recipes for Success
Why Technology Is Leading Us Down the Wrong Road

Jeff Turner
RealEstateShows.com

Jeff Turner is an active blogger, CEO of RealEstateShows.com, and an expert on innovative technology. In this Recipe for Success, Turner explains why he feels that technology is taking us down the wrong road.

Don't get me wrong. There's nobody who loves technology more than I do. In fact, I spend 12 hours per day sitting in front of a computer. I have ten blogs. Our company at RealEstateShows.com provides agents with an inexpensive solution that lets them use digital photos coupled with the Ken Burns technology to display their listings online. (Ken Burns was a documentary film producer who used panning techniques to give still photos the look of being a video.)

So why do I believe that technology is taking us down the wrong road? With over 90 percent of all buyers now beginning their search online, it's easy to think that posting more photos and more videos is the best way to market property. The challenge with this approach is that it is information focused. People don't buy properties based upon information. They buy based upon emotion. The idea that buyers will purchase their primary residence online is nonsense. Sure, there are a few exceptions, but 99.9 percent of all buyers want to come to the house and walk through it. They want to have a sense of what it's like to live there. You can never get that emotional experience from a computer. When people buy houses, they normally buy because they fell in love with the property.

Let me give you an example. When my wife and I were looking for a house 20 years ago, our agent showed us a couple of properties that we didn't like. She then said, "I have a duplex I would like you to see. I believe you'll fall in love with it." I was adamant that I didn't want a duplex. We finally relented and went to see the duplex. Our agent was right. We fell in love with it. Best of all, the rent from the other unit paid our mortgage.

This sale would never have happened if my wife and I had been looking online. We would have never looked at the property because we would have ruled it out when we set up our search criteria. This is exactly the problem with giving web visitors more and more information. The more information you give them, the easier you are making it for them to exclude your listing from the ones they want to see. Your role in web marketing is to get them to come out and see the house—not to give them so much information that they decide not to look at your listing.

The fallacy that many agents have fallen for is that more web information equals more web visitors. Many of the alternative business models believe that a website can substitute for a live agent. I think both of these contentions are wrong. A website is not a replacement for a live agent nor is it a substitute for seeing the property in person.

Yesterday I was blowing bubbles with my kids. I could have produced a video and shown it online, but it would just not be the same as actually holding the jar in your hand and participating with your kids. Buying a home is very similar. It involves all of your emotions—not just what you see and hear on your computer.

At RealEstateShows.com, we've spent a lot of time researching how the brain works when viewing property online. A key point to consider is attention span. There's a reason that television commercials are 30 or 60 seconds. Rather than doing a three or four minute movie or virtual tour, we have found that the brain can absorb about five photos in 30 seconds or nine photos in 60 seconds. If you create a video that is longer than 30 to 60 seconds and that is packed full of pictures, you will exceed the amount that the brain can absorb.

Technology is a powerful tool, but it is no substitute for the personal connection between an agent and their client. Agents should think of technology as being an electronic version of the newspaper. People don't buy properties from newspaper ads, although they will often go to see a property they saw advertised.

The bottom line is that technology works best as a teaser. Photograph the best points of the property. Don't reveal too much. Avoid giving potential buyers a reason for not seeing your property or feeling as if they have already seen it. Ultimately, it's not just the property you're selling; you're selling the entire experience of blowing bubbles as your children's laughter fills the air.

Chapter 13
Web Marketing: the Basics

A sale is not something you pursue, it's what happens to you while you are immersed in serving your customer.
Source Unknown

Skills Check:
Put a checkmark (√) next to what you do now. Leave the remaining items blank. Review the action steps at the end of the chapter to determine the strategies you will implement in your business.

___ 1. My website focuses on a specific target market or niche.

___ 2. I have my own URL that references real estate rather than my name.

___ 3. My website provides access to all MLS listings in my area.

___ 4. My website is easy to navigate, provides visitors with what they want, and allows visitors to "opt in."

___ 5. My website provides access to comparable sales data.

___ 6. My website has a "call to action" with a free report or some other item that motivates the web visitor to provide their personal contact information.

___ 7. I respond quickly to all website inquiries by using text messaging, instant messaging, click-to-talk-technology, or a call center.

___ 8. My website is a rich resource of information about the areas and/or niches that I serve.

___ 9. People who visit my website can find links to community information, service providers, plus access to all the various professionals that they will need to buy or sell a house.

___10. I frequently update the information on my website.

____ 11. I belong to listing syndication service that sends my listings to at least 30 different websites.

Turn Your Website into a Lead Generation Machine

Today there is an extraordinary selection of technology solutions from which to choose. In fact, the rate of innovation is so fast that even those who follow it regularly have a hard time keeping pace. The challenge is which technology solutions are right for your business? Should you have your own website or is having a page on your brokerage site sufficient? Is it possible to obtain top placement on the search engines without spending a fortune? Do you really need a blog or are there other alternatives? What technologies are here for the long haul and which ones will be gone tomorrow? The bottom line is that the right technology is the one that produces the most leads for your business. If you plan to be in the business for at least another five years, sorting through the options is imperative. A great place to begin is with your website.

Knead the Dough Secret #28
A great website is highly targeted,
easy to use, and easy to remember.

A Systematic Approach to Web Marketing

Target marketing is at the heart of web marketing success. The question is what are the best ways to do it? In terms of your website, here are the key steps.

1. **Web marketing actually begins off-line**
   Who are the people in your target market? What are their lifestyles like? What concerns do they have? What types of recreational activities do they enjoy? What are the demographics (average income earned, age, number of people per family, ethnicity, etc.)? Identify a very narrow market segment and become the expert. Interview people from your target market and find out what matters to them. Where are the cool places that your target market congregates? (It could be at the local soccer field to watch their kids play soccer followed by a trip to a local pizza place.) Your website must make people feel, "Wow—this site is all about me and my lifestyle!"

2. **You must have a website, not just a web page**
   The next question you must address is whether you have a true website or a web page that resides on your broker's site or on Realtor.com. To succeed online, it's important that you have your own website with your own unique URL (i.e., web domain or address).

3. **How to select the right URL for your site**
Two of the most highly searched real estate terms are, "real estate" and "homes." For example, the main URL for your site could be 90272RealEstateProperties.com or 90272PacificPalisadeshomes.com. Using the zip code is smart since many people put zip codes into their search. Also, zip code URLs are easier to obtain than other real estate URLs such as PacificPalisadesRealEstate.com. In fact, it would be smart to select several URLs that you direct back to specific pages on your main site. You might have one page at PacificPalisadesCondos90272.com devoted exclusively to the condominiums and condominium living in that zip code. You could also have 90272HuntingtonPalisades.com page devoted exclusively to the properties and lifestyle in that area. Each one of these sites would appear as if it were a home page. Your goal is to have consumers immediately recognize whether your site is a good fit for them. Serving a very specific niche is the best way to do this. It will also enable you to obtain better placement on the search engines.

4. **Easy navigation**
When visitors reach your website, it should be easy to navigate as well as being user-friendly. "Navigation" refers to how easy it is to move from place to place on the site. "User friendly" refers to how quickly and easily your visitor can find what they are searching for on the web. Ask a friend who is not Internet-savvy to locate information on your website while you look over their shoulder. If your friend has difficulty, you need to revamp your site so it is easier to use.

5. **Give them what they want**
According to an extensive research from Z57.com, web visitors only click on three things when they visit agent websites: "buyers," "sellers," and "find a property." To market proactively, you must focus on these three critical areas. There is nothing wrong with including other key phrases for the search engines, but make sure these three areas are prominently displayed on your site.

6. **Be the resource for neighborhood sales data**
Visitors want to know how much properties are selling for in their area. If your Board of REALTORS® allows you to post closed sales to the web, update all the sales for your service area at least once per month. If your Board does not permit posting of addresses and exact sales prices, you can post price ranges and general amenities. For example:

$325,000-$350,000 Shady Hollow Subdivision

3 bedroom, 2.5 bath, pool, family room, 1 story, wooded lot

3 bedroom, 3.5 bath, family room, remodeled, 2 story brick traditional

For additional information, contact us at yourwebsite.com

7. **"Opt-in" is a necessity**
   With the changes in the spam laws, you must offer an "opt-in" feature for any communications you send from your site. "Opt-in" means the visitor voluntarily signs up to receive communications from you. It also means the individual may "opt-out" at any time. People are more receptive to your marketing efforts when they have made a conscious decision to request what you are sending.

8. **Increase your stickiness**
   "Stickiness" refers to how long visitors stay on your site. To have visitors stay on your site longer, have a wide variety of resources visitors may find useful. For example, include a page of "Frequently Asked First-time Buyer Questions," a mortgage calculator, as well as Chamber of Commerce information for the areas you serve. Other ways to increase stickiness include providing information on schools, crime, transportation, and recreation. Also, consider adding aerial maps, videos of the area, or other community information. While all of this may sound complicated, most real estate website providers include these services as part of their website packages.

9. **Change your site frequently**
   Give your visitors reasons to visit your site often. Since mortgage information changes constantly, you may want to provide a link to a lender who publishes today's mortgage rates. Another alternative is to sign up for a daily real estate news feed like the one provided by Inman News Features (Inman.com). Fresh information invites your visitor to return to your site repeatedly. Furthermore, the more professional your content appears, the more likely you are to hear from website visitors.

   The current trend is for websites to become more like blogs. Instead of requiring a web designer to change your site, you will be able to update it as easily as posting information and then clicking on the publish button.

10. **Landing pages with a call to action**
    Many agent websites are simply on-line advertisements since they lack a call to action. A landing page provides web visitors with an incentive that motivates them leave their contact information. For example, include buyer reports such as,

"Avoid the Ten Biggest Seller Mistakes that Can Cost You Thousands" or "Save Thousands with These Little Known Mortgage Secrets." Other calls to action could include an Annual Report, Equity Check-up, or your digital newsletter. Make sure your website asks for the order on every page of your site. The most important place to do this is before and after each listing on your site.

For a private showing or for additional information on this property, please contact me at... (insert your e-mail address, website, and/or cell phone number).

OR, for potential sellers:

Please click here to obtain a no obligation telephone market analysis of your property.

11. One-stop shopping
Provide links to the other products and services that your clients may need when they move including mortgage, title, repair people, moving services, landscaping, etc. Make your site the single resource buyers and sellers will need to close their transaction.

12. Immediacy is the name of the game
If you have a call to action, it's important that you are able to respond quickly to your web visitors' requests. Here are some of the ways to make sure that you address web inquiries quickly.

a. Use an 800 Call Capture Number where your visitors can listen to a pre-recorded message and leave messages for you about their wants and needs. The system captures their contact information so you are able to follow up with them.

b. Add instant messaging (IM) to your site. There are a number of companies that provide this service. Check our RealEstateCoach.com site for a current list of providers.

c. Autoresponders handle requests from website visitors quickly and efficiently. Once you set them up, a consumer could click on a special report that they would like to receive and the system sends it to them automatically. Most systems notify you as well and include the email address of where the report was sent.

d. Click-to-talk systems allow your web visitor to click on an icon on your site. The visitor enters their phone number and the Click-to-talk system calls you and conferences you in with the consumer. RealPing.com, a privately branded version for the real estate industry, allows agents to control the images that the web visitor sees online. The system allows you to take the consumer through listings on your site, simply by using the keypad on your cell phone. You do not need to be at a computer.

e. For high volume agents or teams, a call center is another viable approach. Companies such as LeadQual.com will "scrub" or qualify incoming website leads. If the lead meets the appropriate criteria, the lead is handed off to a live agent in less than five minutes.

f. An in-office assistant or a virtual assistant are other alternatives. Good in-office assistants can be difficult to find and even more difficult for a busy agent to train. In contrast, virtual assistants work with you on an independent contractor basis and are not based in your office. They have their own computer, phone, and other tools required to conduct business. They can be available while you are sleeping or anytime during the day.

13. Syndication

The term "syndication" refers to publishing your listings on other websites. At the time this book went to press, the most robust system available to agents was through Point 2 Agent. (Visit RealEstateCoach.com/point2 to learn more about how to add this important tool to your business.) You will select a template and make a website in less than 10 minutes. Once you have completed that process, you can upload your listings. Please note that this is not a substitute for your existing website, but an additional resource. Once your listings are in the Point 2 system, you can select the sites where you would like to syndicate. Their syndication partners include Craigslist, eBay, Google Base, PropertySmart, Trulia, Yahoo Classifieds, Zillow, and numerous others. You can obtain a downloadable graphic to use on your listing appointments at RealEstateCoach.com/handout that displays their current syndication partners. This is a powerful tool for listing and selling property because of the tremendous exposure it provides. It provides an important justification for earning a full commission.

For buyers, the basic Point2 website provides reports that are sent automatically to your web visitors, numerous calls to action, as well as populating your website with current listings. Again, it only takes about 10 minutes to set up this feature and the cost is minimal.

Once you have done the work to create a website, the next question is how to get people to your website.

Chapter 13
Action Plan

Web marketing is critical to your success, especially as the tidal wave of Gen X and Gen Y clients flood the market. They will find you online and get to know you online. Consequently, managing on your online reputation and image is critical. The next chapter focuses on how to drive people to your site. If you haven't addressed the issues in this chapter, however you are wasting money.

As in previous chapters, begin by identifying the action steps that you would like to take. Rewrite items that may not fit. Circle the number of each strategy that you plan to implement in your business and then record the date you complete the item in the space provided. If you select more than one item, place the items in priority order and work on implementing one item at a time. Your goal is to find an activity that is sustainable over time and that you will feel motivated to do on a regular basis.

Action Steps:

___ 1. I have changed my website so it focuses on a specific target market or niche.

___ 2. I own at least one URL that references real estate rather than my name.

___ 3. My website is easy to navigate and allows visitors to "opt in."

___ 4. My website provides access to all MLS listings in my area including comparable sales.

___ 5. I use free reports, e-coupons, or other items of value as a "call to action" that motivates web visitors to provide their personal contact information.

___ 6. I normally respond immediately to all website inquiries by using instant messaging, click-to-talk-technology, or a call center.

___ 7. My website has fun and interesting information about the areas and/or niches that I serve.

___ 8. My website has links to community information, service providers, and to other professionals viewers will need to buy or sell a house.

___ 9. I have created a strategy that will allow me to update the information on my website frequently.

___10. I have joined a listing syndication service that sends my listings to at least 30 different websites.

Are you ready to achieve on-line dominance? If so, Michael Russer has the Recipe for Success that will show you how.

Recipes for Success
Five Steps to Marketing Successfully Online

Michael Russer
OnLineDominance.com

I first met Michael Russer back in the mid 1990s. He wrote the first book describing how real estate agents could market effectively on the web. Russer has also been a leading advocate of working with virtual assistants to build your business. His message addresses what agents can do to create web traffic and then convert that traffic into signed business. If your website is failing to deliver the results you want, follow the five steps that Russer outlines below to improve the results of your web marketing.

When I'm out on the speaking circuit, agents often ask me, "What can I do to drive more traffic to my website?" Driving traffic to their website is the last thing they should be concerned about. The real issue is what happens once the web visitor gets to their site. There's no point of driving traffic to your website if the visitor stays for a few seconds and leaves.

Step 1: The number one reason that agents fail miserably online

The reason that agents fail to convert their web leads is that they do not target a market. They try to be everything to everyone. This is what virtually all other agents do as well. This means that you are competing with everyone. In contrast, when you target market, you create a specific niche. This specialization is the key to converting more web leads

When agents sign up for my Online Dominance Course, we show them how to identify and evaluate potential target markets. The first step is to choose something that you are passionate about and that you truly enjoy. Second, you must determine how much turnover exists in that particular market and whether it is broad enough to produce the income results that you would like to achieve. For example, one of our clients wanted to specialize in selling horse properties. He did the analysis and learned that he could not make the money he wanted, even if he had 100 percent dominance. Instead, what he did was to become the "outdoor specialist" for this area. This specialization drove tremendous business to him almost immediately.

Many agents are concerned that if they specialize, they will lose business. In most cases, they don't have it anyway, so there's really nothing to lose. Furthermore, it's not a loss if it's the wrong type of client for your business.

Many agents attempt to build their business by targeting their sphere of influence and their past clients. This is a slow way to grow your business and involves a considerable amount of face-to-face time. Even more importantly, this approach provides no insulation from other agents who may know your potential client. In fact, the typical person knows between 6 to 12 people who hold real estate licenses.

In contrast, when you're the known specialist who is the best choice to represent buyers and sellers in your area, the other agents will have difficulties competing against you.

Step 2: You must answer the question, "What's in it for me?" (WIIFM)

This is an area where most agent websites fall short. Your website visitor must know instantly that your website is the perfect fit for them. The goal is to make the visitor to your site say, "WOW—this is the site for me!" To do this, you must put yourself into your web visitors' shoes. You must shift from being in a sales role (i.e., focused on what you want to achieve) to being focused on marketing, which is identifying and fulfilling what the customer wants.

For example, if you are serving a first time buyer niche, ask yourself as well as those around you, "What are the primary concerns that first time buyers have? What are their greatest fears? What do they need to know to close a successful sale? What types of information do they want about the neighborhood? What other needs do they have?

Linda Jefferson, who is one of our clients, has an excellent example of the type of website I am discussing. It's at GoArmyHomes.com. The moment a website visitor views Linda's website, it's clear that she has niched her business for army families. She understands their special needs, which is evident from her site. If an army family is buying or selling in Linda's area, she is the clear choice to represent them.

You can achieve great results by taking as little as 20 minutes to brainstorm with a group of others who have experience with your niche. Don't try to do this alone. Instead, enlist others to brainstorm with you. When you do a brainstorming session, every idea is a good idea. Be complimentary. Avoid criticizing any idea during the brainstorming session since it shuts down the flow. Hold off on evaluating the idea until after your brainstorming group leaves.

Step 3: Powerful branding will make or break your website

An important step in succeeding online is to create a powerful brand for your business. If you don't brand your site effectively or if you use your name to brand, you really have nothing to sell. When you specialize and provide exactly what your clients want, you will create a brand that has a high perceived value. GoArmyHomes.com is a powerful example of how to correctly brand a website. The website has a specific target market and the name reflects that market.

Having a powerful Unique Positioning Statement (UPS) is also critical. A strong UPS clearly states your area of expertise while also causing a gut reaction in your web visitors that you are the agent who really understands what they want and need. A strong UPS also immediately removes about 90 percent of your competition, since very few agents have created a niche that they clearly serve. In fact, a great UPS for the Internal Revenue Service would be, "We've got what it takes to take what you have!" Anyone who hears that UPS immediately knows that it's true. A well written UPS allows consumers to make their own conclusions as opposed to stating the conclusion for them.

Step 4: Engagement vs. information flow

Many agents confuse information or content with engagement. To engage your web visitors, you must write in a conversational tone. Avoid using "I" and focus on using "you." The most important thing that you can do is to make the site about them. You're not telling them about you—you're having a conversation about what matters to them.

One of the most important aspects of web marketing is to have attention grabbing headlines. The best way to do this is to hire a virtual copywriter who understands how to market and yet can still recreate your voice as the agent. By addressing the specific needs of your market and speaking to them in a conversational tone, your conversion rates will increase dramatically.

Once your site is finished, test it out by asking your clients and associates whether the site is powerfully engaging. If not, keep working on it until it is. Again, an excellent way to do this is to brainstorm with your clients about what works for them.

Step 5: How to drive people to your website

Once you have completed the four steps above, you're now ready to drive people to your website. Many people ignore the importance of integrating their web marketing and their print marketing. Use your print marketing to drive people to your website for more information.

In our Online Dominance class, we show our students how to target statistically likely sellers. For example, if the average length of time that someone in your area stays in their home is six years, then we recommend that our agents identify people who have been in their present home five to seven years and market to them. This three year window normally achieves excellent results.

There are two ways to motivate people to visit your site. The first is "pain"—they're unhappy about some aspect of their current living situation and moving is a potential solution. The other way is by using pleasure. In this approach, you highlight an "irresistible offer," something that is so attractive that people will go online or provide their contact information to obtain it.

Using a Privacy Policy Is Critical

When you require web visitors to fill out a form to receive information, most will leave your site. On the other hand, using a privacy policy can help you obtain more information by giving your web visitor the choice. Our privacy policy guarantees that any information that they enter will be private and not shared with any other source. We follow up by explaining that most web visitors are in the information gathering stage and that they prefer to remain anonymous. If the web visitor is uncomfortable providing their information, there is no obligation for them to do so. What's surprising about this approach is that by making the form optional, approximately 80 percent of your web visitors will provide their information.

Regardless of how many leads you generate, following up is critical. Our E-Productivity course shows our clients how to work successfully with virtual consultants to keep their lead generation strong and their conversion rates high.

Chapter 14
Click Your Way to More Real Estate Dough™

Limitations live only in our minds. But if we use or imaginations, our possibilities become limitless.
Jamie Paolinetti

Skills Check:
Put a checkmark (√) next to what you do now. Leave the remaining items blank. Review the action steps at the end of the chapter to determine the strategies that you will implement in your business.

____ 1. I use my print advertising to motivate people to visit my website.

____ 2. My website is optimized for search engine placement.

____ 3. My website is packed with information about the lifestyle in the market areas that I serve.

____ 4. My website has a site map.

____ 5. I use key words and phrases to build traffic on my website.

____ 6. My website comes up on the first pages of most search engines for the specific niche(s) that I serve.

____ 7. I participate in a pay-per-click program.

____ 8. I use videos and/or podcasts to increase the traffic on my website.

____ 9. I post at least 20 photos of each of my listings on my website.

___10. I have a system for tracking analytics on my website and monitor results on a regular basis.

___ 11. I know how to market my listings on over 30 different websites.

How to Get Discovered on the Web

Thousands of agents spend their hard earned commission dollars on their website. Some have stellar success and others have no traffic at all. To maximize the results from your web marketing efforts, follow the guidelines below.

1. **Use print advertising to drive your web traffic**

   The obvious places to include your website address are your business cards, brochures, and any other print advertising that you do. Unless you have an 800 call capture number on your print ads, however, there is no way to monitor how much business the print ads generate. In contrast, it is easy to monitor your website traffic as well as where it originates.

   Use your print ads to motivate people to visit your website by making an offer of service. For example, you can use a postcard campaign to motivate people to go to your site to determine whether they would qualify for a property tax reduction. Outline the guidelines and have the forms available for visitors to download. If your visitor would like the most recent comparable sales information, invite them to contact you. Use your print as a means to be proactive in motivating people to visit your website.

2. **Key word phrases and metatags**

   Search engines "spider" the web by searching for key word phrases and metatags that closely match the requested search terms. Your site will appear based upon how well your key words and metatags match the search parameters. For example, if your niche is selling probate properties in Austin, Texas, key word phrases you could use include, "Austin," "Texas," "real estate," "probate," "probate sellers," "probate listings," "probate buyers," etc. Key words are normally visible on your web page. In contrast, metatags are embedded in the HTML coding and are only visible to the search engines. Your web hosting company or a search engine optimization (SEO) specialist will handle this on your behalf.

   The most highly searched term in our industry is "real estate." Use it often on your site along with plenty of references to the areas where you conduct business. An important point to keep in mind is that your content must match your search terms. If web visitors come to your site and discover that your content does not match their search, they will quickly leave. Your web ranking is dependent upon your content being in alignment with the searches generated.

3. **Site map**

   Site maps enhance search engine placement and may appear at the bottom of your home page. A site map is akin to a table of contents. Search engines target site maps, read them, and then match their searches based upon the keyword phrases or metatags that are on the map. Most professionally designed websites have a site map. The site map is often invisible to your visitors, but is visible to search engines.

4. **Paid search using "pay-per-click"**

   Pay-per-click is tied to key word phrases. You bid on the phrases and top rankings go to the highest bidder. The only time advertisers are charged is when someone clicks through to their website. Most search engines list paid ads first and then list the remaining sites based upon the formula the company uses for web placement. The popularity of the key word phrases determines the pricing. Pay-per-click works much like an auction. The more you bid per click, the better your placement will be.

   For example, if you were searching for a home in Portland, Oregon, you would type in "Portland Oregon homes" or "Portland Oregon real estate." Once your search comes up, you will notice several different types of information on the page. On some pages, you will see two or three sponsored links at the top of the page. These advertisers are usually large institutions that pay sizeable fees for top placement. Directly below the space for the top two or three sponsored results, you will see the balance of the pay-per-click results. These advertisements have priority over people who do not pay for web placement. Advertisers normally set a monthly budget. When advertisers reach their budgeted figure, the search engine drops them until they either replenish their account or until the following month. As a result, search engine rankings constantly change.

5. **Paid advertising**

   As you look at the results of your search, also note the advertisements in the margin. This area is a combination of pay-per-click and traditional print advertising. Unlike the search areas, this area posts short ads much like the classified ads in a newspaper. The cost for the ad is based upon how many visitors click through to your website. Most search engines ads cannot exceed three lines and approximately 100 characters. Before writing your ad, look at the other ads, especially those in major metropolitan areas. This will give you some ideas about the type of ad you can place. Also, remember to make your ad about the consumer as well as identifying the geographical region and niche you service.

6. **Organic or free search**

   Pay-per-click programs can cost thousands of dollars each month. A better alternative is to go for "organic" search placement. Organic search is based upon how many people click through to the site, whether or not they stay on the site, how long the site has been in existence, as well as a host of other complicated factors.

When it comes to organic placement, content is the key. Design various landing pages on your website to serve very small segments of the market. For example, rather than trying to reach every condominium buyer in your city, a better approach would be to provide a specific landing page for three or four large condominium projects. To reach buyers in San Francisco, avoid using "San Francisco homes for sale." A better approach would be to devote a landing page to "San Francisco Victorian homes." Load the page with data about Victorian homes in San Francisco. Topics could include articles on how to restore a Victorian home, information from the local historical society, advertisements from vendors who specialize in providing historically accurate fixtures, etc. You could also host a blog where readers could comment on their favorite Victorian home, pitfalls to avoid when remodeling an older home, as well as reliable contractors. The more data and the more interactivity that you provide on your site, the better the search engines like you. This in turn leads to a higher organic search position.

7. **Turn on the Google juice**
   "Google juice" refers to providing features on your website that Google's algorithms prefer. (An "algorithm" is the formula that the search engine uses to determine their rankings.) Blogging can help you climb to the top of searches as can podcasting and video. The more traffic you create, the higher your rankings will be.

8. **Mash it up and make it sticky**
   Once a web visitor reaches your site, your goal is to keep them there and motivate them to provide their contact information. This is known as "stickiness." One of the best ways to create stickiness is with "mash-ups." A mash-up references multiple applications on a site such as a combination of mapping, video, and a place for people to leave their comments.

Sticky Photos

In July 2008, Point2Agent released a study that examined consumer web viewing patterns for over 100,000 listings in the Point2 system. Listings were from multiple countries and were representative of all price ranges. Their findings replicate similar results from a survey conducted in 2007 as well as results reported by Realtor.com. First, consumers skip over listings with no pictures. Point2's research showed that compared to listings with only one photo, those with 21 or more photos generated more than triple the number of detailed views, more than double the amount of interest, and double the number of leads. In fact, increasing the number of photos on your website from 15 to 16 resulted in a 20 percent increase in the number of leads generated.

Lead Conversion, Not Just Lead Generation

The real estate industry has always been proficient at generating leads. The biggest challenge facing us, however, is how to convert those leads into signed business. The California Association of REALTORS® in their *2007 Study of Internet Buyers and Sellers* reported that 48 percent of Internet leads are being ignored. There are several explanations for this situation. First, Internet leads can take up to 18 months to incubate. This poses a significant challenge since most agents and companies lack the necessary systems to incubate leads for this length of time. Furthermore, the concept of incubating leads flies in the face of the traditional marketing wisdom that focuses on "right now" business such as expired and For-Sale-by-Owner listings. While web leads may take longer to incubate, 68 percent only interview one agent. In contrast, the typical traditional buyer interviews a median of three agents. As a result, the first agent to reach the web consumer has a high probability of closing that business. Speed is the key.

Don't Drip—Predict!

With web leads taking up to 18 months to convert, it's important to have a system that allows you to stay in touch without sending your web leads elsewhere. While drip marketing worked well several years ago, now it's one of the fastest ways to cost you a lead. You can avoid this issue by having a blog where people can subscribe to your RSS (Really Simple Syndication or blog feed).

Another approach is to use predictive marketing. In addition to syndicating listings to over 30 different sites, Point2Agent.com now offers a predictive marketing tool with its premium sites. When buyers sign up to be notified of new listings, the system monitors their browsing patterns and then places homes that fit their preference at the top of what the buyer sees. For example, if a buyer always looks at the kitchen first, the system displays the houses with the best kitchens first. This system is much more effective than drip email since it automatically responds to each web visitor's unique web browsing patterns.

Analyze Analytics

One of the biggest mistakes that both agents and companies make is failing to evaluate their web statistics. Where do leads originate? Which websites generate the most traffic for your listings? What pages on your site cause your visitors to go elsewhere? You can't answer these questions unless you are using tracking. Point2 provides their analysis tool at no charge as part of their basic website package. For your other websites, you can use Google Analytics or GetClicky. What's especially interesting about the GetClicky application is that you can actually monitor the live activity on your site.

Monitoring the patterns of your web visitors allows you to identify what works on your site and what you need to delete. You can experiment with different marketing campaigns and see the results in real time. Monitoring your web traffic is one of the best ways to keep your web business strong.

Single Property Websites

Single property websites are powerful tools to help you convert more listing leads into signed business. When you offer sellers a customized website that uses the property address as the URL (333ElmStreetAustin.com), most will sign the listing agreement on the spot. Initially these sites were priced at about $100, but today they are about one-third that amount. When you post the URL on your sign, visitors can enter it into their cell phone and see the interior of the property without disturbing you or the sellers. These sites also have the following advantages:

1. **A powerful lead conversion tool**
   Single property sites help you convert more listing appointments into signed business. After the property closes, keep the URL active and allow the new buyers to post their pictures on the site. You continue to pay the hosting fees. When the property comes back on the market, the sellers are more likely to list with the agent who has been hosting their home's website as opposed to their past agent who probably hasn't been in touch.

2. **I speak your language**
   You can now obtain single property websites in Spanish as well as English. Having your listings translated manually rather than automatically is a wise decision. Online translation services such as those offered by Google or Babel Fish, often make major errors that show you really don't understand the language. If you do opt to use one of these, always have the translation reviewed by a native speaker.

Remodel with the Click of Your Mouse

One of the best ways to increase your stickiness on any website is to add the new space design tools from Obeo.com. Obeo will photograph your listing and upload the property pictures to their software. The system then generates a property floor plan that allows you or your clients to arrange the furniture long before the movers ever arrive. If your buyers object to a room color or to the lack of hardwood floors, Obeo allows you to change these features, as well as the exterior color, the indoor wall colors, the flooring, the countertops, and the type of wood used in the cabinetry.

This powerful tool keeps your website visitors engaged while also allowing them to envision what the property would be like once they make their desired changes. More importantly, it can prevent them from making a drastic mistake.

Obeo has a new version in development that will allow consumers to not only redo the walls, the flooring, cabinets, and countertops; they will also be able to "furnish" the property with name brand furniture. When users identify what they like, all they have to do is to point and click to order their furniture and other decorating items online.

The Obeo system tracks agent and client page views separately. Fellow speaker Verl Workman described how he used the Obeo features including its room tracking program to persuade all seven of his listings to lower their price and to increase their commission. Using the system, Verl showed one seller how 256 agents had viewed her listing and yet there had been no showings. Clearly, the problem was the combination of the price and the commission. When you can accurately document how much web traffic your site is receiving, it's much easier to persuade sellers to lower their price and/or raise the commission. Verl then went back to each of his sellers, showed them the web statistics, and every one of them opted to increase their commission to gain more attention on-line.

Table 1

How to Market Your Listings on More Than 40 Different Websites

(Visit RealEstateCoach.com/handout for the most up-to-date list)

Are you marketing your listings everywhere you could be marketing them? If not, this quick list will put you on multiple websites at very little cost. In fact, many of these resources are free.

1. When you take a listing, your listing appears on your local MLS, your company's local website, your national website (if with a major firm), and your personal website.

2. If you list with Realtor.com, your listings not only appear there, they also appear on the RealEstateJournal.com.

3. Many local newspapers have a website as well. If you are advertising in print, you may also have free advertising online.

4. If you have a property listed for $1 million or more, UniqueGlobalEstates.com will post your listing at no charge.

5. Use a single property website such as those provided by AgencyLogic.com and ListingDomains.com.

6. Visit RealEstateCoach.com/Point2 to set up a website that will allow you to syndicate your listings to over 30 different websites. This includes Craigslist, eBay, Google Base, Trulia, Yahoo Classifieds, Zillow, and many more. Visit RealEstateCoach.com/handout for the downloadable file you can use in your marketing materials or on listing appointments.

7. Zillow and HomeGain generate millions of unique visits each month and charge nothing for you to place your listings on their sites.

8. At the time we went to press, you could post your virtual tours and HDTV videos on TubeMogul and have your videos broadcast to YouTube, Google Video, Yahoo Video, plus at least ten other video websites. Don't forget to post on iTunes as well. Also look for new video opportunities from cable television companies.

9. Post bankruptcy and foreclosure listings for free at Foreclosure.com and RealtyTrac.com.

Chapter 14
Action Plan

A one page website is no longer enough. Your website must be optimized so that leads can find you on the web and then you must provide services that motivate visitors to work with you. Chapter 15 addresses how to build your online reputation with blogging.

As in previous chapters, begin by identifying the action steps that you would like to take. Rewrite items that may not fit. Circle the number of each strategy that you plan to implement in your business and then record the date you complete the item in the space provided. If you select more than one item, place the items in priority order and work on implementing one item at a time. Your goal is to find an activity that is sustainable over time and that you will feel motivated to do on a regular basis.

Action Steps:

____ 1. I use print advertising to motivate people to visit my website.

____ 2. I have an SEO specialist to optimize my website for me.

____ 3. My website is packed with information about the lifestyle in my market areas.

____ 4. My website has a site map.

____ 5. I use key words and phrases to increase my web traffic.

____ 6. For the niches I serve, my website comes up on the first pages of most search engines.

____ 7. I participate in a pay-per-click program.

____ 8. I use videos and/or podcasts to increase the traffic on my website.

____ 9. I post at least 20 photos of each of my listings on my website.

___ 10. I have a system for tracking analytics on my website and I monitor my results on a regular basis.

___ 11. I know how to market my listings on over 30 different websites.

One of the ways to build your web traffic is to use search engine optimization (SEO). In the next Recipe for Success, Mike Parker explains the basics of SEO as well as how to create more traffic for your website.

Recipes for Success You Have a Website but Are Your Web Visitors Calling You?

Mike Parker
TheBlackwaterCG.com

Coming up on the first page of a Google, Yahoo, MSN, ASK, and AOL search is no small feat. If you're interested in learning about search engine optimization (SEO) and what it can do for your real estate website, Mike Parker is the expert to see. His company, The Blackwater Consulting Group (together with CompassSearch), helps agents build an online presence using search engine optimization. Their REAL SEO™ program also assists agents in converting web visitors into qualified leads. While SEO is important, success results from what happens AFTER visitors come to your site. If you're not getting the results you want from your website, Mike's Recipe for Success gives you some reasons why.

The house purchasing paradigm has changed. In the past, clients would decide that they were going to buy or sell a piece of real estate. The first step would be to contact a real estate broker. Today, the first step for most clients is to go online. According to the National Association of REALTORS®, 84 percent of all residential transactions now involve the Internet. Furthermore, a whopping 74 percent use a search engine to help them decide on an agent. The reason is that search engines are perceived as being a knowledgeable resource that provide straight, objective answers.

In the past, buyers often had no idea what was available. Today, the buyer typically narrows down what they want to see prior to contacting an agent. They will type in the words "real estate" or "homes," the city where they would like to search, and perhaps even the name of the neighborhood.

Just as they selected the homes that they wanted to see online, they will repeat the process when selecting an agent. Consequently, it's critical that you appear in one of the 10 choices they have on the first page of their search. If you're not in this top group of sites, the probability of converting that Internet buyer is zero.

Many agents complain that their websites produce no leads. This often results because the agent's site is not a true website, but a "subdomain" site that resides as a separate area on another company's website. The result is that search engines cannot optimize or index the subdomain site. An excellent example is an agent who has a web page on their company's site. Even if the agent has multiple pages on such a site, web visitors will be unable to find the site unless they have the specific URL (web address). If buyers knew the exact page address they wanted, there would be no need for search engines. If you want to be found on the Internet, begin by obtaining your own URL or domain; don't rely exclusively on a page on your broker's site or on Realtor.com.

In terms of creating your own site, there is a wide variety of excellent template sites that you can customize for as little as $50 per month.

Once you have your site, how do web visitors find you? The two primary ways are through Pay-per-click (PPC) and organic search (i.e., coming up in the results because your website is an excellent fit for the web visitor's search). SEO helps you obtain organic placement. Blogging can help your site be found, but requires a serious commitment to writing regularly. Pay per click is online advertising that can be expensive and that only helps you on the search engines where you advertise.

SEO is no simple matter. There are at least 40 variables involved, each with different weights. Think of the web as a giant file drawer with over 11 billion entries (because there are over 11 billion active web pages today, growing at an astronomical rate). Your website must be properly filed and indexed if Internet buyers are going to have any chance of finding it.

In terms of SEO, the single most important factor is your HTML tags—the file tabs under which your site is filed by the search engines. HTML tags consist of:

1. Your title tag (120 or so characters that specifically states the product you sell).

2. Your meta description tag that provides more details about the niche or market you serve.

3. Your meta keywords tag, which broadens the areas you can be found online.

Tags are extremely important in that they must relate to your home page copy. Examples of key words include the name of the city, state, and community where you do business. Key words could also reference a market niche such as relocation or first time buyers.

Even if potential clients do find you, the question is "now what?" Obviously, it's important that your site is up to date with current listings, that you have fresh content on a monthly basis, and that your site is easy to navigate and understand. It's more important to give those visitors a reason to become people that want to do business with you. This process is sometimes termed "lead capture." It is here that your creativity gets a chance to shine.

For example, one of our clients offered a copy of their family's 100-year-old clam chowder recipe along with a booklet describing their market towns. Visitors voluntarily provided an email address to receive it. The agent's leads soared. The key to generating leads is to give your web visitors something they value, be it specific information or a local item of value.

Even if your site is converting leads, are you tracking your visitors? For example, our system tracks every page click that visitors make and so much more. This is valuable because it lets you know what matters to your clients and what is irrelevant. You can remove the areas that your consumers don't visit and replace them with areas that you know to be more appealing. You can also measure your advertising effectiveness.

Essentially, online lead generation comes down to four steps:

1. Internet buyers must be able to find your website when they search for homes in your town—it must be optimized for that to occur.

2. The visitors must convert to a lead. You must be able to motivate them to give you their contact information.

3. You must contact each lead immediately. A survey from MIT (Massachusetts Institute of Technology) reported that the likelihood of selling an online lead is 500 percent higher if you contact them in minutes as opposed to contacting them in hours.

4. You must maintain regular contact with that Internet client and respond to their messages immediately. To do this, have your leads text messaged to your cell phone. In online marketing, the early bird really does get the worm!

Chapter 15
Blogging: as Simple as 1-2-3

There is no such thing as public opinion.
There is only published opinion.
Winston Churchill

Skills Check:
Put a checkmark (√) next to what you do now. Leave the remaining items blank. Review the action steps at the end of the chapter to determine the strategies that you will implement in your business.

___ 1. I understand the difference between a website and a blog and use both in my business.

___ 2. My real estate blog generates clients on a regular basis.

___ 3. I use my blog to help establish trust in my local market area.

___ 4. I have niched my blog for a specific geographical area, a type of property such as relocation or foreclosure, or for a specific demographic such as people who are retiring.

___ 5. I use pinging and RSS feeds to make sure that my blog reaches search engines such as Google.

___ 6. I never steal content from other people's blogs, use pictures without the photographer's consent or attribution, or use music that I have not properly licensed.

___ 7. I regularly use key terms to help my blog obtain higher search engine placement.

Blogging Basics

Today many agents struggle to find clients. Open house attendance is down nationally. Referrals drop when the market slows and cold calling is harder than ever. Web leads can take 6 to 18 months to convert. The one bright spot in all of this is blogging. Today's consumers love interacting online. They search out little-known facts, current happenings, as well as what's hot and what's not. With print newspaper circulation declining, some people say that blogs are the digital answer to the local newspaper. In fact, blogging is rapidly becoming the leading way for individual agents to establish their credibility as real estate experts as well as to attract new business.

What is a blog? Some people say it's a combination of the word "web" and "log." Many of the earliest blogs were not much more than diaries or journals. Social and political blogging has been around for a number of years. Business blogging, however, is a much newer trend that is already revolutionizing how real estate professionals conduct their business. Blogs are not only the voice of the moment; they are also a way to generate more leads, to interact with potential clients, and to build trust in the communities we serve.

Knead the Dough Secret #29

In virtually all cases, a blog combined with a well designed website will generate more leads than either a blog or a website alone.

Do I Really Need a Blog?

The answer to this question is contingent upon how much business you have. If you have a strong lead generation pipeline, you may be able to maintain that pipeline without a blog. On the other hand, if you want to become the dominant player in a geographical area or reach a national or international audience for your market area, blogging is the best way to achieve that goal.

The Six Primary Benefits from Blogging

1. **Blogging improves web rankings**
   Spiders (the technology that search engines such as Google use to "crawl" and index website information) love the steady stream of fresh content found in blogs. In contrast, websites are static. Once the spider catalogues a website, it only catalogues the site again when the content is updated. Blogs also link to other blogs, posts, and articles whereas most websites do not. By linking your blog and your website, you improve your search engine ranking. Each time that you post an entry to your blog, you create a new URL. This in turn serves as an additional link to your website. The more links that you have and the more fresh content that you generate, the higher your ranking will be. When other bloggers link to your posts, you create even higher rankings.

2. **Blogs are easier to work with than websites**
   Business blogging is at the cutting edge of Web 2.0 and may make many websites obsolete. The reason for this is that websites provide static information. When

you have a blog, it's easy to post updated listings, sales, recent neighborhood information, etc. In contrast, changing your website usually requires a web designer and a change fee. Blogging can be as simple as writing an email and sending it. Best of all, most blog hosting sites are either free or charge a minimal fee. All that is really required is your personal time commitment to do the posts.

3. **Blogging allows consumers to get to know and trust you**
   Given that today's typical web consumer begins their property search 6 to 18 months prior to the time they plan to move, your blog allows the consumer to get to know you in a safe, non-threatening way. Remember, most people prefer to remain anonymous until they are ready to take action. Potential clients who regularly read your blog learn to trust you as a valued source of information. This in turn helps to establish you as an expert in your area.

4. **Blogging lets you establish yourself as an expert in a specific niche**
   If you do geographical farming, starting a neighborhood blog for your farm area is a way to distinguish yourself from competitors who are still relying on postcard and email marketing. What makes your blog different from their marketing is that your farm area now has a forum where they can post meaningful content, comment on local events, or simply let neighbors know about a special birthday or anniversary.

5. **Blogs are an excellent way to reach younger buyers and sellers**
   Blogs are particularly attractive to those under the age of 30. The under 30 crowd grew up with computers and prefers to communicate via texting rather than email or phoning. This group loves digital communication and sharing comments with each other.

6. **Blogs are easier to write and publish than newsletters**
   Just as websites may become less important, blogging may soon replace newsletters as well. Like most websites, newsletters are static and do not allow for interaction. In contrast, blogs thrive on interaction and reader comments. Blogs are also less formal than newsletters, shorter, and easier to write. A typical blog post is 5 to 10 sentences. Some are even shorter. You can make a single observation about an event, provide a useful tidbit of information, or link to another blog post or web article that you believe your readers would enjoy.

The Blogger's Dictionary

To take full advantage of blogging in your business, it's important to know the key concepts and terms. This is by no means a comprehensive list, but it will get you started with some of the basics.

Blog (a more detailed definition)

Wikipedia defines blog as "a type of website where entries are made and displayed in a reverse chronological order." According to Jim Cronin, (RealEstateTomato.com) a blog is written in your own voice and is akin to the editorial page of the newspaper. It's a place to voice your opinions, share the latest business news, create community, and discuss local events. Blogs contain fresh, compelling, and changing content. In contrast, websites are akin to a brochure that contains static information. When you link your blog with your website, you have the best of both tools.

Post

Posting to your blog is merely the process of writing content and then placing what you have written online.

Comments

In blogging, comments refer to additional posts made by those who have something to say about the blogger's original post. This is where people can create a conversation about specific topics. Bloggers have the option of allowing anyone to post to their blog unedited (not a good idea) or to moderate (screen) the posts.

There are several reasons for moderating your posts. First, you have no obligation to post everything that comes in on your blog. Second, some people may use the blog to make remarks that are in violation of the real estate law or that could be slanderous in nature. Third, you may receive requests that are completely irrelevant to your blog and to your readers. Finally, spammers sometimes attempt to use blogs to spread their unwelcome messages. Consequently, it's smart to screen comments before allowing them to post.

RSS

RSS stands for "really simple syndication." If you find a blog that you enjoy and that has an "RSS" symbol, you can subscribe to the "RSS feed." When the blogger updates their content, the RSS feed notifies you of the update and sends it directly to your computer. Many of the newer computer software programs have RSS aggregators as a standard feature.

Regardless of which system you use, the RSS aggregator notifies you when the information you wanted is available. It automatically sends it to you along with a brief description and a link. The system gathers and displays the feeds from each source. The primary reason for using RSS aggregator is to avoid having your email box cluttered with RSS feeds.

Pinging

Bloggers use pinging to notify others that their blog has been updated. You can use a service for this, but most of the major blogging platforms will now handle this for you automatically. Technorati.com is an important site to ping. The reason Technorati is so important is that you cannot ping many of the search engines directly. Nevertheless, these search engines pick up what is posted on Technorati. By using pinging, you speed up the process by which web users can locate your blog. To take advantage of the pinging function on many blogs, merely enter the key words or terms in the space identified for "Technorati tags" or "key words."

Permanent linking (Permalinks)

Most blogging platforms automatically create a separate URL (web address) for each of your posts so that both readers and search engines can find your post at a later date. Permanent linking also allows visitors to return to the post or to link to it from other websites. A key advantage of permanent links is that search engines read them as a new link to your website. This increases your link popularity and helps you to obtain higher search engine placement.

Blog roll

A blog roll is your personal list of the other blog sites that you respect.

What Platform Should I Use?

This is perhaps the most important decision you will make and there's not a single good answer. Typepad is easy to use but does not integrate with your existing website. Since your blog resides on Typepad's server, they get the traffic. You can use the Typepad Permalink feature to link back to your site. Wordpress works with your existing site, but it is too challenging for most agents. The best strategy is to check with other bloggers about what they're using and what works best for them.

Post Your Listings

Your blog is an excellent place to promote your listings. There are two ways to do this. The first option is to integrate your listings into your blog. If you use this approach, segregate listing information from your blog's content. The person searching for listing information may not want to wade through commentary.

You can also create a separate blog for each of your listings. To do this, go to GoDaddy.com and purchase the URL or domain name (i.e., 345 Elm Street) for each separate blog. If you obtain the URL before your listing appointment, it prevents other agents from competing with you to use the seller's address. In the future, it may become common practice for those who visit different listings to post their feedback. If you decide to allow other people to make comments about your listings, be sure to moderate all posts (review them before allowing them to be published on your blog).

Knead the Dough Secret #30
Instead of answering questions by email, post your answers on your blog. Old emails to past clients are a treasure trove of potential blog posts.

What to Write Made Easy

The challenge every blogger faces is what to write. Actually, there are thousands of topics that you could select. The key in successful blogging is to find something that is exciting to you and that will maintain your interest over time. The tips below come from some of the most successful real estate bloggers in the country.

1. **Headlines matter**
   You only have a few seconds to capture the reader's interest. Write powerful headlines that grab the reader's attention. Your headline should reference topics that are compelling to your readers. For example, if you are working in Phoenix and want to attract foreclosure buyers, be sure that your headline includes "Phoenix," "foreclosure" and "real estate buyers." Using these key words in your headline will drive more traffic to your site.

   When you blog about one of your listings or a specific geographical area, it's smart to include the zip code in your headline, in the text of your blog, and in the key words.

2. **Niches for riches**
   Creating a niche that serves a segment of the market is an excellent way to begin blogging. Niches to consider include specific demographic groups, market niches, or your personal recreational interests. Another strategy is to identify a problem that people in your niche regularly encounter and then provide solutions. Many people also enjoy reading blogs about the lifestyle in the area where they are considering moving. Focus on the benefits of living in your market area, because emotional benefits sell houses. If you represent first time buyer properties, create a blog for first time buyers. Other niches include blogs for non-native speakers, investors, and resort properties. Whatever you elect to blog about, make sure that it ignites your passion. If not, you will find it difficult to blog regularly.

3. **Local color**
   In Austin, Texas, residents proudly proclaim, "Keep Austin Weird." Bumper stickers and T-shirts all over town convey this message. In fact, there is an annual "Keep Austin Weird" street festival. This is an example of what could be a regular category for a blog. Instead of just writing about it, however, make your posts come alive by taking your own pictures. In this case, you could run the "Keep Austin Weird Photo of the Week" and post it with a brief description. You could also invite your readers to submit their own photos. Either way you're building readership and having fun as well.

4. **Fun spots**
   Are there any free concerts in your city or special plays for children? If so, provide your readers with tips on where to obtain a gourmet picnic basket to make the outing extra special. Build your business by interviewing the owners of different entertainment venues in town. Share your favorite picks for the best local brews and burgers. Take the time to interview the owners, find out about how they started their business, and send them the link to your blog post. Don't forget to take pictures. This is a terrific way to build your referral network while supporting your local business community.

5. **Live like a local**
   People who live in an area often don't visit local tourist attractions. On the other hand, many visitors want to discover where the hidden local gems are. Where do the locals go when they want a great meal? Who has the best patio dining? Share your city's best kept secrets with your audience, ask for their feedback, and you'll have them sharing their tips as well.

Knead the Dough Secret #31

Ripping off other people's website content or blogging content can cost you plenty—both in copyright fines and by landing in "Google Hell."

6. **Linking is the proper etiquette for using another blogger's content—not copying.**
   One of the most important things you can do in any blog post is to link to other bloggers whenever possible. When you reference them in your blog, the best bloggers will link back to you. This helps to build your search engine ranking. Furthermore, rather than requiring your reader to cut and paste an address into your web browser, all the reader has to do is click on the link.

Do not copy other people's content. If you're going to reference someone else's work, do so with a link rather than copying it. The link builds your search engine placement. Copying someone else's posts, however, can get your blog banned by the search engines. This is known as "Google Hell" since your blog will no longer come up in their searches. You can reference someone else's work by providing a brief excerpt from the original source and then create a hyperlink to that resource.

It's also important to avoid using music that you have not licensed as well as pictures taken by other people. Remember that radio stations pay a fee to the record label to play the songs you hear. Rather than risk using music on your site, a better approach would be to use a video or audio greeting from you. It's more personal and you don't have to worry about copyright infringement.

Avoid using search engines to locate pictures. Search engines pull pictures from a variety of sites. In fact, a site may have used a picture with the appropriate license. If you copy a licensed photo to your site without paying the necessary fees, you will have violated the owner's copyright. Many professional photography companies now track their copyrighted photos in order to protect the photographers they represent. Avoid thousands of dollars of fines and potential litigation by simply taking your own photos.

Help! I'm Not a Writer!

If your writing skills are poor, you can still blog without hiring someone to do it for you. A simple approach is to record your comments and have them transcribed. You can also use "voice to text" systems such as Jott.com that will allow you to post your voice message as an audio or text file directly to your blog. A different alternative is to hire a writer to place your ideas in grammatical form. Keep in mind, however, that it's your blog. It must reflect your personality.

A different approach is to invite guest contributors to share their expertise. For example, you might have a CPA do a post about changes in the tax law or have a probate expert discuss trusts. Provide information about changes in zoning laws, new construction in the area, neighborhood watch, etc. You could also include restaurant reviews from your readers, information on upcoming garage sales, or the sports schedule for local schools. Invite your local PTA, Chamber of Commerce, or charitable fundraising groups to participate as well. Again, be a resource for all that is local in your market area.

Blogging can be a highly enjoyable way to build your business. Imagine the fun you can have taking pictures and doing nifty things all in the name of creating your local blog. Sure beats licking stamps, cold calling, and knocking on doors.

Chapter 15
Action Plan

Blogging is rapidly becoming a tried and true way to build your business. While it's not for everyone, it is one of the new ways to have clients learn to trust you. The key point to remember is that your blog must be about something that ignites your passion and is focused on a very narrow market segment. Your goal is to be the go-to expert for that niche.

As in previous chapters, identify the action steps that you would like to take. Rewrite items that may not fit. Remember to circle the number of each strategy that you plan to implement in your business and then record the date you complete the item in the space provided. If you select more than one item, place the items in priority order and work on implementing one item at a time. Once you complete the items you have selected, move on to the next chapter.

Action Steps:

___ 1. I have both a blog and a website for my business.

___ 2. My real estate blog generates clients for my business on a regular basis.

___ 3. I will use my blog to help establish trust and credibility in my local market area.

___ 4. The niche that my blog will serve is: ______________________________

___ 5. I plan to use key words as well as Technorati to make sure that my blog reaches search engines such as Google.

___ 6. In the future, I will never steal content from other people's blogs, use pictures without the photographer's consent or attribution, or use music that has not been properly licensed.

If you're ready to explore blogging for your business, Teresa Boardman provides important insights about how to do this in the next Recipe for Success.

Recipes for Success
Obituary Marketing
Teresa Boardman
StPaulRealEstateBlog.com

While there are thousands of real estate bloggers, two of my favorite blogs belong to Teresa Boardman (St. Paul Real Estate blog and the blog she started for fun, The Real Estate Weenie). Teresa has become one of the most successful bloggers in the country, not only due to her excellent photography skills, but also due to her ability to capture the essence of living in St. Paul, and to have fun in the process. Teresa has managed to climb to a first page ranking on Google for "St. Paul real estate." In fact, her ranking comes up higher than the major real estate companies that serve her area.

What's her secret? Fresh content every day that is specific to the St. Paul area. Teresa carries her camera wherever she goes. She takes pictures of historical buildings, houses with interesting histories, and local street culture. Her goal is to capture what it's like to live in St. Paul. It's relatively simple to take a picture of something and write a brief description. She mixes this with at least one fun post per week that lets her readers know who she is as a person. Her other posts are business based. Below you will find an example of one of Teresa's fun posts.

Real Estate Company Websites and the Obituaries

When I read the Sunday paper, I always take a peak at the obituaries, mostly to see if I am listed. This past Sunday I got to thinking about how similar the obituary section of the paper is to real estate company websites.

Real estate company websites usually include a page with pictures of agents, a brief bio, and maybe some details about the services they provide. There is a banner across the top, with the name of the real estate company on it. The obituary pages of the paper are similar; there is a banner across the top and then pictures of people with a brief bio, and details about services.

There are other similarities. I look at the dates in an obituary and see that the person who passed away was born in the 1920s. This means they would be in their 80s today, yet the person in the picture looks to be in their 20s or 30s. This seems to be true with the photos of agents on real estate company websites too. I have met agents who are 10 to 20 years older than the website photo. Yet the pictures in the obituaries some how look more natural than those of agents on real estate websites.

Not all obituaries have pictures with them. The same is true with agent bios on real estate websites. For the obituaries the picture section is simply left blank: on the real estate website the place where the picture should go will have a shadow of a face, the company logo, or a for sale sign.

I often wonder who made the rules about real estate company websites. Did they get their ideas one Sunday morning as they were reading the obituaries?

In a subsequent post, Teresa suggested that an entirely untapped place for agents to post their pictures was on the back of tombstones. Her posts work because of her humor and astute observations. Today's web savvy consumer wants competence but many also want to do business with someone who is fun. A blog is an ideal place to demonstrate both.

Chapter 16
Lights, Camera, Action!

The more informative your advertising, the more persuasive it will be.
David Ogilvy

Skills Check:
Put a checkmark (√) next to what you do now. Leave the remaining items blank. Review the action steps at the end of the chapter to determine the strategies that you will implement in your business.

___ 1. I produce an online video for each of my listings.

___ 2. I regularly post my videos to my website and/or blog.

___ 3. I advertise on cable television.

___ 4. I target my cable television advertising to specific niches or market areas.

___ 5. I use a video syndication service to publish my listings on multiple video sites including YouTube.

___ 6. I use video email.

___ 7. I use video testimonials from past clients on my website.

___ 8. I use video to help relocation clients save time in determining where to purchase.

___ 9. I use video to record physical inspections.

___10. I use video to illustrate how houses look before and after they have been staged.

Knead the Dough Secret #32
Video messaging will soon make text messaging obsolete.

Video Apps—THE Marketing Tool of the Future

Video applications are one of the hot new options in real estate marketing. If you're not promoting your listings using video, you're missing a huge opportunity to differentiate yourself from the competition, provide a higher level of service to your clients, and reach the hot Gen X and Gen Y markets.

Perhaps the most challenging question is where to begin and how much to spend. Not only are some of the names confusing, so is selecting the services that will work best with your business. The price points range from very little to very expensive, depending upon the level of quality that you want.

1. **Easy ways to get started**

   There are a number of excellent video applications that have a minimum cost. Many agents already market their listings with a virtual tour. If you would like to make your own 30 or 60 second commercial, there are numerous alternatives.

   One of the simplest approaches is to use a service that uses from five to nine still photos in conjunction with the Ken Burns technology. Burns technology allows the agent to control where the camera moves as well as allowing the agent to pan in and out. The result is similar to actual video tours. Once the agent uploads the pictures, depending upon the system, the agent may select licensed music, a professional voiceover, or create their own voiceover.

   According to Jeff Turner, the CEO of RealEstateShows.com, one of the challenges with virtual tours is that you would have to redo the entire tour if you want to change pictures as the seasons change or if you want to include additional shots at a later date. With his program, agents can easily change their show by changing the pictures. Once the agent creates the show, the agent can embed it into a blog post or even into the Multiple Listing Service.

2. **Upgrade from brochure marketing to video marketing**

   If a picture is worth a thousand words, then a video is worth ten thousand. While it may not be practical financially to shoot a video for every listing, it's an important option for expensive properties.

   An excellent way to use video is to shoot a tour of your local community. Rather than promoting yourself, give a guided tour of your market area that demonstrates what makes your area unique. Use the video to introduce future residents to unusual things to do or the best kept secrets that even locals may not know. Also, don't be afraid to do something fun. People love being entertained. Post your video brochure to your website or blog. You can also record it on an inexpensive travel drive that you can give out to clients you meet face-to-face.

3. High quality video/HDTV

If your commercial is only going to appear on the web, you do not need superb quality. On the other hand, if you plan to use your video on television, hire a professional production company such as InmanStories.com or TurnHere.com. One of the hot trends is to shoot your virtual tours in HDTV. It's a powerful way to show your listings, especially if someone has a big screen television.

4. Video syndication

Once you have produced your video, the question is how to get it out there. The best choice is to use the universal upload tool at TubeMogul.com. Rather than uploading your listing videos separately to various sites, TubeMogul does all the work. They also track how many page views you receive for each site where your video is syndicated. Their website claims, "Users of the Universal Upload have witnessed up to 3X more views per video." Part of the reason is that they currently syndicate videos to 15 different sites, including YouTube, Google Video, and Yahoo Video.

Knead the Dough Secret #33

Television gives you instant credibility.

Cable Television

Due to the proliferation of cable and satellite television, cable television advertising costs have declined dramatically. Cable operators actively seek local advertisers as an additional revenue source. When the cable operator lacks local advertising, they run national ads to fill space. The local cable company receives no revenue from running these ads. Thus, local cable television operators are eager to do business with agents because agent advertising represents more revenue for them. In fact, 30- to 60-second ads can be as little as $6 to $12 per spot. Furthermore, cable television allows you to target specific geographical areas at a minimal cost. Compared to classified advertising costs, cable television is a real bargain.

1. Choose your audience

Before investing in cable television advertising, carefully evaluate the commercials on the channels where you would like to advertise. For example, if you're working with luxury homes, look for shows that have commercials for luxury cars, expensive travel, or premium credit cards. If you're marketing golf properties, consider advertising on the Golf Channel. If you want to reach stay-at-home moms, advertise on stations running large numbers of baby commercials. Your goal is to match your commercial to the shows your target audience is most likely to watch.

2. **Placing your commercial**
   Cable television lets you advertise by zip code or by a given radius from a central location. In terms of the cost, cable advertisers usually sell "blocks" of users. (A typical block might be 50,000-75,000 users.) You can also advertise by county, state, or region. Depending on the size of your viewing area, you could be advertising on CNN, Discovery, or ESPN for only a few dollars per ad.

3. **Cable has a new "Front Door"**
   In 2008, two new cable network players emerged on the real estate scene. Scripps Networks, the owners of HGTV, the Food Channel, and a host of other lifestyle cable television channels, launched "Front Door" as a new real estate channel designed to tap into the growing interest in real estate programming. Better Homes and Gardens also seeks to capitalize on the cable television market through their relationship with Meredith. Meredith is one of the nation's leading media and marketing companies with businesses centering on magazine and book publishing, television broadcasting, integrated marketing, and interactive media. Look for both of these companies to continue to create innovative ways to integrate video, print, and online marketing throughout their multi-million viewer networks.

4. **The best solution for your business**
   The best solution for your business depends upon the quality you want and your pocketbook. It's probably not a good idea to shoot your own shaky, poorly lit video, even though many Gen X and Gen Y users are OK with the grainy quality that is common on YouTube. When it comes to marketing properties, especially those with hefty price tags, it's smart to go with the best quality that you can afford.

   As compared to high quality print ads that can cost you anywhere from $2,500 to $5,000, having just one excellent video can land you on hundreds of sites on the Internet. In a time where more people are becoming increasingly careful about their advertising budget, video can provide one of the best sources for a high return on your advertising dollar.

Other Cool Ways to Incorporate Video in Your Business

You can do much more with video than just producing commercials. Video has numerous other applications. All you need is a little creativity. Here are some other ways to incorporate video into your business.

1. **Video mail, not email**
   Create your own video emails using your webcam. You can purchase a great webcam for under $100. There are a number of services that allow you to create video emails. Most are free, work on any browser, and require no download or

installation. Simply login, record or upload your video, and send it. The recipient is notified by email or text that there is a new video message. To watch, all they have to do is click on the link.

2. **Live like a local**
   Professionally produce a video about the specific geographical area(s) that you serve. In the video, conduct a "live like a local" tour. Show the local farmer's market, your favorite place for coffee, or the view from a favorite restaurant at sunset. Whet their appetite for more by showing people having fun and enjoying life in your area. Avoid doing an infomercial about you.

3. **Video testimonials**
   A video testimonial is an excellent way to create trust and credibility. Using videos of happy clients singing your praises is a compelling way to market your services. More importantly, video testimonials are a powerful risk management tool. If you are ever involved in litigation, there's nothing better than having the person who is suing you saying how wonderful you were in handling their transaction.

4. **Save gas with video caravans**
   For years, agents have jumped in their cars every week to view their company's new listings. A great alternative is to have each listing agent video their new listings and then show them at your weekly office meeting. In addition to more agents seeing the interiors of company listings, your office will save hundreds of gallons of gas every month.

5. **Preview neighborhoods and houses for relocation clients**
   One of the most time-intensive activities in the real estate business is helping relocation buyers decide on a specific neighborhood in which to purchase. Rather than driving them everywhere, take videos of the various areas where they are looking. Video the traffic at rush hour as well as what it's like on a weekend morning or afternoon. You can also video the inside of the houses that they would like to see (provided you have the seller's permission). Post the video on a passcode-protected part of your site. Once you have made a video of the general areas, all you have to do with future clients is to video the houses they want to see.

6. **Go mobile**
   In the very near future, our mobile phones will be our connection point for virtually everything that we do. You'll watch your favorite TV shows, receive video messages from vendors about specials as you walk past their stores, and

experience a wide array of other applications. To take advantage of this trend, obtain a "dot-mobi" address in addition to your "dot-com" address. On your dot-mobi site, provide a series of links to your listing videos plus any other high interest videos about local restaurants, theaters, or other recreational activities.

7. **Get a jump on the competition**
   Whether you're at an open house or are previewing properties for clients, if you find a terrific property, make a quick video using your PDA or iPhone and send it to your clients. If the property is one where there may be multiple offers, you greatly increase the odds that your clients will be first in line with their offer.

8. **Architectural tour**
   Most areas have historical homes as well as architectural styles that are unique to the region. Make a video of 5 to 10 of the best examples of the various architectural styles that are prevalent in your market. Conduct a guided video tour of the major historical homes as well. If you are in a resort area, use video to show the different types of second homes or vacation rentals as well as nearby amenities.

9. **Before-and-after staging videos**
   An important step in selling property quickly is to stage it properly. Sometimes sellers are reluctant to do this. Showing them a video of properties that were staged and then successfully sold can motivate them to take this important step.

10. **Inspection videos**
    Make a video of your home inspections. Rather than having to rely on a verbal description of a particular problem, having it on video is much smarter. You can also use video to illustrate how to operate the appliances, sprinklers, air conditioning, and other systems.

As our current bandwidth continues to expand, video will become increasingly important in both our personal and our business communications. Static pictures and text messaging will no longer be satisfactory to the next generation of web users. Instead, they will expect a full range of video applications that create the experience of "being there." In fact, we already have the technology to create three-dimensional virtual tours. Once the bandwidth is in place, it may not be long before we are doing our showings from our mobile phones and a set of 3-D goggles. Now that would be a true revolution in how we conduct our business.

Chapter 16
Action Plan

If you want to be competitive, video is an important addition to your business, especially if you are representing younger clients or luxury properties. A simple place to start is to produce a video about your area or to take videos of your listings and post them on sites such as TubeMogul.

As in previous chapters, identify the action steps that you would like to take and rewrite items that may not fit. Circle the number of each strategy that you plan to implement in your business and then record the date you complete the item in the space provided. Remember, making too many changes at once can be overwhelming. Instead, make one or two changes at a time and integrate them into your business before making any other changes.

Action Steps:

___ 1. In the future, I will produce an online video for each of my listings.

___ 2. I will regularly post my videos to my website and/or blog.

___ 3. I have put together an ad for cable television.

___ 4. My cable television advertising serves specific market niches or areas.

___ 5. In the future, I will use a video syndication service to publish my listings on multiple video sites including YouTube.

___ 6. I currently use video email.

___ 7. I will use video testimonials from past clients on my website.

___ 8. In the future, I will send relocation clients a video showing different areas to help them save time deciding where to purchase.

___ 9. In the future, I will use video to record physical inspections.

___10. I have created a video that I give to sellers illustrating how houses look before and after they have been staged.

The increase in bandwidth coupled with increased downloading speeds means that video applications are going to continue to grow. On the other end of the spectrum is the "short and sweet tweets" of sites like Twitter.

Chapter 17
Make Your "Tweets" Short and Sweet*

Call it a clan, call it a network, call it a tribe, or call it a family. Whatever you call it, whoever you are, you need one.
Jane Howard

Skills Check:
Put a checkmark (√) next to what you do now. Leave the remaining items blank. Review the action steps at the end of the chapter to determine the strategies that you will implement in your business.

___ 1. I belong to at least one business-to-business social networking site such as LinkedIn.

___ 2. I currently have an active account on MySpace or Facebook.

___ 3. I am active in at least one real estate social networking site such as ActiveRain or RealTown.

___ 4. I have an active account on Twitter.

___ 5. I have created my own community website, blog, or social network.

___ 6. I have posted a profile on Trulia and/or Zillow and regularly answer questions on their forums.

___ 7. I am currently an active member at SecondLife.

___ 8. I have my social networking activities organized in one place.

*Technology changes continually and rapidly. The best way to stay current on technology changes is to subscribe to our audio podcast program at ListenAndLearnRealEstate.com.

Knead the Dough Secret #34
Want to eliminate spam? Send and receive your messages through social networking sites such as LinkedIn, Facebook, and Twitter.

Network Your Way to Web Success

Social networking may soon overtake virtually every other source as being the most important strategy for lead generation. If you're not engaged in Web 2.0 social networking strategies, there's no better time than now to start. The names and jargon may be confusing. Nevertheless, it only takes a small amount of time to "friend" yourself to web success.

What is a social network? According to Wikipedia, social networks are online communities where people can explore interests or activities that they share with others. The key point is that social networks allow participants to interact through chat rooms, instant messaging, traditional email, video, video email, file sharing, blogging, and discussion groups. Wikipedia identifies three primary types of social networking services:

1. Directories such as former classmates

2. Means to connect with friends (Facebook, MySpace, Twitter, and YouTube)

3. Recommendation systems linked to trust (LinkedIn)

For example, social networks are a great way to stay in contact with family, friends, and clients. Many agents who have lost track of past clients and friends have found them through these networks. These sites also allow you to share pictures of your listings, videos, links to interesting articles, as well as important information for potential clients. Granted, there are certain risks associated with being online. Whatever you post is there for posterity, even if you take it down. Identity thieves can check your work history. Nevertheless, the benefits of participating far outweigh the potential risks.

For Gen X and Gen Y, Web 2.0 applications are now the primary way that they connect. While this may seem like a new approach, Web 2.0 is akin to the general store from 100 years ago. People came there to discuss politics, hear the latest gossip, and to personally connect with others in their community. The way that you participated was by being there. Today, places such as Facebook, MySpace, LinkedIn, Twitter, and YouTube serve essentially the same function.

In today's Web 2.0 environment, having a website with your bio, a branding statement, and cool technology tools is no longer enough. Today's consumer wants to get to know you through the actions you take online, not just through the static content that you post on your website.

If you're new to social networking, it can be overwhelming. Where do you start? What social networks are really worthwhile? How much time should you spend and where should you spend it? Should social networking take priority over other real estate related activities? Do you need a blog or is a profile on Trulia and Zillow a better alternative? Can spending all this time online actually translate into closed sales?

The answer to these questions depends upon what you want to achieve online, how proficient you are with technology, how well you write, and how diligent you intend to be in terms of regularly participating. Much like the individual who sits at home and avoids interacting in face-to-face activities, if you're not willing to "be there," and be actively engaged in the social networking process, then this is probably not a good venue for your business development. On the other hand, given the huge proportion of younger buyers and sellers that frequent these various sites, not participating will cause your business to gradually erode as the next generation of buyers and sellers shifts to Web 2.0 solutions for their real estate needs.

The great news about the Web 2.0 environment is that most of the real estate specific services are either free or very low cost. This means that you can experiment with different services and determine which ones are the best fit for your business.

Knead the Dough Secret #35
Online reputation tools are rapidly becoming the preferred way for consumers to select the people with whom they choose to do business.

How to Begin?

There are numerous ways to become active in social networking. Below you'll find some of the most commonly used methods.

1. **Recommendation systems linked to trust**
   LinkedIn is the most widely used business-to-business recommendation system. There is a robust free version of the site as well as a paid version. When you post your profile, you also post the other places that you have worked as well as where you attended college. Based upon this information, the system automatically makes suggestions about people you may know. The beauty of the system is that you can easily send invitations to people in your current address book to join your network. Once someone agrees to be in your network, you can then view all the members of their network.

   These types of recommendation systems are a powerful tool for building referrals. For example, when you start working with a client, invite them to join. If the client is already a member, you will then have access to their network. If there is someone that you would like to meet on your client's network, all you have to do is to ask for an introduction. A slightly different application is to invite your preferred vendors to join your network. Inform your clients that only your best resources are on your network. Carefully monitor the quality because your good reputation is critical.

2. **Broker-to-broker social networking**
   If you want to connect with other agents, develop referrals elsewhere in the country, seek help, or just stay up to date on blog posts from leading agents, ActiveRain and RealTown are excellent choices. These are two of the most frequently visited social networking sites in the real estate business.

3. **Facebook and MySpace**
   Of the major social networking sites, Facebook is probably the most important one to consider if you want to have an active presence in your community without having to write a blog. If you're younger, having a MySpace account is also smart. In June, 2008, MySpace launched a new application designed to motivate "non techie" users to join the MySpace network. Although neither of these sites is real estate specific, they both afford great opportunities to meet people in your community and engage in a meaningful conversation.

   The first step is to complete a profile. You can then add "friends" (i.e., people you know, have done business with, or who may have an interest in sharing information with you). Both Facebook and MySpace allow you to post in your geographical area. To build credibility as an agent, post interesting information about the area, not about you or even real estate in general. Instead, focus on participating in the community conversation. Pushing your real estate listings or marketing yourself will cause you to lose "friends" instantaneously. Instead, find people who have interests similar to yours, whether it's kids, the local football team, or a hobby that you enjoy regularly.

4. **Twitter**
   Some people have likened Twitter to a mini-blog. You post what you're doing throughout the day so your friends/clients can stay in touch. Most of what is on Twitter is "Hi! Here's what I'm doing—bye!" Nevertheless, it is becoming an important way for people to share information and stay in contact. For example, assume that you're out previewing open houses and you see one that is perfect for two of your clients. You could send them a "tweet" to come see the house while it was open. You can also track well known authors such as Seth Godin on Twitter. Regular Twitter users run their "Twhirl" all day. This keeps them updated on any "tweets" they receive. In fact, many Gen X and Gen Y users use Twitter or Facebook to send their communications. Remember, "tweets" are short and sweet.

5. **Create your own community**
Community websites and blogs have been around for several years. If you would like to create a private social networking site that has functionality similar to MySpace and Facebook, you can use a service such as Ning.com. These new private social networking sites are the next generation of message boards or chat rooms. Ning has hundreds of thousands of private social networks on a wide variety of topics. In many respects, this system is easier to use than blogging. For example, you can open a "forum" topic and any of your members can comment on them. Possible uses include creating a private network of people who are interested in historical homes or who live in a particular high rise condominium. You can share information pertinent to the area as well as restaurant reviews, upcoming events, or funny stories. Remember, social networking is about the conversation.

6. **Profiles on major real estate sites such as Trulia and Zillow**
For those who are not comfortable with writing blog posts several times per week, an entirely different approach is to complete a profile on Trulia and Zillow. Each of these sites has millions of unique visitors every month. Once your profile is complete, both companies have discussion forums where you can answer questions posed by visitors. If you answer only one question each week, at the end of the six months you will have 26 posts on those sites. This strengthens your credibility as an expert in a specific market. The advantage here is that these sites are specific to a single zip code or location. Thus, your posts appear when people from your area visit these sites.

7. **Virtual real estate gets real**
Did you know that there is an alternative real estate reality where virtual real estate is traded for real money? If you haven't heard of "Second Life," this hot new community may take you by surprise (http://secondlife.com/whatis/). People trade their real dollars for Lindens. They can then purchase virtual web real estate and develop houses, hotels, stores, or anything they want on their virtual land. In fact, Second Life has its own currency exchange. You can also buy and sell real products and services. Think that this is not serious? Second Life has already created its first millionaires and that's in real U.S. currency. Companies with brick and mortar stores are now making their products available through their virtual store on Second Life. Coldwell Banker and RE/MAX have a presence on Second Life. Are you up to joining the virtual property party?

8. **Yoono, you don't need to get overwhelmed**
   Does all of this seem overwhelming? The good news is that like other web trends, consolidation of services is taking place. In terms of social networking, Yoono.com has made handling social networking easy, especially if you are using the widely used tools such as Facebook, Twitter, and Flickr.com (Yahoo's photo site).The system is an add-on to your browser. Simply click on it to view your messages, pictures, or tweets from your network. Yoono organizes them all in one place. Furthermore, it lets you prioritize all the incoming information so you can focus on the input that you want to receive and ignore the rest. It also lets you move from site to site with just one click rather than having to leave one site and then navigate to another site. It's a simple way to organize your online social life.

Social networking can become addictive, running into hours each day. Explore different networks and experiment with participating. If it works for you and you're having fun, stay involved in the conversation. If not, move on to a site that supports both your business and your personal interests. If you plan to be in business for the long term, social networking is a trend that you cannot afford to ignore.

Chapter 17
Action Plan

Social networking is one of the most powerful ways to market on the web. The goal is not to focus on advertising. Instead, successful social networking is about contributing to others, being engaged in an on-going conversation, and having them learn to trust you over time through the actions you take online.

Identify the action steps that you would like to take and rewrite items that may not fit. Circle the number of each strategy that you plan to implement in your business and then record the date you complete the item in the space provided. Decide which social networking strategies will work for you and experiment to see what fits.

Action Steps:

___ 1. I have an active account on at least one business-to-business social networking site such as LinkedIn.

___ 2. I have a MySpace or Facebook account.

___ 3. I am actively participating in at least one real estate social networking site such as ActiveRain or RealTown.

___ 4. I have learned how to tweet on Twitter.

___ 5. I have created my own community website, blog, or social network.

___ 6. I have posted a profile on Trulia and/or Zillow and will regularly answer questions on their forums.

___ 7. I have visited Second Life and am participating in the on-line virtual real estate world.

___ 8. I will use Yoono to organize my online social life.

Social networking has its roots in old fashioned neighborhood gatherings. In the next Recipe for Success, Marc Davison explains the secrets involved in putting social networking to use in your business.

Recipes for Success
Being There: Generating Loyalty the Old Fashioned Way

Marc Davison
1000 Watt Consulting

Marc Davison is one of the most knowledgeable and forward thinking experts in the real estate industry. His work has been a constant source of inspiration and insight for our business. In addition to being a regular columnist for Inman News, Marc is one of the co-founders of 1000 Watt, a firm that provides consulting to the top real estate firms in the country. In this Recipe for Success Marc explains that the be-all, end-all is not technology, but personal connection.

If you think your customers know you by reading your Website bio, think again.

If you think you create loyalty from a simple brand statement, think again.

If you think all this innovation separates you from tradition, please think again.

The past

Every Friday morning, as a boy, I joined grandma on her weekly trek to the butcher. Shelly knew exactly what kind of chicken grandma preferred for the Sabbath meal.

It was bagged when we arrived. Her name, scribbled across the wrapping. A few marrow bones thrown in for her soup. No charge. And a sugary bow tie cookie for me.

Every so often as a boy, I'd join grandpa going to the shoe repair store. Mario, the owner, was a tiny man dwarfed by stacks of shoes and shoe parts. His olive skin held a shiny patina from all the polish he handled. "Marco Polo!" he'd scream as I entered his shop. "Looka how bigga you get." Even if he hadn't seen me for a year. Even though I had hardly grown.

Back then, New York's Lower East Side was our Internet. These shops were our destination sites of choice. The owners garnered loyalty the old fashioned way—by being there. Holding court. Playing to the crowd of visitors, customers, members.

They'd talk and joke—share their opinions about anything.

Shelly and Mario were yesterday's webmasters. Social networks' architects. They epitomized the very essence of what "local" meant. When I think of them, memories overtake me. They had an intimate relationship with their customers. Chicken is chicken, but there was only one Shelly.

Sometimes, the conversations inside their stores were about politics. Sometimes it was about sports. Often, it was about the neighborhood. Who did what to whom. Who bought a new car. What home was for sale. Sometimes, it was idle banter. But it was always real. Honest. It mimicked life. And it was the foundation of their business.

Today

Meet Tony—Zappo's resident shopkeeper. Standing behind his counter, like Shelly, garnering loyalty the old fashioned way—by being there. Sharing his thoughts. Playing to the Zappos crowd.

I received a Twitter message last week regarding his thoughts on service. It prompted me to go to his website. I shopped around and ordered three pairs of Doc Martins—sneaker shoes and a pair of summer sandals. Asked for 3-4 day delivery. They arrived the next day, just like his tweet suggested.

Tomorrow

I know this whole Web 2.0 stuff is seemingly fleeting, trendy, and difficult to measure.

I know it can be argued that so much of what is being twittered about—especially in real estate—is hardly quotable and borderline rubbish.

I know that discounting many of Web 2.0's higher possibilities is a predominant sensibility in real estate especially among die-hard traditionalists holding onto old-fashioned ways.

But I submit that what you are discounting is deeply rooted in good old-fashioned tradition. I submit that if applied correctly, blogs, Twitter and the like could very well be the vehicle by which those old-fashioned ideologies we honor so dearly can be resurrected.

I submit that these Web 2.0 tools stand to better connect you with your customers than the template, static, boilerplate Web tools you have been using for the last 10 years.

Nostalgia

Shelly or Mario never said anything all that memorable. But the social experiences inside their establishments have lingered for 40 years.

Your establishment is online. This is where conversations must now take place. To fight this inevitability is to buck the very tradition you hold dear. Real estate begins with a conversation and what better way to start and carry one than with the array of free 2.0 tools at your fingertips.

Granted, learning how to properly use these tools might be an arduous swim upstream. But sometimes a trip back to the past is where you can birth a new future What have you got to lose?

Chapter 18
Why Didn't You Just Text Me? Multi-Generational Marketing

*Each generation imagines itself to be more intelligent than
the one that went before it, and wiser than
the one that comes after it.*
George Orwell

Skills Check:
Put a checkmark (√) next to what you do now. Leave the remaining items blank. Review the action steps at the end of the chapter to determine the strategies that you will implement in your business.

___ 1. I always ask my clients how they want me to communicate with them and adjust my style accordingly.

___ 2. I know how Traditionalists, Boomers, Gen X, and Gen Y differ and how to work effectively with each group.

___ 3. I use voice-to-text systems to communicate more effectively with my clients.

___ 4. When I work with people born before 1964, I take the time to build a relationship with them.

___ 5. When I work with Gen X, I understand that they prefer to do their own research and are not usually concerned about having a personal relationship with their agent.

___ 6. When I work with Gen Y, I feel comfortable having them invite their friends and family to participate in the buying or selling decision.

___ 7. I use social networking sites such as LinkedIn, Facebook, or SecondLife to develop my business.

Knead the Dough Secret #36
For the first time in history, you must adjust your communication and your marketing messages to fit the age of your client.

Bridging the Generational Communication Gap

Whether you are writing an ad or negotiating a transaction, understanding your clients' preferred communication style is critical. Today, the way that we communicate depends upon the generation into which we were born. While there may be exceptions to these general trends, a large proportion of each generation exhibits many of the behaviors outlined below.

I first encountered the generational communication gap when my husband and I were on a delayed flight into Seattle. Our 16 year old nephew was going to pick us up at the airport. We called and emailed him to let him know that we would be about an hour late. Nevertheless, when we arrived, he had been waiting over an hour. When we let him know that we had tried to reach him, his response was, "Why didn't you just text me?" The truth of the matter is that it never crossed either of our minds that he wouldn't check his messages or his email.

A few months later at our Annual Really Awesome Women in Real Estate Conference, several Boomers asked about how to work more effectively with Gen X and Gen Y agents and staff. We had a panel of Gen X and Gen Y women, and their comments were quite enlightening. What was readily apparent is that there is a substantial difference in each generation in terms of how they approach the work place, how they cope with life, and how they communicate.

In today's changing real estate environment, it's important to match our communication styles to those of our clients. Each generation has very different styles of communicating. The only way you'll know for sure how to best serve each of your clients is to ask how they would like you to communicate with them.

Traditionalists (Born Before 1946)

Traditionalists are also sometimes known as the "Greatest Generation." Currently there are about 59 million members in this age group in the United States. Their core values are respect for tradition and authority, playing by the rules, and self sacrifice. Unlike members of the younger generations, Traditionalists believe in duty before pleasure. Work hard, save your money, delay gratification, and eventually you will get want you want.

When working with any client, the most important question you can ask is, "How would you like me to communicate with you?" It's important to adapt to the client's style of communication rather than expecting your client to adapt to your style. This is especially true for Traditionalists. While a Gen X could call or email, a large number of Traditionalists do not know how to use a computer.

To market to Traditionalists, use face-to-face, telephone, or print communication. Handwritten thank you notes are particularly effective. Respect the Traditionalist's experience.

When working with them in person, ask about past properties that they have owned as well as what they liked or didn't like about their past selling or buying experiences. Since they value stability and security, most will refuse to stretch to buy something outside their price range. They tend to be careful with their money and in many cases will prefer to buy less than they can afford. Your marketing messages will work best when you stress safety and security.

To the greatest extent possible, focus on how to make the buying or selling process safe for your Traditionalist clients. Take care of the details—most will appreciate it. Be patient when you explain how the processes work. The way that real estate is conducted today is substantially different from how it was conducted in the past. Sit down with them face-to-face and answer their questions. While it may not be the most convenient way for you to communicate or market, your Traditionalist clients will definitely appreciate it.

Baby Boomers (1946 to 1964)

The Baby Boom Generation currently dominates the real estate business both in terms of real estate professionals and in terms of which age group owns the most property. According to NAR, the median age of REALTORS® has been hovering around 51 for several years. In 2007, 54 percent of all listings were with sellers between the ages of 50 and 60. This is the same percentage that we saw in 2006.

Part of the reason the Boomer generation is so influential is due to its size. There are over 78 million Boomers according to the U.S. Census. There is some speculation that Gen Y's numbers may have surpassed the Boomers, but the exact count will not be known until the 2010 census data is available.

In terms of their characteristics, the generation that spawned the "Summer of Love" and communal living is still interested in their community. This is an important point to remember when working and marketing to Boomers: their community is an important aspect of their existence.

In terms of their work, the Hippies of the 1960s became the Yuppies of the 1980s. Proving themselves is a core value, as is idealism and optimism. Boomers want to make a difference, whether it's being involved in charitable causes or saving the planet. While Boomers are not usually interested in self sacrifice, most will go the extra mile to do a deal or to meet a work commitment. In fact, many Boomers are workaholics whose work is their identity. While they can be self-centered and competitive (the original "Me" generation), they are also good at building communities and creating relationships.

Most Boomers prefer email, print, and telephone communication. A great way to meet Boomer clients is by becoming involved in charity work or doing work for your local community.

Both Boomers and Traditionalists love to discuss all aspects of the real estate process. As my 16 year old nephew described it, "You old people sure like to talk a lot."

Furthermore, most Boomers prefer to develop a relationship before they will trust you with their business. Just giving them information is not enough to motivate them to hire you. If you want their business, listen and communicate with them by phone, email, or snail mail.

Marketing to potential second or retirement home buyers can be a powerful new niche for your business. According to NAR, approximately 17 percent of the Boomers plan to purchase real estate in the near term. Furthermore, the peak buying time for second homes is between the ages of 50 and 60. The census data shows that the peak of the Baby Boom was in 1960. What this means is that the second home and the retirement community market should continue to be highly active for at least the next ten years. Many Boomers and Traditionalists will purchase a second home prior to their retirement. They test out the new community to determine whether they want to make their second home their primary residence when they retire.

In terms of where to focus, communities with mild weather, a low cost of living, reasonable tax and insurance rates, plus proximity to health care are great places to niche your business for at least the next decade. Golf course communities should continue to be popular as well as senior communities that cater to affluent and active seniors who want minimal property maintenance. If you are a Boomer, moving to one of these communities and becoming the local real estate expert could be a great way to market your business for years to come.

Another offshoot of this same trend is the explosion of vacation club properties as well as fractional ownerships (where several people own a percentage of a property and have the right to use it for a specific amount of time each year).

Today these opportunities are often affiliated with major luxury hotel chains in prime locations. Owners have the advantage of being able to trade their property for stays at prime properties elsewhere in the system. In fact, one hotel chain actually allows you to switch your unit for points at any of their worldwide resorts.

Gen X: The Latch Key Generation (1965 to 1976)

Gen X, born between 1965 and 1976, is the smallest generation, with a population of approximately 48 million. When the Boomers went off to work, this generation was left at home to fend for themselves. Gen X was born into the highest divorce and abortion rates in history. Over half were raised in one-parent homes. It's no surprise that many have elected to delay marriage and having children. Over 50 percent are single. Current predictions are that a typical Gen X'er will have 10 to 12 jobs during their lifetimes. More importantly, they actively seek to have real life balance. Unlike Boomers and Traditionalists who will work extra hours to complete a project, Gen X is much more likely to walk away at the end of the day to be with friends and family. For them, their personal time is more important than their jobs.

In fact, here's how one Gen X'er described her approach to her job with a major real estate company.

> *My friends and I used to talk about getting married and having children when we turned 30. Now that we're in our late 20s, we're thinking about waiting until we're 35 or perhaps even 40.*
>
> *In terms of my job, when I was first hired, I immediately went to the web and researched everything I could find out about the company where I would be working. I'm constantly researching information on the web to improve my performance. I want to know everything I can about what works for our people. Although I love my current job, I'll probably stay for a few more years and then move to a new job with different challenges.*
>
> *One of the interesting things that I discovered about our generation and the older people I report to is that they sometimes don't understand the reasons that I'm always asking "Why?" Sometimes they perceive it as being confrontational. All I'm really trying to do is to understand how things work.*

Because many Gen X'ers did not spend that much time with their parents and used technology to connect rather than being face-to-face, they often lack people skills. Here's how one CEO described the situation:

> *I'm really having trouble with our younger (Gen X) sales staff. They seem to think that providing information should be adequate motivation for their clients to do business with our company. Most of our clients are Boomers. I've talked to our younger sales staff about creating relationships and have even taken them on appointments with me so that they could see how to build relationships. They just don't get it. They have an order taker mentality. Our clients want to feel they have a personal relationship with us—they don't want to work with someone who just dishes out information.*

Unlike Boomers, with whom trust and a personal relationship is critical, Gen X relies more on information. They are direct, pragmatic, results oriented, and have no tolerance for phonies. Your marketing messages must take a "you decide" approach. Your role is to be a rich resource for information. Your Gen X clients will definitely want to make their own decisions.

Gen X is fiercely independent and often has little use for authority. Boomers often have difficulty understanding why Gen X behaves the way that they do. Here's how one Boomer agent described one of his closings with a Gen X buyer:

> *I can't believe what happened at our closing last week. I had a Gen X buyer and when we went to the closing table, he insisted on reading all 108 pages of the loan documents. I can understand not wanting to sign documents until you have read them. What I couldn't believe, however, was that he wanted to rewrite the loan documents. The title officer, the mortgage broker, and I were all supposed to sit there while he argued with us why he should be able to make the changes that he wanted.*

While the other agents in the room were amused by this tale, several others jumped in to say that they had encountered similar types of behaviors in their Gen X clients as well.

When you work with Gen X, don't be surprised if they have done extensive research on virtually every real estate website that serves your area. Market to them by having your website and/or blog be so content rich that they will always go to your site first for information.

Gen X may challenge and confront you. In most cases, they simply want to understand the process. They will also go online to verify what you tell them. If your data conflicts with their data, they will challenge you to explain the difference.

Gen X has had computers since elementary school. Mobile access is a way of life. "Email is the new snail mail." Both Gen X and Gen Y prefer text messages. When they contact you, they also expect instantaneous response.

The best way to work with Gen X is to be a conduit of information. Give them lists of real estate sites and blogs where they can do their own investigation. Avoid being attached to what they decide. Under no circumstances should you use, "I'm the expert" approach or try to parent them. Instead, use the phrase, "It's your house and it's your decision. My role is to provide you with as much information as possible so that you can make the best possible decision."

Marketing to Gen X (and Gen Y) is very different from marketing to Traditionalists or Boomers. According to a study from California State University at Chico,

It's more important to be interactive and to show people having fun. Gen X and Gen Y want to be marketed with a strong dose of the truth coupled with irony and humor. (Martin, 2005)

While Boomers and Traditionalists respond well to brand marketing, Gen X and Gen Y prefer lifestyle marketing. Their jobs are less important than their family and friends.

Gen X clients don't want to "pay their dues" or "go the extra mile to make the deal." They also respond poorly to fear-based tactics such as, "If you don't buy now, they will sell to someone else." Because they are so independent, micromanagement or indirect communication will undermine your relationship.

Ultimately, Gen X wants to trust you. To gain that trust, be genuinely caring about what they want. Ask their opinions and listen carefully to what they tell you. You must also be direct and honest. Avoid promising more than you can deliver.

Another important strategy is to use "que-gestions" (i.e., a question that makes a suggestion). For example:

Home ownership is the first step toward financial independence. Are you ready to fire your landlord?

Gen Y: The Millennials (1977 to 1994)

Current estimates are that there are 73 million people who are in Gen Y. As a group, they are the most educated generation. They are confident, fun, optimistic, and collaborative. They place a high value on "doing the right thing."

Many people now refer to both Boomers and Gen Y as being the "Me generations." Throughout their lives, members of Gen Y have been told that they are "special" and "unique." They are motivated by money and success. They are impatient about waiting to achieve their goals. Furthermore, a study conducted by Twenge (2007) found that 67 percent of Gen Y college students were 30 percent more narcissistic as compared to college students in 1982.

Gen Y wants it now. Climbing the corporate ladder and paying their dues are foreign concepts to this generation. Bill Gates summed it up when he said, "Don't expect a corner office, a six figure income, and a company car fresh out of school—you have to earn it!" Boomers believe you have to earn privileges, whereas Gen Y wants those privileges now.

While Gen X'ers are eager to exercise their independence, Gen Y is often content to graduate from college and return home. The problem has become so widespread in Japan that Japanese parents now call this age group "the parasite generation."

These factors have contributed to an important trend that we're seeing among first time buyers. Many young people are electing to stay at home or to rent in desirable areas. Because Gen Y is highly motivated by money, their first real estate purchase may be an investment property rather than a personal residence. In fact, aggressive Gen Y's are purchasing property in their teens and early twenties provided they can obtain financing.

Because Gen Y places such a high value on collaboration, they normally prefer to make decisions based upon input from their peer group. This often leads to "group think," where the conclusions drawn among their peer group outweigh expert advice from the outside. Consequently, if you are working with someone from Gen Y, shift from the "expert approach" that works with Boomers and Traditionalists. Instead, be a resource for information. Although it can be difficult, the best course of action is to allow your clients to navigate through the process with the help of their peer group rather than offering your advice and expertise.

Also, don't expect Gen Y clients to be forthcoming about anything that is bothering them. Unlike members of Gen X who have no issue about confrontation, Gen Y has difficulty confronting. For example, one woman I spoke with suggested that her niece call a mutual friend to get some help with a project. The friend would have welcomed the call. Her niece's response, "Call? That's way too confrontational!" A primary reason text messaging is so popular with this group is the recipient has time to consider how or when to respond to the text message. Texting entirely circumvents confrontation.

Marketing to Gen X and Gen Y

Gen X and Gen Y are changing how REALTORS® will market in the future. While a study conducted in the United Kingdom (Revoir, 2007) showed web use had increased among "Silver Surfers," web use has declined among 18 to 24 year olds. Since 2005, there has been a 20 percent decline in the number of adults and children who listen to the radio or who watch DVDs and video. Young people are spending less time in front of their computers and more time using their mobile phones, MP3 players, and iPods. Each of the following strategies is an emerging way to market more effectively to younger clients.

1. "Dot-mobile"

One of the most important new trends is "dot-mobile." Many major companies have already launched secondary websites that are a condensed version of their main site. These sites work specifically with mobile devices making navigation to key features simple. Merely tap on the feature you want and it appears. In fact, in the Netherlands you can actually purchase a house with your cell phone.

Because consumers remember mobile ads at a rate three times higher than other advertising, expect an increase in the number of ads that you will see on your mobile. In the future, retailers will detect that you are a previous customer as you walk by their stores. Your mobile device will receive a coupon that is good if you stop by their store at that moment. Consequently, to reach more Gen X and Gen Y clients, consider setting up a separate dot-mobile version of your website.

2. **Interactivity**

   A key feature in marketing to Gen X and Gen Y is interactivity. While many older clients have no interest in connecting online, Gen X and Gen Y actively interact and co-create on the web. This is one of the most important reasons for having a blog, a community website, or becoming involved in social networking. Each of these venues allows your users to interact.

   One of the latest trends is to create games where users can interact with the website's content. For example, in mid-2008, Zillow launched an application that allows web visitors to rate different rooms in competing houses. The site brings up two kitchens and the user picks their favorite. The site then brings up a different kitchen to compare with the favorite from the last pair. At the end of the sequence, you can see how your choices fared when compared to choices made by other players. Any steps that you can take to make your website more interactive will strengthen your marketing efforts to Gen X and Gen Y.

3. **Connection plus anonymity**

   Gen X and Gen Y enjoy being active online, however, many prefer to remain anonymous. They will surf to another website if you require them to reveal personal information before they are ready to do so. This has resulted in the use of "avatars," i.e., an online identity that is separate from your real world identity. A classic example of an avatar is the character you may elect to represent you in a video game.

   Even though Gen X and Gen Y may want privacy at times, they are equally willing to post very personal information on places such as MySpace, Facebook, iTunes, and YouTube. If you're representing a specific zip code or demographic, checking these sites periodically is an excellent way to learn what the online community has to say. Join the conversation and you will increase your business.

4. **Communicate their way**

   Texting is difficult for older agents. The keys on cell phones may be hard to see and sometimes difficult to press, especially if the person has arthritis. Fortunately, new voice-to-text technologies (e.g., Jott.com) allow you to send message via email, text, or MP3 audio file from the convenience of your cell phone or land line. The system automatically converts your message into the format your user prefers. Best of all, with a single phone call, you can deliver the same message to multiple users as well as specifying the time that you would like the message to be delivered. The real advantage, however, is that those who receive your marketing messages can receive information in a way that best suits them.

Chapter 18
Action Plan

One of the most important steps that you can take to improve your business is to adjust your marketing and your communication style to fit the way that your clients prefer to communicate. Remember to ask them how they would like to communicate with you and then communicate in their preferred way. Recent innovations make this easier than ever.

As in previous chapters, identify the action steps that you would like to take. Rewrite items that may not fit. Circle the number of each strategy that you plan to implement in your business and then record the date you complete the item in the space provided. If you select more than one item, place the items in priority order and work on implementing one item at a time. Once you complete the items you have selected, move on to the next chapter.

Action Steps:

___ 1. In the future, I will always ask my clients how they would like me to communicate with them and adjust my style accordingly.

___ 2. I will create a strategy to work with each of the following groups (put an "X" by all that apply):

_____ Traditionalists

_____ Boomers

_____ Gen X

_____ Gen Y

___ 3. I will use voice-to-text systems to communicate more effectively with my clients.

___ 4. When I work with people born before 1964, I will take the time to build a relationship with them.

___ 5. When I work with Gen X, I will provide them with a list of resources so they can do their own research.

___ 6. When I work with Gen X and Gen Y, I will avoid acting like the expert or parent.

___ 7. When I work with Gen Y, I will encourage them to invite their friends and family to participate in the buying or selling decision.

Gen X and Gen Y demand a new type of "floortime." In the next Recipe for Success, Joel Burslem shares his secrets for reaching Gen X and Gen Y.

Recipes for Success
21st Century "Floor Time"
Joel Burslem
FutureofRealEstateMarketing.com

Joel Burslem is part of the next generation of marketing specialists and bloggers who are reshaping the real estate industry. As the tidal wave of Gen X and Gen Y clients enter the market, agents who recognize and serve their needs will prosper. Those who don't will watch their business erode. While many Boomer and Traditionalist agents struggle with Web 2.0 technologies, Gen X and Gen Y live and breathe them. If you plan to stay in the business for the long haul, then heed the advice Joel provides below.

Agents across the country still take "floor time" or "opportunity time" where they wait for leads to call them on the phone. Gen X and Gen Y clients are unlikely to contact you by phone. Instead, up to 90 percent of their communication is by text message. In fact, my niece who is graduating from high school routinely sends 10,000-15,000 text messages per month. If you want to connect with the buyers and sellers of the future, you need an entirely different approach to "floor time" in the 21st century. Here are some of the basics.

1. **We want it our way!**
   Ultimately, real estate is still about great customer service. Technology is merely a way to streamline the process. Blogging, Twitter, video—today's consumers demand that agents use their methods. If you want to fish, you need to go where the fish are.

2. **Authenticity matters**
   Gen X and Gen Y want a hands-off approach. To them, transparency (i.e., being completely forthcoming and open about all aspects of the transaction) is a necessity. Instead of the typical canned messages from the past, younger consumers demand honesty and authenticity.

3. **Instantaneous communication**
   While some people are saying that you must respond to your messages within 15 minutes, I think the expectation among younger clients is that you respond immediately. Who wants to wait for someone to return an email or a phone message? Texting gives us instantaneous communication.

4. **Social networking is useless unless you are willing to engage with the community**
   Two places that are excellent for agents of any age to start social networking are Facebook and Twitter. I currently send all my messages using these two sites. They allow me to stay connected no matter where I am. Getting started is as easy as filling out a profile. Next, look at the different communities and decide whom you would like to follow. More importantly, make sure that you contribute to the conversation. Talking about yourself or sending marketing messages does not work in this environment. What does work is joining in conversations with others and providing information that is interesting to the community.

5. **Build your "social graph"**
   The notion of "friends" when it comes to social networking is a misnomer. The term "social graph" is similar to "sphere of influence." You really don't need to be friends in the traditional sense of the word. Being a "friend" means that you follow the person's posts or share an interest in the same community. In fact, the way to build your social network is to create a community rather than marketing your personal brand. Consequently, whenever someone invites you to be a "friend," it's time to "friend-up!"

6. **Content management platforms replace websites**
   Your website is still very important. What is changing is how it will be created in the future. Look for websites to become more like blogs in the future. The days of having to wait for your web designer to change your website are about to disappear. New technologies allow you to make changes on your website as easily as doing a blog post. In fact, a blog is simply an online publishing tool that doesn't require changes to be made through a webmaster.

7. **An hour a day drives business your way**
   Just posting a profile on Facebook or Twitter isn't going to lead to any business. On the other hand, if you will spend an hour per day engaging in online conversations, you will be sowing the seeds for doing future transactions. For example, if you are waiting for a client or have a slow open house, use your mobile phone to send and receive "tweets" (messages on Twitter). Short messages work and they take only seconds to create. We all have short gaps in our schedules. Use them to engage in online conversations.

8. Incorporate video in your business

One of the agents I work with has a Flip video camera. He uses it to shoot video walk-throughs of properties for clients who live outside the area. (Always obtain a written consent from the seller before shooting the interior of any property.) He then uploads the video to a private account where his clients can view it.

If you are working with sellers, here are four pointers to help you understand how to better work with video.

1. Make sure that you have a human guide to "walk" your visitors through the property.

2. Avoid wasting time giving out the bedroom-bath count, square footage, or other details that are generic and are adequately described in writing. Instead, show the viewer what is unique about the property, whether it's the claw foot bath tub or the terrific view. Your goal is to create an emotional response that creates the excitement that will motivate them to view the property in person.

3. Purchase "site work lights." Don't rely on the ambient lighting when you shoot video. Instead, purchase a cheap pair of work site lights from Home Depot or Lowe's. There's nothing worse than seeing a very dark video of a property. One caveat, however; the work site lights can be a fire hazard. Be careful not to place them near anything flammable.

4. Keep it short. Take no more than two minutes to emphasize key features.

Having a solid web presence is critical to long term success. Using video, online chat, and sites such as Facebook and Twitter are excellent ways to join the conversation and to tap into the buyers and sellers of tomorrow.

Knead More Buyer Dough

Chapter 19
Are Buyers Really Liars?

Sales are contingent upon the attitude of the salesman—not the attitude of the prospect.
W. Clement Stone

Skills Check:
Put a checkmark (√) next to what you do now. Leave the remaining items blank. Review the action steps at the end of the chapter to determine the strategies that you will implement in your business.

___ 1. I interview buyers before taking them out to look at property.

___ 2. I have buyers pre-approved before I begin to work with them.

___ 3. I prepare a "Buyer's Book" for each of my buyers that includes copies of the contracts, neighborhood information, and a list of websites where they can find useful information on financing and other purchase related issues.

___ 4. I provide my buyers with a "Buyer's Service Guarantee," a written commitment of the services I provide to my clients.

___ 5. I obtain a commitment from the buyers to work with me exclusively either with a handshake or a Buyer's Agency Agreement.

___ 6. When I work with buyers, I normally ask open-ended rather than closed-ended questions.

___ 7. As part of the Buyer's Interview, I obtain the buyers' permission to close them after each showing.

___ 8. When I set appointments to show property, I know how to set up "decoys" that assist the buyer in deciding which property to buy.

___ 9. When I show property, I keep my opinions to myself and wait to respond to what the buyer says.

___ 10. After each showing, I ask the buyers whether they intend to write an offer on the property they have just seen.

___ 11. When we finish viewing properties, I ask the buyer to rank the properties that we have viewed.

Knead the Dough Secret #37
Emotions, not logic, sell houses.

Benefits, Not Just Features

Are you tired of working with buyers who don't buy from you? Do you believe those people who say "buyers are liars?" If so, your buyer skills can probably use improvement. The reason that many agents have trouble working with buyers is that they don't take the time to discover what really matters to their clients. Agents usually ask about the area, the schools, bedroom-bath count, and price range. They may also ask about the number of garages, whether there is a family room, a formal dining room, and perhaps a pool. Each of these items is a feature.

Features are a physical aspect of the property. People don't buy sticks and bricks. They buy the benefits they perceive the property will have. Benefits are emotional. You may show your buyers a wonderful listing that seems to be perfect for them and yet they walk away. The reason they didn't purchase was that the emotional value was not there for them.

How can you uncover the emotional benefits that your buyers are searching for as opposed to only working with the features that the buyers say they want? The answer is to conduct an in-depth Buyer Interview.

A thorough Buyer's Interview allows you to tap into their emotional motivation for buying. You can do this by asking them questions about their lifestyle, where they spend time when they're at home, and what they enjoy doing. To uncover what truly matters to your buyers, use the following process.

Ten Steps for Creating Loyal, Truth-Telling Buyers

1. **Make an appointment to conduct a Buyer's Interview**
   Explain that the purpose of this appointment is to help find the best possible home for them and to avoid wasting their time showing them properties that are not a good fit.

2. **Ask the buyers to be pre-approved by a lender prior to coming into the office**
   If possible, encourage your buyers to obtain pre-approval rather than just pre-qualification. Pre-approval means the borrower's credit has been checked and all that is required to fund the loan is an appraisal and the appropriate title work. Be sure to let the buyers know how being pre-approved is a major benefit to them. Here's a script that outlines the benefits:

   Buyer Pre-approval Script

   Agent: *Mr. and Mrs. Buyer, prior to our meeting, I strongly recommend that you contact a lender to obtain pre-approval for your loan and here's why:*

   First, you will know exactly what price range is right for you.

   Second, if there are errors on your credit, and unfortunately, these are quite common, you won't be putting your earnest money deposit at risk while you're waiting for the credit reporting agencies to resolve the problem.

   Third, sellers are more likely to be flexible on their price when they have a buyer who is pre-approved.

   Fourth, if there are multiple offers on the property, being pre-approved will give you an advantage over other buyers who are not pre-approved.

   Finally, some purchase contracts require the buyer to be pre-approved within a few days of acceptance. Do you have a lender that you would like to work with or would you like some names from me?

   If your buyers are paying all cash, request a letter from their bank, investment advisor, or CPA stating they have sufficient funds to cover the price.

3. **Prepare a Buyer's Book to give your buyers either in person or downloadable from your website**
   A "Buyer's Book" can include copies of the contracts, neighborhood information, and a list of websites where they can find useful information on financing and other purchase related issues. It's also smart to include links to current listings that have virtual tours or videos.

4. **Conduct the "lottery" exercise**

This is a great tool to uncover what buyers really want when they purchase. Tell your buyers that they have just inherited $10,000,000 from a long lost relative or won the lottery. To really have fun, order play money in million dollar denominations and give them that.

Next, have the buyers describe the perfect house for them. In most cases, they will have a hard time going beyond what they can currently afford. Using this approach creates a number of benefits. First, when someone hands you money, even if it's play money, there's an automatic good feeling about the person who gave it to you. Neurolinguistic Programming calls this "anchoring." Using the play money anchors a good feeling about you at the beginning of the process. Also, even though the buyers are discussing a much more expensive house, you will hear common themes. Are they visual? Is a view important? Are they kinesthetic or auditory? If you listen carefully, you'll be able to discern much more about what matters to them rather than asking directly about what they want to buy.

This exercise only takes a few minutes and it provides a wealth of information about what matters to your buyers. Remember to write down what they say.

5. **Questions to ask on the Buyer's Interview**

a. First, focus on asking "how" and "what" questions rather than "why?"

b. Ask about the number of people in their household, their names, and any special needs. Don't forget to ask about their pets.

c. Ask about the financial aspects of their purchase including the price range as well as what other types of properties they have owned in the past.

d. It's smart to discover who will be involved in the purchase and who will be qualifying for the loan. Sometimes, they're not the same people. Especially with younger buyers, it's important to know who will be involved in the decision making process. It may be a number of their friends in addition to family members.

e. Inquire about their lifestyle, including where they spend time as well as the activities they engage in when they're at home.

f. Have the buyers tell you in as much detail as possible about the features they like in their present home, what they like about those features, as well as what they dislike.

g. Ask them about their favorite types of floor plans as well as about floor plans that they don't like. Be sure to explore the bedroom/bath count and other features they will want in their next home.

h. Ask them to describe their favorite house from when they were a child and what it was about the house that they really liked. This may be the most important information they give you in terms of tapping unconscious motivation to purchase.

i. It's important to discover their timing, including when they would like to begin looking as well as when they would like to be in their new home.

j. Determine how long they have been looking for a new home and whether they are looking with any other agents. Regardless of how they answer these questions, write down their response and move to the next question. You will ask for an exclusive commitment later in the process once you have established your value.

k. The last three questions are the most important. "Of all the things we have discussed, what are the five things a house must have in order for you to buy it?" This question forces the buyer to prioritize what is most important. You will use this list of priorities when the buyer is ready to make their purchase or if they are having trouble finding the right house for them. For example, if the buyer doesn't mention a formal dining room as one of their top five priorities, and then they object to a house because it does not have a formal dining room, then you would respond by asking whether the formal dining room has taken priority over one of the other top five items and if so, which one.

l. The next question is, "We find that our buyers have different strategies for looking at houses. To avoid wasting your valuable time, would you prefer for me to preview the homes and show you the top five homes, would you prefer to look on the multiple listing service with me to determine your preferences, or would you prefer to look online and let me know which houses you would like to see?"

m. This is the most important question, "When we look at property, it is very important that you tell me what you like and what you don't like. Consequently, after we look at each house, unless you tell me that you want to write an offer, I'm going to ask 'What are the reasons that you are not buying this property?' Is that okay with you?"

The final question on the Buyer's Interview actually allows you to close the buyer after every single showing. Needless to say, most agents are reluctant to ask closing questions. This simple question takes care of that issue in addition to helping the buyers to clarify what they truly want.

By using this approach, you will uncover the buyer's motivation and determine the features and benefits that will have the greatest probability of motivating the buyer to write an offer. You will also set up a scenario where you are working as the buyers' partner in helping them find the best property to fit their needs. This whole process will take about 20 minutes, but this is 20 minutes well spent.

Knead the Dough Secret #38
There's no such thing as a 100 percent house.

6. **Set up your closing process**
   Encourage the buyers to look online and let them know that properties can be quite different in person. Invite them to look at houses that you feel may be a good fit.

   A major trap for buyers is expecting to find the perfect house. The key point to make during this discussion is that even if you custom build, "There's no such thing as a 100 percent house." To address this issue, one of the most important questions on the Buyer's Interview asks, "Of all the things that we have discussed, what are the five things a house must have in order for you to buy it?"

   Explain that if the buyers find a house that has all five of the key features that they want, they should be prepared to place an offer on that property. Another way of approaching this issue is to tell the buyers that if they find a house that meets 90 percent of their key criteria, it's probably time to write an offer.

   For those who are married, you can also use the following analogy that usually creates a good laugh:

   There's no such thing as a 100 percent house, just as there's no such thing as a 100 percent spouse. You just have to determine which set of warts you're willing to tolerate.

   Of all the questions on the Buyer's Interview, the most important one is the final question that asks, "What are the reasons that you are not buying this property?"

   Setting up this process during the Buyer's Interview allows you to close the buyers after every property you show. If the buyers are unwilling to write an offer, listen carefully to what they say doesn't work for them. You may have to reassess their top five priorities. For example, if they haven't mentioned that having a large back yard is important and yet they reject every house that lacks a large yard, ask whether the yard has taken precedence over one of the other top five factors on the list. If so, you can alter your search criteria to focus on their revised top five preferences.

It's extremely important to keep them focused on these top five preferences. If they want more, you can ask,

Would you prefer to look in a less desirable area to find the properties that have all the features that you want or would you prefer to pay more?

If they still want all the features in the same price range, remember to remind them that, "There's no such thing as a 100 percent house."

7. **Give the buyers your "Buyer's Pledge"**
   Many buyers do not understand how many forms and the number of actions it takes to close a transaction. Make a list of every step you take plus at least five customer service items that you promise to deliver. For example, responding to their inquiries on the same day, monitoring their transaction daily while their property is under contract, or immediately contacting them when new properties that fit their criteria come on the market. Ask the buyers to review your Pledge and answer any questions that they may have. Once you have done that, sign the pledge and give it to them.

8. **Obtain the buyer's agreement to work exclusively with you.**
   This is where you will address whether they are working with other agents. When you give them the Pledge, here's what to say:

My Buyer's Pledge is quite extensive. All that I ask in exchange is that you work with me exclusively. Is that a strategy that works for you?

If the buyer(s) seem reluctant, it's better to discover now that they want to work with other agents. Assuming they are not comfortable working with you exclusively, here's what to say:

Because of the level of service that I provide, I only work with buyers who agree to work exclusively with me. (Stand up and extend your hand.) I wish you the best in finding the right home for you with the other agents. Thank you for meeting with me today.

The buyers may be surprised and agree to work with you. If not, you have saved yourself a considerable amount of time and effort.

If the buyers agree to work with you exclusively, extend your hand and say:

Let's shake hands on that.

In Western society, shaking hands is more binding than many contracts. The reason is that it taps into our anchors about keeping our word as well as our integrity. While it's not a guarantee that the buyer won't go elsewhere, it is a much easier way to close the buyer on this important issue.

9. **Review agency requirements and sign appropriate agency documentation** Most states require some sort of Agency Disclosure. If you are working with a Buyer's Agreement, this is the time to discuss it. If you are using the handshake process and still need to have Agency documents signed, explain to the buyers that your State requires that you disclose the nature of your Agency agreement.

10. **Begin the search process**

Knead the Dough Secret #39
Always plan to finish your showings earlier than the time you tell the buyers you will be finished.

Keep the Men Happy

Once you confirm your appointments, you're ready to start your showings. An important guideline to follow is to make sure that you have your buyers back either on time or earlier than they expected. For example, if you believe that you will be finished with your showings in two hours, tell the buyers you will take 2.5 hours. While being on time is both good manners and good business, there's an even more important reason for following this advice. Men and women approach time differently. While there are always exceptions to the rule, the following differences are common.

Women are usually comfortable taking as much time as needed to get a job done. For them, time is fluid. In contrast, men usually allocate specific amounts of time to complete each task. Thus, when you take more time than a man has scheduled, you are interfering with another activity. The result can be anger and frustration. On the other hand, when you finish early, the buyers will perceive you as being efficient and competent. By scheduling extra time, you allow for traffic delays, extra time to see a property of special interest to the buyers, or anything else that may come up over the course of showing them property.

Knead the Dough Secret #40
Only open your mouth to ask a question
or to reconfirm something the buyers said.

Another way of saying this is "shut up and sell." The hardest job for many agents is keeping their opinions to themselves. The feature that you point out may be the very thing the buyers hate most. Remember, the only opinion that counts is the buyer's opinion. It's their house and it's their decision. Your role is to provide them with the best information possible so they can make the best decision possible in terms of purchasing a property.

When showing property, avoid making statements. Instead, ask questions to probe their level of interest. For example, if the buyer says, "I hate this gold carpet," don't launch into an explanation on how they can change it or tell them they can ask for a carpet allowance in their offer. Instead, ask a question.

Would you replace the carpet or expose the hardwood floors?

When you ask whether the buyers will replace the carpet or expose the hardwood floors, the moment they choose a response, they have mentally pictured themselves as living in the property. In other words, you have mentally "moved them into the property."

Another way to use questions is to reconfirm what the buyer is experiencing by using a "tie down." For example, if the buyer says, "What a pretty house," respond by saying, "It is a pretty house, isn't it?" Repeating the positive statements that buyers make increases the probability that they will write an offer.

Knead the Dough Secret #41
Use "decoys" to assist the buyers in making decisions

Dan Ariely in his book, *Predictably Irrational* (2008), reports on a study that reveals some surprising aspects of human decision making behavior. Ariely's study demonstrates that we are much more likely to purchase when we have some means to compare two or more items. For example, buyers opted not to buy a bread maker priced at $275, but sales sky rocketed when the same machine was placed next to a larger model with a much higher price.

In terms of real estate, Ariely gives the example of showing buyers a contemporary and a colonial house. The two houses are so different that the buyers cannot decide. When you add a "decoy," that is, a third house that is slightly less than one of the other houses in terms of quality, the buyers normally make the decision relatively rapidly. In Ariely's example, the decoy could be a second colonial style house that needs a new roof.

To assist your buyers in making a decision, identify the house(s) that are closest to what they want. Then, include one that has a similar price with a flaw the other property lacks. Avoid showing all "perfect" houses since buyers choose based upon their ability to make a comparison.

Knead the Dough Secret #42
Avoid manipulative closing techniques. Instead, look for buying signs that tell you they are ready to purchase.

The buyer's body language can tell you whether a buyer is ready to be closed. Body language communicates much more information than speech. If you're walking in front of your buyers, it's virtually impossible to observe the subtle clues their body language provides. Whenever possible, stay in back of your buyers so you can better observe their unconscious buying signs. Here are some of the most common ones:

1. Slowing down their pace as they walk through the property.

2. Touching a wall or opening cabinets.

3. Looking at a feature two or more times.

4. Taking a second look at the property brochure.

5. Objecting to a feature—people normally don't object to specific features unless they see themselves living in the property.

In terms of preparing the buyer to write an offer, if you followed each of the steps on the Buyer's Interview, you can now ask the buyers after each showing, "Is this a house that you would like to write an offer on, and if not, what about this house does not work?" Take notes on their comments to determine whether you need to change your search criteria.

At the end of the day as you're driving your buyers back, ask them to rank the properties they saw. If you have had them out on previous occasions, ask them to share the best two or three houses in their opinion. If any of these houses meet 90 percent or more of their criteria, remind them of the conversation you had about writing an offer on houses that meet this percentage of their criteria. Also, don't be shy about reminding them that "There's no such thing as a 100 percent house."

If the clients have definitely located the right property for them, all you have to say is,

> *Well, I guess all we need to do now is to go back to the office and take care of the paperwork.*

Chapter 19
Action Plan

Buyers aren't liars if you earn their trust and take the time to discover what matters to them. If you work with buyers, using the steps in this chapter will save you both time and money. The result will be less work to convert more sales.

Begin by identifying the action steps that you would like to take. Rewrite items that may not fit. Remember to circle the number of each strategy that you plan to implement in your business and then record the date you complete the item in the space provided. If you select more than one item, place the items in priority order and work on implementing one item at a time. Your goal is to find an activity that is sustainable over time and that you will feel motivated to do on a regular basis.

Action Steps:

___ 1. I will conduct a Buyer's Interview as a regular part of my buyer in-take process.

___ 2. I will have buyers pre-approved before I begin to work with them.

___ 3. I will prepare a "Buyer's Book" for each of my buyers that includes copies of the contracts, neighborhood information, and a list of websites where they can find useful information on financing and other purchase related issues.

___ 4. I will provide my buyers with a "Buyer's Service Guarantee," a written commitment of the services that I provide to all of my clients.

___ 5. I will obtain a commitment from the buyers to work with me exclusively either with a handshake or a Buyer's Agency Agreement.

___ 6. When I work with buyers, I will ask open-ended questions that help me understand what is motivating the buyer to purchase.

___ 7. When I conduct a Buyer's Interview, I will obtain the buyers' permission to close them after each showing.

___ 8. When I show property, I will keep my opinions to myself and wait to respond to what the buyer says.

___ 9. In the future, when I set appointments to show property, I will set up "decoys" that assist the buyer in deciding which property to buy.

___10. After each showing, I will ask buyers whether they intend to write an offer on the property they have just seen.

___11. When we finish viewing properties, I will ask the buyer to rank the properties that we have viewed.

Are you ready to make more buyer dough? If so, the next Recipe for Success will show you how.

Recipes for Success
Five Creative Ways to Make More Buyer Dough

When sales are sluggish, you can hope that things will get better or you can actively generate your own buyer leads. All it takes is a little bit of creativity. Special thanks to our valued clients who shared these tips.

1. **Too many distressed properties**
   When the market is slow, buyers are looking for great deals. Take advantage of this by creating a separate website with a "Best Buy" URL. For example, you could use "YourTownBestHomeBuys.com" or "91456BestRealEstateDeals.com" (using the zip code). On this site, list the best real estate buys in all categories including short sales, foreclosures, REOs, as well as other properties that are a good value.

2. **"Your language spoken here"**
   The dollar's weakness against other currencies makes American real estate a great buy. If you are fluent in another language, hold first time buyer seminars in your other language(s). If you work in an area where there is substantial number of foreign buyers, hold your seminar as a teleconference or webinar. This allows you to reach potential clients anywhere in the world. It's also smart to translate key parts of your website into any language in which you are fluent.

3. **Hold mortgage seminars**
   Many buyers don't understand the financing options available to them, especially with the new changes in FHA. As compared to the subprime loans of the past, FHA loans have lower foreclosure rates and are usually available at a considerable savings. Invite a loan officer to answer questions. Hold seminars at your Chamber of Commerce, place of worship, or even a local school. Market to renters with materials explaining how these various programs work.

4. **Market to parents of college students**
   Dorm costs are expensive. Many parents and grandparents have realized the wisdom of buying a condominium or investment property where their children/grandchildren can live while attending college. A great way to market to this group is to mail to parents who have children graduating from your local high school. Hold a seminar on "How to Buy Your First Investment Home and Save a Bundle on Dorm Costs." Another approach is to help parents with young

children to create a college fund for their children by purchasing an investment property. Illustrate how purchasing a property with a strong cash flow allows them to pay the mortgage off in 10 to 15 years. By the time the child reaches college, chances are the property will be free and clear. This means that the cash flow alone may be enough to pay college expenses.

5. **Relocation strategies**
   Watch your local newspaper for information on companies that may be relocating in your area. Also, pay special attention to new commercial construction that may attract people from outside the area. For example, a new luxury hotel can generate one to three jobs per room. It's also smart to establish relationships with local head hunters to stay abreast of who may be relocating into your area.

Chapter 20
Get Your Buyers Off the Fence and Under Contract

Obstacles are necessary for success because in selling, as in all careers of importance, victory comes only after many struggles and countless defeats.
Og Mandino

Skills Check:
Put a checkmark (√) next to what you do now. Leave the remaining items blank. Review the action steps at the end of the chapter to determine the strategies that you will implement in your business.

___ 1. I know how to use a mortgage calculator to illustrate the benefits of buying now rather than waiting.

___ 2. I know how to demonstrate to nervous or reluctant buyers the reasons it may be smart to write an offer now.

___ 3. I can address the buyer's concerns about the possibility that market values may decline.

Buyer's Markets—There Is an Upside

As this book went to press, most places in the United States were in the midst of the best buyer's market in over 30 years—plenty of inventory, historically low interest rates, and a considerable number of great bargains due to foreclosures.

One of the most important questions agents and brokers are asking today is, "How can we persuade our buyers to take action now rather than waiting?" Many buyers are convinced that waiting will allow them to buy the property at a lower cost. This flawed thinking fails to consider the true costs of homeownership, not only in terms of tax consequences, but also in terms of wealth accumulation.

Knead the Dough Secret #43
The smartest real estate investors are contrarians—they sell when others are buying and buy when others are selling.

One trait that almost all smart real estate investors share is that they are contrarians. When there are multiple offers on properties and dramatic run-ups in prices, they're selling. When prices are falling, they're buying. In contrast, the general buying public tends to jump into the market when prices are going up and sell when prices are going down.

In fact, the current buyer's market is the best in over 30 years. The reason? During the previous buyer's markets of the 1980s and 1990s, we had double digit interest rates. In fact, I remember our office manager standing up and saying, "Home Savings has a great fixed rate of 16.5 percent." Furthermore, prices are down in many markets and inventory is up. Buyers who miss the opportunity today will end up lamenting the fact that they didn't take advantage of this market.

The Ideal Move-up Market

If you are in a market where there is price depreciation, this is an ideal time for your move-up owners to purchase a more expensive home. Assume that your buyers paid $300,000 for their property and the market has declined by 10 percent. Their property is currently worth $270,000. If your clients are going to purchase a property that was $600,000 a year ago, it's now worth $540,000. By purchasing this year, your clients have an instant $30,000 in savings as compared to a year ago. Furthermore, their mortgage and property taxes over the next 30 years will be substantially lower.

If your buyers are retiring or trading down, most real estate cycles are approximately 10 years in length (i.e., it takes 10 years to cycle through a seller's market to a buyer's market and then back to a seller's market). If your seller can afford to wait a few years, they may be able to pick up some appreciation later. On the other hand, they have the cost of maintaining the larger property rather than having lower overhead and more cash. To understand the exact financial ramifications, advise them to meet with their CPA, tax attorney, or financial advisor before listing their property.

It's Cheaper for Me to Rent!

How many times have you heard that objection? Granted, that if people live in a pricey area, renting may make sense for a large proportion of them. On the other hand, the interest rates are so low that purchasing usually makes more sense.

To illustrate this point, follow these steps:

1. Determine the rate of inflation in your local area for the last 10 years or use the national figure of 2.54 percent.

2. Check your local census data to determine how much properties have appreciated over the last 10 years. If it exceeds that national average of 25.4 percent, then use that number in your calculations.

3. Go online and use one of the "rent vs. buy" calculators. You will need the rate of appreciation in your local area and/or the inflation rate, the cost of the buyer's current rent, the loan amount, and the interest rate.

The examples below illustrate why buying your home is usually better than renting.

Example 1:
Assume that your first time buyer currently pays $1,500 per month rent and plans to purchase a $300,000 property with $30,000 down and a $270,000 loan for 30 years at 6 percent. Your buyer is in 28 percent tax bracket and will own the property for 8 years. Appreciation only keeps pace with inflation at 2.54 percent per year. The estimated cost of renting is $142,015 vs. the estimated cost of buying (due to appreciation and equity build up) is $117,754. The buyer saves $24,261 by purchasing rather than renting.

Example 2:
Your buyer currently pays $2,000 per month rent. The buyer plans to purchase a $400,000 property with $40,000 down and a $360,000 loan at 6.25 percent. The buyer is in the 28 percent tax bracket and will keep the property for 10 years. The property will appreciate at 5 percent per year. During the 10-year period, the estimated cost of renting is $241,189 as compared to the estimated cost of buying (due to appreciation and equity build up) is $68,905. The buyer saves $172,284 by buying rather than renting.

Here's an important point to note about how you present this information. If you are discussing this with Boomers or Traditionalists, give them the data and go over it with them. They will appreciate your expertise. In contrast, with Gen X and Gen Y, give them the link so that they can uncover the information themselves. They won't trust your numbers anyway. Be sure to ask if they would like some help on how to do the calculations. If so, give them an example that uses numbers that are different from the property that they are considering.

What If the Prices Go Down?

If your buyers are sitting on the fence, help them understand the benefits of taking action in today's market. The best way to do that is to show them the true cost of home ownership and how taking action now benefits their long-term wealth accumulation. Table 2 illustrates this point. Please note that on a $200,000 loan, if the interest rate increases one percentage point from 6 to 7 percent, the borrower will pay an extra $47,340 over the life of the loan. If the interest rate increases two percentage points, the buyer will pay approximately $100,000 in extra interest or almost 50 percent of the original loan amount.

Table 2

Interest Rates and the Cost of Waiting to Purchase

$200,000 loan (numbers rounded to the nearest whole dollar)

Interest Rate	Monthly Payment	Monthly cost for 1% interest increase	Annual cost for 1% interest increase	30 year cost for 1% interest increase	30 year cost for 2% interest increase
6% to 7%	$1199 $1331	$132	$1578	$47,340	
7% to 8%	$1331 $1468	$137	$1643	$49,280	$96,620 (6% to 8%)
8% to 9%	$1468 $1609	$141	$1692	$50,760	$100,040 (7% to 9%)

$400,000 loan (numbers rounded to the nearest whole dollar)

Interest Rate	Monthly Payment	Monthly cost for 1% interest increase	Annual cost for 1% interest increase	30 year cost for 1% interest increase	30 year cost for 2% interest increase
6% to 7%	$2398 $2661	$263	$3,156	$94,680	
7% to 8%	$2661 $2935	$274	$3,288	$98,640	$193,321 (6% to 8%)
8% to 9%	$2935 $3218	$283	$3,396	$101,880	$200,520 7% to 9%)

Laurence Yun, Chief Economist for NAR, points out an additional cost of waiting to purchase that most buyers do not know about. The following chart illustrates how renters actually lost wealth while homeowners experienced a substantial increase in wealth.

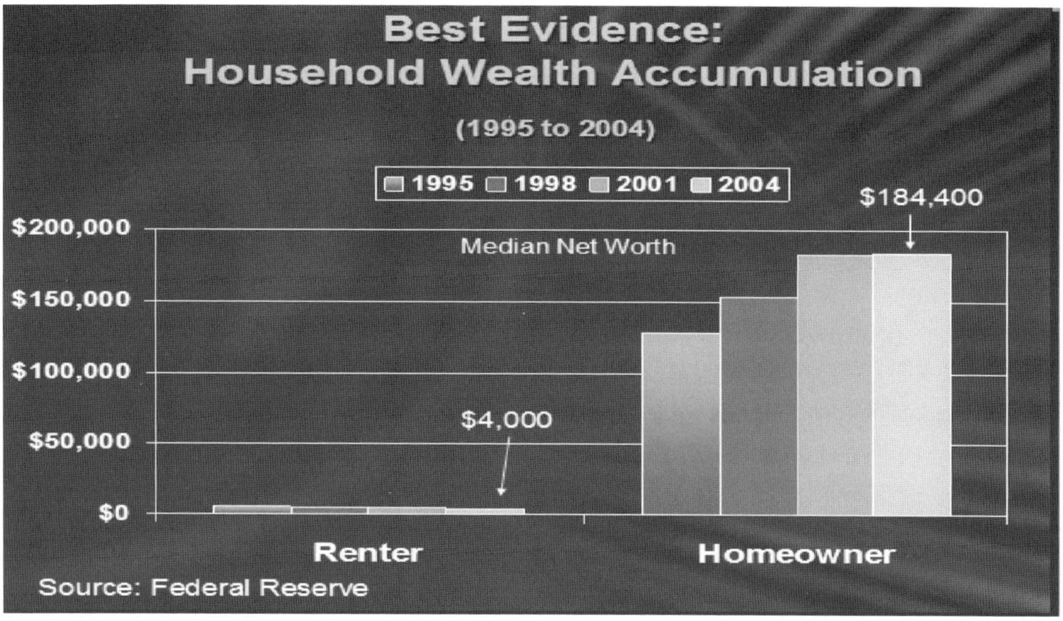

Many people fail to realize that homeowners accumulate wealth by paying down their mortgage, even if their house does not increase in value. Renters lose additional wealth as their rental payments increase over time, whereas a homeowner with a fixed rate loan has locked in their mortgage amount for the next 30 years. If there is inflation, the homeowner pays off their loan with inflated dollars. Rents, in contrast, keep pace with inflation.

Thus, buyers who elect to wait or those who are planning to move up may be leaving money on the table in two different ways. First, if the interest rates increase, they will end up paying more over the term of their loan. Second, by waiting to take action, they will accumulate less wealth, experience less appreciation, and eliminate their mortgage debt at a later date.

Chapter 20
Action Plan

Developing strong buyer dialogues is crucial when the market is tough. A buyer's market is filled with opportunities for those who want to purchase their first home, trade up, or who are considering purchasing residential investment properties. Prospect these types of buyers and your business will remain strong regardless of how others are doing.

Begin by identifying the action steps that you would like to take. Rewrite items that may not fit. Circle the number of each strategy that you plan to implement in your business and then record the date you complete the item in the space provided. If you select more than one item, place the items in priority order. Work on one step at a time until you have completely integrated it into your business before moving to the next step. Remember, your goal is to find an activity that is sustainable over time and that you will feel motivated to do on a regular basis. Once you complete the items you have selected, move on to the next chapter.

Action Steps:

___ 1. I will learn how to use a mortgage calculator to illustrate the benefits of buying now rather than waiting.

___ 2. I have mastered how to show reluctant buyers the reasons it may be smart to write an offer now.

___ 3. I know how to answer buyers' concerns about the possibility that market values may decline by showing them the cost of waiting.

You have done all the work to place a property under contract and the lender says "No," to your buyer's loan. The next chapter shares the secrets of how to close the deal anyway.

Chapter 21
When the Lender Says "No"
Secrets for Closing the Deal Anyway

Neither a borrower nor a lender be.
Shakespeare

Skills Check:
Put a checkmark (√) next to what you do now. Leave the remaining items blank. Review the action steps at the end of the chapter to determine the strategies that you will implement in your business.

___ 1. When I write an offer, I always place the buyer's interest rate one half point higher than the current rates.

___ 2. When I write an offer, I never use the term "prevailing rate" to specify the interest rate that the buyers are willing to accept.

___ 3. When lending conditions are tight, I encourage my buyers to apply at a mortgage broker who has access to multiple lending sources or to apply at two different lenders.

___ 4. When I place a property under contract, I always do a thorough comparable market analysis to give to the appraiser.

___ 5. I know how to use secondary financing to keep transactions together if the appraisal comes in low.

___ 6. I know how to use interest rate buy-downs to keep my transactions together.

Crunching the Credit Crunch

According to Lou Barnes in his July 27, 2007 column in *Inman News:*

> *A "credit crunch" is a lender strike, and a bad one is a common initiator of recession: not just raising rates for risky deals, but choking off credit altogether.*

In other words, the people who make loans stop making them. The 2007-2008 credit crunch resulted from lenders being unable to sell the loans they made on the secondary market. The result was a lending situation different from what anyone had ever experienced before. A+ borrowers found it nearly impossible to obtain jumbo loans, regardless of their excellent credit or large down payment. Foreclosures soared as investors walked away from properties with subprime loans. In a historical turnaround from previous slow markets, the high end of the market continued to be strong while the first time buyer market stalled. As the credit crunch eases and inflationary pressures rise due to high gas and food prices, look for interest rates to increase again. There may still be some rocky times ahead in terms of closing loans.

When prices are increasing and interest rates are declining, appraisals are usually not an issue. On the other hand, if the rates are climbing and/or the prices are declining, closing the loan often becomes the biggest hurdle to overcome in closing the transaction. This is where your negotiation skills can make or break your deal.

Below you'll find a number of strategies to help you avoid most lending problems. The old saying, "The best defense is a good offense," is true. The more you can do on the front end of the process to avert loan problems, the easier it will be to close the transaction.

Secrets to Closing the Loan Anyway

If you are representing the seller and the buyer's agent writes in an interest rate of 6 percent, it's smart to counter that the buyer will accept up to a 7 percent interest rate. Be sure to request documentation that the buyer can qualify for a loan at the higher rate. It's also smart to counter that they will take an adjustable rate mortgage in case they don't qualify for a fixed rate mortgage. Remember, if the interest rate exceeds the amount in the contract, the buyer has the right to cancel the transaction. Second, never write in "prevailing rate." You don't want your buyer applying for a seven percent loan and learning they have to take a nine or ten percent loan because they have poor credit.

Pray for Sunshine, Be Prepared for Rain

When property values increase, lenders are open to appraising property higher than the comparable sales, especially if there were multiple offers on the property. When prices are declining, however, the price the buyer agrees to today could be higher than the property will be worth at closing. Competent appraisers generally consider all market conditions and make the appraisal based upon what the market is doing. Thus, in a declining market, appraisals can come in at less than what the buyers agreed to pay. When the appraisal comes in low, most buyers walk away from the transaction to avoid overpaying. To circumvent this challenge, begin by advising buyers about what could happen. If they're prepared for a low appraisal due to changing market conditions, they will be more willing to stay in the transaction.

One of the best strategies to circumvent getting a low appraisal is to make sure that you provide the appraiser with the most complete set of comparable sales available. Many times the appraiser is relying on closed sales data and may not include properties that are still under contract. Be sure to include both sets of data, even if the appraiser elects to use only closed sales.

Comparable sales data must be as detailed as possible. Determine if there was a virtual tour for each of the properties that you included in the comparable sales. If so, include a link or any pictures that are available online. If the pictures are no longer available, contact the listing agent to see if he or she can provide them. The more data you give the appraiser, the less likely you are to have problems.

When prices are declining, appraisers tend to be conservative. Since the buyer generally pays for the appraisal, most lenders will provide the buyer with a copy if asked. It's an excellent practice to see what comparable sales were used in the appraisal. Sometimes, out of area appraisers will select comparable sales that are in two completely different market areas, even though they may be close to each other geographically. There may be new comparable sales since the appraisal was completed. If this is the case, submit the updated comparable sales to the lender along with a letter explaining the reasons the property should be appraised for more. Again, you can avoid these hassles by making sure that the appraiser has the best comparable sales available prior to making the appraisal.

Knead the Dough Secret #44
Seller financing can save the day.

When the Appraisal Comes in Low

If the appraisal comes in low, you may be able to save your transaction by asking the seller to carry a second trust deed for the difference. If possible, avoid showing properties where there is no equity.

A different alternative is to seek a home equity line from a credit union or business bank. For example, if the buyers planned to make any renovations or to replace major items such as the air conditioning, carpets, or appliances after the closing of the transaction, they may be able to obtain a home equity loan for the amount, thus freeing up additional funds to put toward the down payment. Another approach would be to seek financing from a private lender who does "hard money" loans.

These loans are typically much more expensive. In a severe crunch, private financing may be your only alternative. When times are really bad, agents may have to carry their commissions as a second or third mortgage secured against the property.

Knead the Dough Secret #45
Interest rate buy-downs create a
win-win for both sellers and buyers.

A third alternative is an interest rate buy- down. Interest rate buy-downs work well when interest rates increase while the property is under contract but has yet to close. Permanent buy-down programs are the hardest to find and the most beneficial to the parties, since the reduced interest rate is good for the life of the loan. For example, assume that a buyer is purchasing a $500,000 property with $50,000 down, and a loan of $450,000 at 6.5 percent. For $18,000, the buyers' loan is reduced by $290 per month. To reduce payments to this level by lowering the price would require a price reduction of $45,800. This creates a win for both parties. The buyer gets a monthly payment equivalent to a 10 percent reduction in the loan amount and the sellers net $27,800 more than if they had lowered the price an equivalent amount.

Many lenders also offer buy-down programs to help borrowers qualify as well. The most common buy-down is known as "2-1." Assume that the rates are at 8 percent. A typical buy down would be 6 percent for year 1 and then 7 percent for year 2. At the beginning of the third year, through year 30, the rate would go back to 8 percent. At closing, the borrower or the seller prepays the difference in interest for the first two years.

For example, if the borrower is taking a loan of $300,000, the buy-down amount would be two percentage points, or $6,000, the first year, and $3,000 the second year, for a total of $9,000. The $9,000 may be added to the purchase price, provided the comparable sales are high enough to support the higher valuation. In the example above where the buy down is only a .50 percent, the buy-down amount on a $300,000 mortgage for the first year would be approximately $1,500.

A slightly different approach is to keep the loan fees the same, but to raise the overall interest rate once the buy-down period has passed. For example, if the borrower above was unable to prepay the buy-down amount, the lender could help out with the equivalent of an adjustable rate mortgage. Assume the interest rate is 7.5 percent with 1.0 point. To keep the points at 1.0, the borrower could qualify at a rate of 6.25 percent. The second year the interest rate would be at 7.25 percent and years 3 through 30 would be at 8.25 percent. There are multiple variations on this theme. The simplest solution may be for the borrower to take a traditional adjustable rate mortgage rather than working with the buy-down.

Working in today's new lending environment requires skill and preparation. Take the necessary steps to outline the current lending situation to your buyers and sellers before writing or presenting an offer. Prepare your sellers for the possibility of carrying the financing. Also, be sure to advise both buyers and sellers that the property may appraise lower than the contract price due to shifting mortgage conditions. Having these conversations ahead of time will help you to close more transactions, even when obtaining financing is a struggle.

Chapter 21
Action Plan

Mastering mortgage negotiation skills is one of the most important steps that you can take to close more transactions. Take the time to learn how to use online mortgage calculators that allow you to demonstrate the cost of waiting to purchase as well as how buy-downs work.

As in previous chapters, begin by identifying the action steps that you would like to take. Rewrite items that may not fit. Remember to circle the number of each strategy that you plan to implement in your business and then record the date you complete the item in the space provided. If you select more than one item, place the items in priority order and work on implementing one item at a time. Once you complete the items you have selected, move on to the next chapter.

Action Steps:

___ 1. In the future when I write an offer, I will protect my buyers by putting a cap on the interest rates.

___ 2. To increase the probability of closing my transactions, I will recommend that my buyers either submit at least two loan applications to different lenders or apply at a mortgage broker who has access to multiple lending sources.

___ 3. When I place a property under contract, I will provide the appraiser with a detailed comparable market analysis, regardless of whether I represent the seller or the buyer.

___ 4. I know how to use secondary financing to keep transactions together if the appraisal comes in low.

___ 5. I know how to use interest rate buy-downs to keep my transactions together.

In a slowing market, it makes sense to work with buyers. Nevertheless, listings are still the name of the game. The key is pricing them right and achieving maximum exposure that results in the maximum price for the sellers.

Listing Dough: Are You Ready to Rise to the Top?

Chapter 22
Listening Consultations, Not Listing Presentations

The single biggest problem in communication
is the illusion that it has taken place.
George Bernard Shaw

Skills Check:
Put a checkmark (√) next to what you do now. Leave the remaining items blank. Review the action steps at the end of the chapter to determine the strategies that you will implement in your business.

___ 1. On my last listing appointment, I focused on the seller rather than discussing my accomplishments or how good my company is.

___ 2. I take written notes on what the sellers say is important to them about the marketing of their property.

___ 3. I can effectively build a personal connection with the seller during the first five minutes of my listing appointment.

___ 4. I always ask to represent the sellers on the purchase of their next property or for the relocation referral if the sellers are moving out of the area.

___ 5. I always offer a "Seller's Guarantee of Services" that allows the seller to give the listing to someone else in my firm if I don't live up to what I promise.

___ 6. I create a customized Ninety-Day Marketing Plan for each of my listings.

___ 7. During each listing appointment, I explain at least three services that differentiate me from other agents.

___ 8. I explain how the services that my company provides are a benefit to the sellers in helping them achieve their goals.

___9. I give sellers the names and phone numbers of at least three satisfied past clients.

Never Do Another Listing Presentation

The most important strategy that you can use during any client meeting is to ask questions. For years, we trained agents to do "listing presentations." Today's consumer wants to know how you're going to meet their needs. They're not interested in hearing about how great your company is or about your personal sales achievements. Consequently, the shift to make is from doing listing presentations to doing "listening consultations" where you ask questions and focus on what the seller says.

An important part of this process is to take written notes. This sends a nonverbal message to the sellers that what they say is important enough for you to write it down. It also is a good way to keep focused by asking questions rather than shifting into presentation mode.

Before discussing the eight key listing questions that will help you convert more listings, it's important to be prepared for your listening consultation experience. The first question you must ask yourself is whether you will have time prior to your meeting with the seller to prepare a brochure, web page, and other key materials. This will determine whether a one-step or a two-step listening consultation will work best for you.

One-Step or Two-Step, Digital or Traditional—What Works for You and Your Clients?

A one-step listening consultation involves pricing and listing the property in a single seller visit. A two-step listening consultation allows you to preview the property and drop off your pre-listing package prior to meeting with the sellers. When possible, it is better to use a two step listening consultation because it gives you the time to review the comparable sales after viewing the property. Nevertheless, you must be prepared to do your consultation on the spot.

In the two-step process, you will have to determine whether you will use traditional paper materials or whether you will go digital. An important factor to consider is how technologically sophisticated your clients are likely to be. If they are members of Gen X or Gen Y, digital is your best choice. For Boomers and Traditionalists, paper may be preferable. The key point is to match your consultation with the sellers' preferred communication style.

If you're using a paper pre-listing package, drop it off prior to your face-to-face consultation with the sellers. You may also send it as an email attachment, however there's a chance that it may be caught in their spam filters. Also, many will not remember to print it before you arrive. Because this initial step is so important, dropping off a hard copy is definitely worth the effort. If you don't have time to deliver it personally, send it via messenger or overnight it.

If you're doing a digital pre-list package, post it on a private page on your website or social network. All you have to do is to send them the link. Again, they may not click through to look at everything, but it's easier to access digitally than carrying around the paper version.

What Should I Include in My Pre-Listing Package?

If you are using the paper version, prepare a number of pre-listing packages at the same time. This is a great job for an assistant. Your time is better spent on evaluating the comparable market analysis (CMA) to determine the price and making sure that you are prepared to discuss the comparable sales. You must also be prepared to explain how your marketing plan helps the seller achieve the highest possible price in the shortest amount of time. By having the packages prepared ahead of time, all you have to do when you receive a listing lead is prepare your CMA, take your digital photo so you can do the brochure, and customize the letter by typing in the seller's name. Pop those three additional pieces into your proposal and you're ready to go on the appointment.

It's also smart to include copies of all the contracts and disclosures in your pre-listing package. This allows the seller to have time to review the documentation. If you are using hard copies, write the word "Sample" across all the documents you provide. This prevents someone else from using your documentation and limits your liability.

If the sellers request the digital pre-list package, send them the links to your website or transaction management site where they can download the documents. Also, provide them with links to virtual tours, videos, plus a sample of your tracking data if you're using a system such as Point2Agent that tracks web hits from various sources.

Below you will find a list of what to include as well as some examples.

1. The first page should always be a color brochure of the seller's property. This sends a strong message to the seller that you are organized and thorough.

2. Cover letter explaining what's in the marketing proposal (Table 3).

3. A copy of *Get Your Property Sold Now!* with the chart (Table 4) completed. This provides a list of the "Premium Services" that you provide and will help you distinguish yourself from other competitors. (Order this booklet at RealEstateCoach.com.)

4. A copy of your Seller Services Guarantee. This is a list of all the steps that you take to sell a property. Be as detailed as possible. It's also smart to include at least five customer service items in this list such as weekly seller updates, monitoring of the buyer's loan process, and coordinating all inspections.

5. Staging guidelines. If you're not hiring someone to stage the property, give the sellers a handout or provide a video that explains the staging process.

6. A sample Ninety-Day Marketing Plan. This outlines when you will complete the various marketing tasks that you will employ to sell the property. Be sure to include the dates the property will appear in the Multiple Listing Service, when it will be posted on other real estate sites, when the brochures will be ready, when the sign will go up, when you will hold open houses, etc.

7. Comparable market analysis (CMA) if you have time to prepare it.

8. Supply and demand data (Table 5).

9. Your personal contact information including your email and the URL for your website.

10. A single property website using the seller's address as the URL (e.g., 345MainStreet.com).

11. Testimonials from past clients including their contact information. Be sure you have permission from your past clients to do this. Another excellent way to do this is to invite past customers to post their testimonials on social networking sites such as LinkedIn or Facebook. If past clients are willing, use a video camera to get their testimonial and send the sellers the link.

While this may seem like a lot, once you put the forms together, it's simply a matter of printing them from your computer or sending a link to the sellers. You may be wondering whether the seller will read all of this. The answer depends upon the seller's personality and behavioral style. Detail people will carefully review everything you send. Those who are high-powered, get-it-done types may not even look at what you have provided. Nevertheless, this approach sends a strong nonverbal message that you are a well-prepared professional. Agents who do not take these extra steps will have a hard time competing with you.

No matter whether you do a one-step or two-step listening consultation, you must be prepared to explain what you have provided to the sellers. People are busy. While they may intend to look at the material, they may not have time to do so.

T*able 3*

Sample Cover Letter

The letter below outlines the important items to include in your pre-listing package. It also helps you to properly set the sellers' expectations about your respective roles in pricing and marketing the property.

Date

Dear ***********

Thank you for the opportunity to discuss the marketing and sale of your property located at ***********. Our goal at ABC Real Estate is to assist you in netting the highest possible price from the sale of your property.

While your agent controls the marketing, you as the seller control the condition of the property as well as the "positioning" or price. Each factor below will influence how quickly you will sell as well as how much you can expect to net from your real estate sale.

1. Location: This includes the community where your property is situated, proximity to schools and transportation, attractiveness of the street, and overall convenience to shopping and work.

2. Competing Properties: How do the features and amenities of your property compare to other properties in the same price range?

3. Condition: How well have you maintained your property as compared to competing properties? Today, staging is usually a necessity in order to obtain the highest possible price.

4. Accessibility: It's sometimes challenging to have your house ready to show at all times. The more accessible your property is, the easier it will be for buyers to see it. Maximum exposure equals maximum price.

5. Your Agent: The agent's marketing plan, web expertise, and use of print media will determine the exposure your property receives. The agent's ability to negotiate also strongly influences how much you will ultimately net from your sale.

6. Supply and Demand Statistics: These statistics tell you how quickly properties are selling. Pay special attention to the amount of inventory on the market. Six months or less means a more rapid sale whereas eight months or more means downward pressure on prices and longer market times.

These factors directly affect the value of your property. Another important consideration is the Comparable Market Analysis. This gives you the best indication of how much your property will sell for as well as how much lenders may allow buyers to borrow on your property.

In this package, there is also a copy of *Get Your Property Sold Now!* This simple guide shows you the services your listing agent should provide to get your property sold for the highest possible price in the shortest amount of time. Also included are a sample Ninety-Day Marketing Plan, sample marketing materials, as well as our Seller Service Pledge. If you need additional information or have any questions regarding the marketing of your property, please feel free to contact me. I look forward to working with you.

Sincerely yours,

Table 4

Sample Premium Marketing Plan

Remember that when you are creating your Premium Marketing Plan, it's important that you do not promise more than you can deliver. Part of the purpose of this document is to help sellers understand the amount of work that is required behind the scenes to help them close their property. You can also use this tool to justify your full commission. It provides an objective way for the sellers to compare your services with those provided by your competitors.

Create Your Premium Marketing Plan Using

Get Your Property Sold Now!
Copyright 2008, Bernice L. Ross
Reprinted with permission

Fourteen Key Strategies to Net You the Most Money	Your Co.	1	2	3
1. Top list-to-sell price ratio				
2. Listing posted to local MLS				
3. Premium marketing plan to reach the brokerage community				
4. 800 Call Capture System on all advertising media				
5. Customized print marketing plan including targeted, niche marketing strategies				
6. Web marketing strategy publishes your listing on over 40 different websites				
7. Customized website for your listing promoted through YourPropertyAddress.com				
8. Agent provides video tour of property marketed on at least 15 video sites including YouTube				
9. Company and/or agent appears on the first page of major search engines for your area				
10. Agent's website provides mapping, mortgage, and other important community information for your neighborhood				
11. Agent has click-to-talk, instant messaging, or a call center to respond immediately to buyer leads for your property				
12. Staging services to make your home look its best				
13. Corporate risk management program limits exposure to costly litigation				
14. Written Agent Performance Guarantee assures your satisfaction				

Staging Guidelines

Your goal when staging a property is to make it as attractive as possible to potential buyers. Especially in a slowing market, every showing counts. When there are plenty of other competing properties, the sellers must not only have the best price, their property must also be in excellent condition. Otherwise, they may end up taking much less for the property.

If you're not good at staging properties, hire someone who is. Some quick hints include reducing the amount of furniture so that the house looks more spacious. Have sellers remove all personal items. If the furniture is looking tired, buy two or three throws plus additional pillows and place them on the furniture to make it look better. Paint where necessary and make sure that everything is working properly. Also, dated fixtures can make the property look older than it is. The seller doesn't have to replace them with anything expensive. The idea is to go for an up-to-date look, especially if you're competing with new construction.

To construct a staging calendar, meet with the seller and decide which items they are willing to address. If possible, provide them with a referral to a decorator and/or other service providers such as painters, finish carpenters, plumbers, gardeners, etc. Next, outline the dates various items are to be completed.

Some sellers may resist doing anything that is different from their current style. A good approach is to remind them, "It's not your house " or "We want potential buyers to see this as *their* house, not as *your* house." Help them to look forward to personalizing their next property. Also, if the house is crammed with stuff, remind them that they will have to pack it anyway when they move. Handling this now will protect the cherished possessions from being broken accidentally.

If the property will be competing with new construction, take the sellers to see the newer homes prior to putting their home on the market. Have them note the decorating ideas and how the new properties were staged to create an impression of a lifestyle. Then explain that's the same goal they should take with staging their own home.

Finally, don't forget about the importance of scent, taste, and sound. Use scented candles or bake cinnamon rolls to provide an attractive aroma. Serve coffee or hot chocolate on cold days or lemonade or cold bottled water when it's warm. Minimize outside noises with a fountain or soft music. Remember, your goal is to help the sellers show their home in the most favorable way possible.

Chapter 22
Action Plan

If you already use a pre-listing package, compare your existing package to the one outlined in this chapter. Given the huge number of Gen X and Gen Y buyers in today's market, it's smart to prepare a digital version of your pre-listing package as well.

Identify the action steps that you would like to take and rewrite items that may not fit. Circle the number of each strategy that you plan to implement in your business and then record the date you complete the item in the space provided. Make and integrate one or two changes at a time. Making too many changes at once can be overwhelming.

Action Steps:

___ 1. On my future listening consultations, I will focus on the seller rather than discussing my accomplishments and how good my company is.

___ 2. I will take written notes on what the sellers say is important to them about their property.

___ 3. As part of my pre-listing package, I will take digital photos of the property and make a color brochure that can be printed or displayed online.

___ 4. I will include a cover letter in part of my pre-listing package explaining what's in the marketing proposal.

___ 5. I will create a Premium Marketing Plan using the services outlined in *Get Your Property Sold Now!*

___ 6. I will use a Seller Services Guarantee on all of my listing appointments.

___ 7. I will assist sellers in staging their property.

___ 8. I will include a sample Ninety-Day Marketing Plan as part of my pre-listing package.

___ 9. I will provide my listing leads with testimonials from past clients as well as their contact information.

While these points are all important, ultimately the price is what will drive the sale. The next chapter looks at the key steps to help sellers to set a realistic asking price.

Chapter 23
The Eight Key Listening Consultation Questions

Quality questions create a quality life. Successful people ask better questions, and as a result, they get better answers.
Tony Robbins

Skills Check:
Put a checkmark (√) next to what you do now. Leave the remaining items blank. Review the action steps at the end of the chapter to determine the strategies that you will implement in your business.

___ 1. During my last listing appointment, I took written notes on what the seller said was important to them about their property.

___ 2. When I meet with a seller, I always inquire about their motivation for selling.

___ 3. During my last listing appointment, I asked the sellers if I could represent them on the purchase of their next home.

___ 4. If the sellers are relocating outside our area, I always ask if I can assist them by giving them a relocation referral.

___ 5. My listing appointments usually take 30 minutes or less.

___ 6. I provide sellers with a copy of my Premium Marketing Plan that includes a written guarantee of my services.

___ 7. During my listing consultation, I discuss three or four key services that I provide that will help the seller obtain the highest possible price for the property in the shortest amount of time.

___ 8. I know how to explain the value of the services that I provide for sellers and, as a result, almost always earn a full commission.

Knead the Dough Secret #46
Listen and ask questions—don't talk and present.

The Eight Key Listening Questions

The collaborative model proposed in this book assumes a give and take between all parties involved in the transaction. The acronym for "Together everyone achieves more," is "TEAM." You will experience the best results if you use this approach in all aspects of your business.

Asking questions is at the heart of the collaborative model. Having a meaningful dialogue with both sellers and buyers creates trust. It's also the first step in establishing a long lasting relationship where you will receive future referrals. Questions shift the focus from you to your client. Once you master the eight questions in this chapter, you will find that your listing appointments will go much more smoothly. Best of all, over 90 percent of the time you will secure the listing provided you ask these questions and can clearly articulate your value proposition.

Before discussing each question in detail, here are the eight questions:

1. What have you enjoyed about living in this property?

2. What's motivating you to sell?

3. Will these features be important in your next property as well?

4. If staying in the area, would you like me to check the Multiple Listing Service to see how many homes in your price range have these features?

5. If relocating, would you like me to interview agents in the area where you are planning to move?

6. Is it correct to assume that you would like to obtain the highest possible net price for your property?

7. To obtain the highest possible net price, you must have maximum exposure to the market. May I show you how our Premium Marketing Plan provides you with maximum exposure that results in maximum price? (Discuss primary points of differentiation.)

8. Which of these services would you like to use in marketing your property?

Question 1: What have you enjoyed about living in this property?
After you have done your initial greetings, take out a pen and a pad of paper to take notes or use your tablet computer. Now you're ready to launch into your listening consultation.

Neurolinguistic Programming (NLP) tells us that if we ask a question that causes a pleasant response, the good feeling will be anchored in the person who answers the question. By asking sellers what they have enjoyed about living in their property, you are tapping into the good feelings they have about their home. This good feeling is associated with you since you asked the question. Here's the exact language to use:

> **Agent:** *An important step in effectively marketing your property is to understand what is most important to you about your home. With your permission, I would like to make a list now of the things you have enjoyed about living in this property. Making a list now will help me to provide more accurate information to prospective buyers and help me prepare a more effective ad. So tell me, what should I put on my list now of the things that you have enjoyed about your home?*

Once your client answers, be prepared to "dig deeper." Ask about the neighborhood, any improvements that the sellers may have made, or special features that may not be visible to buyers when they walk through the property. It's also important to ask about their past experience in listing or buying a home. This will allow you to identify what matters most in terms of marketing their property. Be sure to write down what they tell you. This is extremely important since it sends a nonverbal message that you care about what they say. It also sets the stage for Questions 2 and 3.

Question 2: What's motivating you to sell?
An important part of your listening consultation will be to uncover the seller's motivation. A simple way to do this is to compliment the sellers on their home (provided what you say is true). Follow this up by asking about what's motivating them to sell. Here's an example of how to do it:

> **Agent:** *John and Terry, you have such a beautiful home and the view is wonderful. What's motivating you to sell?*

Listen carefully to the response to determine how motivated they are. Are they just testing the water? Are they in a forced sale situation? Are they moving because of a happy or unhappy circumstance? It's important to have a sense of what is going on before you reach the pricing part of the discussion.

This question also sets up the opportunity for the first closing question of your listening consultation. In our model, closing works by making an offer of service and then asking whether the client would like to use that service. Questions 3, 4, and 5 illustrate this approach.

Question 3: Will these features be important in your next property as well?
This question opens the door to asking the sellers whether you can represent them on the purchase of their next property or help them with an out-going relocation referral. The way to do this will be to review the list of characteristics that they enjoyed about living in their present property and then to determine whether the same features will be important in their next property. In cases where people are relocating, they may be leaving a two-story Colonial home in the Northeast with the idea of purchasing a Mediterranean home in the Sunbelt. Again, this is an excellent opportunity to dig deeper and discover more about what the sellers want. Here's an example of how to do it:

> **Agent:** *You have told me about the wonderful neighborhood here, about how much you enjoy your private backyard and your pool, how much fun you have entertaining, especially with your great open floor plan. Will these features be important in your next property as well?*

If the sellers answer that these features are important, proceed to the next question. If the seller says that these features are not important, inquire about which features will be important in their next purchase.

Question 4: Would you like me to check the Multiple Listing Service to see how many homes in your price range have these features?
This question is an offer of service and will be the opening to your first closing question. Before you can ask this question, however, you must know whether the sellers will be staying in the area or relocating. If the sellers are staying in the area, ask Question 4. If the sellers are relocating, proceed to Question 5.

Many sellers have already begun an Internet search for their new home. Nevertheless, as an agent who knows the inventory well, you can still help sellers determine which properties may be best for them. Often how something looks on the web is very different from how it appears in person. Furthermore, you may know about distressed properties or new listings that the seller may not have seen. Here's what to say:

> **Agent:** *In addition to these features, what other features will be important in your next home?* (Wait for answer.)

And what price range will you be searching in for your next property?
(Wait for answer.)

Would you like me to check the Multiple Listing Service to see how many homes in your price range have these features?

In most cases, the sellers will say, "Yes." If they do, then you are that much closer to obtaining the listing. You may have also secured the purchase side of their transaction. Each time a client answers "Yes" to a question, you move them closer to working with you.

If they answer "No," follow up by inquiring what their plans are in terms of moving. They may have already purchased their next home or they may not feel comfortable agreeing to look until they have sold their present property. It's important not to take this personally or to push them to work with you. Instead, offer the service and if they don't agree to use it, go on to the next part of your consultation.

Question 5: Would you like me to interview other agents in the area where you are relocating?

This question provides a different offer of service for people who are relocating outside your service area. You can use your company's relocation service if it is available. If your company does not offer such a service, we strongly recommend joining a real estate social network such as the ones hosted at ActiveRain, CRS (Council of Residential Specialists), Point2Agent, or RealTown. Each of these organizations has huge memberships. Once you locate several potential agents, contact them to see whether the agent quickly replies to your request. Look for testimonials and other evidence that the agent has an excellent record in the community where the sellers are going. Here's how to introduce the idea:

Agent: *Would you like me to interview three agents in the area where you are relocating so that you can receive the best possible customer service?*

If the sellers answer your offer of service with a "No," you can follow up with a second offer of service. For example, many sellers work through their company's relocation service. As a result, they will already be working with an agent in their new area. Here's a second offer of service that you can make, regardless of whether the person is working with your relocation referral or with another relocation agent:

Agent: *Oh, by the way, would you like me to send the broker a copy of the list we made today as well as some pictures of your present property? That way, the broker will know exactly what to look for in your new home.*

Wait for the sellers to respond. If they say "Yes," follow up with your relocation division and don't forget to send those pictures. If they say "No," continue your consultation moving to how your services are different from the competition.

Question 6: Is it correct to assume that you would like to obtain the highest possible net price for your property?
One of the reasons that agents end up cutting commissions is that they have not demonstrated their value to the seller. Another important reason that sellers ask agents to cut commissions is that sellers believe that a lower commission will net them more money. In truth, higher commissions result in better market exposure. This is particularly true in slow markets. The listings with the highest commissions attract more showings. Additional exposure results in a better bottom line price.

In a strong seller's market, agents who charge higher commissions generally net their sellers more money. The key point to emphasize is how much the seller **nets** at the end of the day—not the amount of commission.

At this point in your listening consultation, you're not going to discuss the commission. Instead, all you need to do is to ask:

> **Agent:** *Is it correct to assume that you would like to get the highest possible net price for your property?*

Wait for the seller to respond. (Occasionally, a seller may not want to net the most from their sale, especially if there is a contentious a divorce.)

Question 7: To obtain the highest possible net price, you must have maximum exposure to the market. May I show you how our premium marketing plan provides you with maximum exposure that results in maximum price?
The next part of your listening consultation differentiates your services from those provided by your competitors. A simple way to think about this is to discuss what all brokers do, what your company does that is different, and what you do that is different. Using *Get Your Property Sold Now!* is one of the easiest ways to do this.

> *To obtain the highest price possible, you must have maximum exposure to the market place. You can achieve maximum exposure by doing the following. All brokers will place your property in the MLS, put a sign in the front yard, run newspaper ads, and market to other agents through brochures, the Multiple Listing Service, and other advertising. With your permission may I show you how my Premium Marketing Plan helps you to earn the highest price possible in the shortest amount of time?*

The next step is to outline the key points of your Premium Marketing Plan. Maximum exposure includes both print and web media. Key points to discuss on your premium marketing plan include placing their property on over 40 different real estate websites and at least 15 web-based video channels. Also, discuss how you will create a customized website for the sellers using their property address as the URL as well as any open house or print media campaigns you may elect to run. Limit your explanation to three or four key points. Outline the other services that you provide in your Premium Marketing Plan.

Question 8: Which of these services would you like to use in marketing your property?

After you explain each service in your Premium Marketing Plan ask, "Is this a service you want?" This is "give-to-get marketing." If the seller challenges you on the commission, use the following script:

> **Agent:** *Mr. and Mrs. Seller, this is our premium marketing package that will help you obtain the highest possible price for your property. If you would like to reduce the commission, I can give you a referral to an agent who does not provide this level of service.*

In most cases, the seller will want the services that you offered and will relent on the commission.

Chapter 23
Action Plan

If you feel nervous about remembering the questions, it's all right to take them with you. Simply print them up and use the same sheet to take notes. You can also use a tablet computer. Again, this approach is simple to use and will differentiate you from other agents who are still using outdated techniques.

Identify the action steps that you would like to take and rewrite items that may not fit. Circle the number of each strategy that you plan to implement in your business and then record the date you complete the item in the space provided. Make one or two changes at a time. Making too many changes at once can be overwhelming. Keep in mind that your goal is to find an activity that is both motivating and sustainable over time.

Action Steps:

___ 1. On my future listening consultations, I will take written notes on what the seller tells me is important to them about their property.

___ 2. Whenever I meet with a seller, I will inquire about their motivation for selling.

___ 3. In the future, I will ask sellers if I can represent them on the purchase of their next home.

___ 4. During each of my listening consultations, I will offer to search for properties for the seller to purchase or assist them in finding a relocation agent in the area where they are moving.

___ 5. I will provide each of my sellers with a copy of my Premium Marketing Plan that includes a written guarantee of my services.

___ 6. I have identified the key services that I want to discuss during my listening consultation. I can demonstrate how each of these services helps the seller obtain the highest possible price for their property in the shortest amount of time.

___ 7. I know how to explain the value of the services that I provide for sellers and, as a result, almost always earn a full commission.

___ 8. If I am still having trouble earning full commissions, I will order and read *Waging War on Real Estate's Discounters* from RealEstateCoach.com.

Need more help on listings? If so, sink your teeth into the next Recipe for Success that shares seven additional strategies that will help you convert more listings into closed transactions.

Recipes for Success
Make More Listing Dough
In Any Market!

The strategies below come from agents who are prospering in the midst of very tough markets. If you need additional help getting your listings sold, experiment with these proven top producer strategies.

1. **Make your listings stand out**
   Staging is critical, especially if you're competing with new product. The question you must address is how much budget does your seller have and what is absolutely necessary. A simple approach is to divide the work into four categories. The first category includes basic maintenance items that must be addressed. In general, these will show up on the inspection report and not addressing them will result in the seller receiving a lower price. The second category is de-cluttering and staging using existing items in the property or staging items that you loan to the seller. The third category is making the house more competitive by painting, replacing the carpets, or doing other basic improvement items. The fourth category includes desirable changes provided the seller has sufficient budget. Sellers are often overwhelmed at how much they may have to do to make their houses saleable. This strategy allows the sellers to identify what is absolutely critical as compared to what is desirable.

2. **Provide financial incentives**
   Many agents encourage their sellers to use financial incentives to attract buyers. Strategies include contributing money to closing costs, offering a higher cooperating commission to buyers' brokers, and paying the buyers' Homeowner Association dues for one year. Two additional strategies are to buy down the buyer's interest rate for one to three years or to purchase a home warranty for the buyer.

3. **Four strategies to keep from chasing the market down**
   One of the greatest challenges in a tough market is persuading sellers to be realistic. Here are four ways to do it.

   a. Discuss the supply and demand data.

   b. Ask the sellers, "If you don't sell, what are your alternatives?" In other words, do the sellers have the time and money to wait for their property to sell or do they really need to sell now?

c. Show the sellers market times for properties at various price points. Then ask whether they want to get ahead of the price declines by being aggressive or linger on the market and slowly see their equity erode.

d. A final approach is to ask them where they want to be in the Multiple Listing Service next month—in the sold properties or in the still-listed properties.

4. **Offer strategies**
A tried and true strategy is to obtain a price reduction whenever the seller writes a counteroffer at less than asking price. This puts additional pressure on the buyers to act. Also, many sellers become discouraged when they receive an especially low offer. Instead of becoming discouraged, tell them to feel good about generating an offer in this market.

5. **Show the sellers how much they're saving**
When the seller is purchasing a less expensive property, calculate how much the seller will save each month in their new property. For example, if the seller's mortgage will be reduced by $1,000 per month, that represents a $12,000 savings per year. Each month they don't sell costs them another $1,000. On the other hand, when prices are going up, show them how much they gain by buying a trade-up property. If your clients are listing a $300,000 property and they are purchasing a $500,000 property, calculate how much your current market has declined. Assume the market has declined by five percent. The sellers will reduce their price on their $300,000 property by $15,000. The same five percent reduction results in $25,000 on the $500,000 property. Thus, the seller picks up an additional $10,000 in appreciation by purchasing a more expensive property.

6. **Reverse contracts**
In *Real Estate in 2008*, one of the contributors to the book suggested using "reverse contracts" as a way to get reluctant buyers to begin the negotiation process. When the buyer is having difficulty deciding about purchasing a specific property, the listing agent can launch the negotiation by asking the seller to issue a "reverse contract." This involves the seller drafting an offer to the buyer, generally at a price slightly under asking price. While this may not always work, it is an excellent way to see whether the buyer is actually serious about purchasing.

7. **Shift your mindset**
Another agent in *Real Estate in 2008* had this suggestion that addresses the most important factor when it comes to dealing with market shifts:

Let's stop talking about the boom days and lamenting the bust days. Let's start talking about the benefits of home ownership, the pride in neighborhoods, and taking a positive approach to the market and to life in general.

Regardless of what type of market you are in, overpriced listings don't sell. The next chapter reveals the secrets of how to set realistic asking prices.

Chapter 24
My Property Is Worth More! How to Persuade Sellers to Set Realistic Asking Prices

What you have to do and the way you have to do it is incredibly simple. Whether you are willing to do it, that's another matter.
Peter F. Drucker

Skills Check:
Put a checkmark (√) next to what you do now. Leave the remaining items blank. Review the action steps at the end of the chapter to determine the strategies that you will implement in your business.

___ 1. I know how many months of inventory are currently on the market in each of the areas that I serve.

___ 2. I can show sellers whether we are in a seller's market, transitional market or buyer's market based upon how much inventory is on the market.

___ 3. When I do a comparable market analysis, I only use properties where the square footage of both the lots and the improvements are within 10 percent of those of the subject property.

___ 4. I know how to use the amount of inventory on the market to help sellers realistically price their property.

___ 5. I know how to persuade sellers to be realistic about their asking prices.

Did You Know that Your House Has to Qualify?

You have reviewed what differentiates your services from the competition and how you're going to help the seller achieve the highest possible price for their property through your aggressive traditional and web marketing plans. The next step in the process is to assist the seller in setting the price. Prior to introducing the Comparable Market Analysis and the Supply and Demand data, make the transition to the pricing discussion by asking the following question:

> *Mr. and Mrs. Seller, you probably know that in order to sell your home you have to have a qualified buyer. Did you know that your house also has to qualify?*

Most sellers are prepared to discuss "list prices" when they consider where to price their property. In contrast, the best comparable sales are those that have closed and "qualified" with a lender for a loan. Asking the question above helps you to circumvent the list price discussion and focus completely on sold prices.

Prior to giving the sellers your CMA material, use the following dialogue to introduce the idea that not only does the buyer have to qualify with the lender, so does their house:

> *You already know that in order to close the transaction, you must first have a qualified buyer, but did you know that your house also has to qualify? How do you determine whether or not your house will qualify? Well, the way that the appraisers do this is based upon the same data that we use called a comparable market analysis. So let's take a look at what properties are qualifying for in your neighborhood.*

There are two advantages to using this approach. By changing the conversation to what properties have "qualified for," you have shifted the conversation from list prices to sold prices. A common way sellers overprice their property is by focusing on the current list prices. This strategy keeps the dialogue focused on sold prices and can help you avoid the list price conversation entirely. Also, using the phrase "what properties have qualified for," places the responsibility for the appraisal on the lenders rather than on you, the agent.

Unhook Their Anchors

Using the approach above has another important advantage. Neurolinguistic programming (NLP) uses the term "anchor" to refer to the process of associating an internal response or feeling with an external trigger. Anchors may occur naturally or may be set intentionally.

Anchors have important implications for real estate. Ariely (2008) demonstrates how difficult it is for people to change existing property price anchors. For example, people who move to a less expensive area spend about the same amount for their new home as they received for their previous property. In other words, even though a property with comparable amenities would cost less, they still opt to buy a property priced at the same level as their original property.

Economists note that prices are "sticky" when values are decreasing. In other words, prices are much more resistant to downward movement as opposed to upward movement. Once sellers or buyers have established a price that they believe a property is worth, their anchors make it difficult to accept a different price. To bypass this anchor, use a price-per-square-foot CMA. (Calculate price per square foot by dividing the sales price by the number of square feet in the property.) Sellers are normally prepared to discuss the list prices, but not square foot prices. This approach helps sellers be more realistic since they have no preconceived basis of comparison.

What Makes an Effective Comparable Market Analysis?

The most important decision in terms of how quickly a home will sell will be where the seller decides to price or "position" the property in the marketplace. This is where knowing market statistics is critical. The two critical documents in this process are your Comparable Market Analysis (CMA) and your Supply and Demand worksheet.

If you are doing a two-step listening consultation, you will probably have time to complete a thorough CMA after viewing the property. In contrast, when you are in a one-step situation, your knowledge of the inventory is critical. A one-step consultation requires that you to commit to a price during your initial meeting with the sellers. You must be able to help the sellers set a realistic price without going back for additional documentation.

The best way to be prepared for either a one-step or a two-step consultation is to gather your CMA information as well as your Supply and Demand information prior to your first appointment. This way you are prepared no matter what the sellers decide to do. These two tools are the most powerful way to persuade sellers to list their house at a realistic price.

Choosing the Right Comparable Sales: The Ten Percent Rule

The Ten Percent Rule addresses how you select the properties to include in your analysis. Whether you are determining how much inventory is on the market or are doing a Comparable Market Analysis (CMA), you can distort the results if you do not follow this rule.

According to the Ten Percent Rule, the properties you select for your CMA must be within 10 percent of both the lot size and the square footage of the seller's property. For example, if you are listing a property with a 6,000 square foot lot and the improvements are 2,500 square feet, all of your comparable sales should range from 5,400 to 6,600 square feet for the lot sizes and 2,250 to 2,750 square feet for the improvements.

As a rule of thumb, smaller improvements command a higher price per square foot than do larger improvements. If you are in an area where the value is in the land rather than the improvements, selecting a property with a significantly larger lot can seriously distort the outcome. Consequently, pay special attention to this guideline so that your calculations and the data that you share with your clients is as accurate as possible.

It's also important to realize that you may be in a seller's market in certain price ranges and a buyer's market in other price ranges, especially if the market is in transition. The luxury and move-up markets are normally the first to experience slowdown. The first time buyer market is normally the last to feel the pinch. In our most recent buyer's market, however, this has not necessarily been the case. The only way to know for sure is to track the market statistics and how much inventory is currently on the market.

What Market Statistics Do I Need to Use During My Listing Consultations?

Other than your Comparable Market Analysis, the most important statistic that you will need to persuade sellers to be realistic is the "Supply and Demand" sheet as illustrated in Table 5. The concept is simple. The higher the supply is, the lower the prices will be. The lower the supply is, the higher the prices will be. Generally, you can find out how much inventory is on the market from your local Multiple Listing Service or from a title company.

Table 5

Supply and Demand in a Major Metropolitan Area*

Please note that the prices reflect a $50,000 range. For example, the $250,000 line contains properties priced from $250,000 to $299,999.

Price Range	Under Contract	Currently Listed	Supply vs. Demand Ratio	Percent Selling	Months of Inventory
$20,000,000	1	5	5 to 1	17.0%	6
$10,000,000	1	47	47 to 1	2.1%	48
$5,000,000	97	1,209	12 to 1	7.7%	13
$1,000,000	34	324	10 to 1	9.1%	11
$900,000	35	523	15 to 1	6.7%	16
$800,000	52	695	13 to 1	7.7%	14
$700,000	111	1,104	10 to 1	9.1%	11
$600,000	144	1,709	12 to 1	7.7%	13
$500,000	124	1,351	11 to 1	8.5%	12
$450,000	175	1,546	9 to 1	10.0%	10
$400,000	276	2,696	10 to 1	9.1%	11
$350,000	254	1,947	8 to 1	11.1%	9
$300,000	380	2,720	8 to 1	11.1%	9
$250,000	408	2,400	6 to 1	14.3%	7
$200,000	190	1,304	6 to 1	14.3%	7
$150,000	69	411	5 to 1	16.7%	6
$100,000	17	124	7 to 1	12.5%	8
Total	2,368	20,114	11.4 to 1	8.1%	12.4

**If this data is not readily available to you, instructions on how to calculate it are located in our List and Sell Real Estate Like Crazy Audio CD program or in our "Listen and Learn" catalogue of 24-7 online courses. Look for the "Rate of Absorption." You will find both of these programs at our website at RealEstateCoach.com.*

The chart in Table 5 provides a wealth of information. Before going on to discuss the specifics of what this data means in a given price range, let's take a look at each category.

How Can I Tell If We're in a Buyer's, Seller's, or Flat Market?

Remember, if there are six or less months of inventory on the market, you are in a seller's market with too little inventory and upward pressure on prices. If there are seven or eight months of inventory on the market, you are in a flat or transitional market with stable prices. If there are nine or more months of inventory on the market, you are in a buyer's market with downward pressure on prices.

Table 5 illustrates all three types of markets—a seller's market, a flat or transitioning market, and a buyer's market. Using the data from the example above, we can draw the following conclusions from the supply and demand data.

1. The overall data for the entire market shows that this city is experiencing a buyer's market. The average amount of inventory on the market is 12.1 months, far above the nine months needed to create a buyer's market.

2. The only price ranges experiencing a sellers market are from $150,000 to $200,000 and over $20 million.

3. Properties priced under $100,000 and between $200,000 and $300,000 are in a flat or transitioning market.

4. The balance of the market is in a buyer's market.

5. Overall sales are down by 33 percent from the preceding year. Usually, a decrease in the number of sales coupled with more than eight months of inventory results in a decline in prices. This market should be experiencing price declines in properties priced over $350,000 if the current trends continue.

6. Decreasing prices usually result in more foreclosures, bankruptcies, and short sales. Builders will be unable to move their inventory. This will result in a downward spiral in prices as sellers become desperate. This spiral will continue until the inventory reverts back to eight months or less.

7. Based upon this particular supply and demand chart, the listings that are most likely to sell are those priced under $350,000. It would be smart for agents in this market to be working this price range in terms of prospecting expired listings, For-Sale-by-Owners, cold calling, door-knocking, or geographical farming. On the other hand, the best deals for buyers will be in the upper price ranges where there is a glut of inventory.

8. The data also demonstrate the "move up buyer squeeze." For example, there is 11 months of inventory for properties priced at $400,000 to $450,000. If these owners would like to purchase an $800,000 house, they have a 9 percent (1/11) chance of selling in any given month. The probability they will not sell is 91 percent (10/11). The good news is that once the owners of a less expensive house close their property, there is 14 months of inventory in the $800,000 price range, so there should be a wide variety of excellent buys.

When markets decline, the last part of the market to experience a slowdown is usually the entry level market. Often the ultra high end is not affected. Although it seems attractive to represent very expensive listings, this data shows that your time would be best spent working in the lower end of the market. This is one of the most important reasons to track this data. It tells you which price ranges are the most likely to experience activity. Spend your time and your marketing dollars where you will achieve the best results.

Giving a detailed chart such as the one in Table 5 may confuse some sellers. The best tactic is to provide the data for the specific price range in which the property should sell. If the seller is an accountant, engineer, or someone who loves numbers, providing the entire chart is often helpful.

A key part of your discussion will be to address what the probability is that the sellers will place their property under contract within a given month. This is a simple calculation. Most Multiple Listing Services track how much inventory is on the market. For example, if there is a six-month supply of inventory on the market, then the probability that the seller will sell this month is 1 out of 6, or 17 percent. The probability that the seller will not sell this month is 83 percent. If there is a 12-month supply of inventory on the market, the probability is 1/12 or 8.5 percent that the seller will sell this month. The probability the seller won't sell this month is 91.5 percent. Here's the dialogue to use:

Mr. and Mrs. Seller, you have an important decision to make. Are you going to position your property where it will be under contract next month or are you going to position (price) it where it will still be listed next month? It's your choice, what would you like to do?

Here's a slightly different approach.

Mr. and Mrs. Seller, you have an important decision to make. Are you going to select a price that will allow your property to sell in one month, three months, six months, or a year or more?

The most powerful approach, however, is this one:

> *Mr. and Mrs. Seller, as you can see from this table, only 8.5 percent of the properties that are listed will sell this month. The probability that you won't sell this month is 91.5 percent. Thus, you have an important decision to make. Are you going to position your property where it will be part of the 8.5 percent that will sell or will you position your property where you will be part of the 91.5 percent that will still be listed next month? The choice is yours, what would you like to do?*

Remember, it's their house and it's their decision. If the sellers are unrealistic, graciously thank them for their time and leave. When sellers see you stand up to leave because you think their price is too high, many will call you back. If not, you just avoided wasting your time and money on a listing that won't sell.

Four Strategies for Coping with Declining Prices

The subprime fiasco, higher foreclosure rates, interest rate increases, and tougher underwriting standards all exert pressure on the market. Buyers may be reluctant to purchase because they fear that prices will decrease further. Sellers are unable to sell, which results in more foreclosures. Lenders end up taking back more property and brokers end up doing fewer transactions. If your market is declining, here are four steps that you can take to avoid being caught in the downward price spiral.

1. **Price properties below the comparable sales**
   Declining prices make obtaining an accurate CMA difficult. Assume that a seller's property is currently worth $400,000 and they want to list at $410,000. If property is declining at an annual rate of five percent per year ($20,000), then the seller's property 180 days from now is only worth $390,000. Given that few sellers price their property exactly at market value, their list price of $410,000 is now $20,000 higher than the property's value. Thus, even with a $10,000 price reduction, the list price would still be $10,000 over the new market value. This is exactly where the seller started at the beginning of the listing period. If a price that was $10,000 over market value did not result in a successful sale, it is even less likely to produce a sale as the market continues to decline.

   To avoid this trap, list the property below the comparable sales. The reason for this is simple—today's comparable sales represent what the prices were 60 to 90 days ago. If the market is declining, then the property is actually worth less than the comparable sales suggest.

Knead the Dough Secret #47
Make every effort to sell your listings during the "honeymoon period."

2. **Avoid letting the sellers "test the market"**
   Persuading your sellers to be realistic is challenging in any market. This is especially true when the market has been very good and is transitioning into a buyer's market. As a result, sellers often want to "test the market." This is a huge mistake. Many sellers mistakenly believe that the initial activity on their property will continue throughout the listing period. Nothing could be further from the truth. When they first list their property, there is pent-up demand among the current buyers who haven't found a property. Once this initial surge ceases, showings will be limited to new buyers coming into the market. Missing this initial "honeymoon period," which normally lasts the first 21 days a property is listed, often results in longer market time and a substantially lower price. Do everything within your power to keep sellers from making this costly mistake.

3. **When it comes to price reductions, you need a chain saw, not a pair of nail clippers**
   When property values are declining, reducing the price to the current market value is not sufficient. Instead, you must be slightly below market value to sell the property. To persuade the sellers about the wisdom of this approach, show them how much they lose each month they hold their property. To illustrate this point, assume that a seller is paying $3,000 per month in principal, interest, taxes, and insurance (PITI) and that the prices are decreasing by $1,000 per month. The actual cost to the seller of not being accurately priced is $4,000 per month ($3,000 in PITI + $1,000 in depreciation).

4. **Tap into the seller's motivation to sell**
   In a declining market, many people are selling because they must. It may be a divorce, financial difficulties, a job transfer, or some other event in which the seller has no choice. An important part of providing the seller with excellent service is to understand their motivation. While sellers' markets are difficult for buyers because prices are constantly climbing, buyers' markets are tough on sellers because prices are declining. If the sellers have to sell and are reluctant to accept a reasonable offer, you can ask, "Which is more important, getting on with your life or waiting for the real estate market to improve?"

If the sellers are purchasing a more expensive home, remind them that they will be making additional money on the deal. For example, the owner of a home worth $300,000 who experiences a five percent price decline will see a $15,000 reduction in value. If that same individual is purchasing a $600,000 home, that home will experience a $30,000 reduction in value. Thus, the seller comes out $15,000 ahead. In fact, the higher price ranges usually experience greater drops than entry level homes.

Helping your clients understand the psychology of a changing market will make the job of selling their home easier. More importantly, it can save your clients money as well.

Chapter 24
Action Plan

To make sure that you are prepared for market shifts, use the suggestions below or rewrite them so they fit the action that you would like to take. Circle the number of each strategy that you plan to implement in your business and then record the date you complete the item in the space provided. If you select more than one item, place the items in priority order and work on implementing one item at a time. Once you complete the items you have selected, move on to the next chapter.

Action Steps:

___ 1. I know how many months of inventory are currently on the market in each of the areas that I serve.

___ 2. I can show sellers whether we are in a seller's market, transitional market or buyer's market based upon how much inventory is on the market.

___ 3. I will use the Ten Percent Rule when I calculate market statistics or when I do a Comparable Market Analysis.

___ 4. In order to help sellers be more realistic about their asking prices, I will show them the Supply and Demand data.

___ 5. I know how to use the "Supply and Demand" approach to persuade sellers to be realistic about their asking prices.

___ 6. My current listings are priced realistically.

One of the greatest challenges listing agents face in declining markets is "chasing the market down." Mike Kelly shares how to avoid this in the next Recipe for Success.

Recipes for Success
Avoid Chasing the Market Down

Mike Kelly
Keller Williams
MikesRealEstateShow.com

Mike Kelly is a superstar agent and hosts a weekly real estate show from Sonoma, California. You have probably heard of the five major food groups. Mike outlines how the same approach applies to sellers. He also shares his Recipe for Success to avoid "chasing the market down."

Everyone has heard of the five major food groups. The same principle applies to sellers as well.

1. **Regular consumers:** these are the normal real estate buyers we have in every market. They get married, have children, relocate, and retire. The challenge we face to today is that up to 40 percent of the properties are owned by speculators rather than regular consumers. Sadly, we're in a "bubble zone" where the prices have been dropping and killing the regular consumer.

2. **Investors:** These people often own multiple properties. If they bought several years ago, they probably still have some equity left. The challenge for this group is that in many cases, their investment properties have a negative cash flow. When they can't rent them, they're willing to dump them for a loss just to rid themselves of the negative cash flow.

3. **REOs:** These are properties that have gone through the foreclosure process. Banks are now one of our seller food groups. They have the power to provide financing to the buyers of their listings as well as to provide other types of incentives. When it comes down to a regular consumer vs. a bank, the institution usually wins.

4. **Short sales:** These sellers are going to walk away from their property if their short sale doesn't go through. I understand that in Michigan, up to 80 percent of the sellers bring money to close the transaction. Here, most sellers walk away. Short sales tend to drain off the good buyers. They can tie them up for months and then the transaction doesn't close.

5. **Pre-foreclosure:** Many of these sellers are facing increases in their adjustable rate mortgages that they can't afford. They're trying to sell their home before they lose it in foreclosure.

It's important for sellers to understand who the competition is, what the market statistics mean, as well as the tax and credit ramifications of doing a short sale or going through a foreclosure. It is absolutely imperative that sellers who are facing foreclosure or who are considering doing a short sale consult their tax attorney. For example, assume that a seller refinanced their property and pulled out a $100,000. They then sell their property for $100,000 less than the loan amount. The IRS views this as "debt relief," which is a taxable event. Assuming that they paid $10,000 in closing costs when they refinanced, they would have $90,000 of taxable income.

I train agents to avoid being discouraged by the numbers. Instead, they must understand that by helping the sellers get ahead of the price reductions, they actually can help them save money. To do this, you must be able to show clients the trends. What is the average market time? What is the rate of absorption? For example, we currently have eight months of inventory on the market. That means that if no new listings were to come on the market, it would take eight months to sell everything that is currently listed.

This is why it's critical that sellers understand how important it is to avoid "chasing the market down." Sellers end up getting less when they price their property at the same level as the competition. To sell in these circumstances, owners must be willing to lead the pack on price reductions. This allows them to sell quickly. The result is that they actually net more than if they stayed on the market and had to repeatedly lower their price.

Even though 90 percent of marketing today is tied to price, properties still have to be perfectly staged, sparkling clean, and in impeccable condition.

To succeed in today's market, research your seller leads before taking a listing. Many are in trouble and they don't know what a NOD (Notice of Default) is or what to do about it. Make sure you know your market statistics and advise your sellers to see their tax advisor before committing to a short sale or allowing their house to go through foreclosure.

Chapter 25
Expired Listings:
Converting Someone Else's Failure into Your Success

Patience, persistence, and perspiration make an unbeatable combination for success.
Napoleon Hill

CAVEAT: It is a violation of the REALTORS® Code of Ethics to solicit another company's listing during the term of its exclusive right to sell agreement. It is extremely important that you take special care to avoid soliciting properties that are listed with other companies, even if the seller approaches you. Remember, sellers and buyers work with you for a few months and then they're gone. In contrast, your reputation in the brokerage community as an ethical and trustworthy person is worth much more and lasts much longer than any single transaction.

Skills Check:
Put a checkmark (√) next to what you do now. Leave the remaining items blank. Review the action steps at the end of this chapter to determine the strategies you will implement in your business.

___ 1. I regularly prospect expired listings.

___ 2. I can easily handle the objection, "How come you didn't show my home while it was listed?"

___ 3. I prospect expired listings by personally contacting them rather than relying on snail mail or email.

___ 4. I prospect owners of expired listings who live outside our area.

___ 5. I prospect old expireds and expired lease listings.

___ 6. I have an expired listing script that persuades sellers to allow me to conduct a listening consultation.

___ 7. I use a Premium Marketing Plan on my expired listening consultations.

___ 8. I never criticize the other agent, regardless of what the seller says.

___ 9. During my expired listening consultation, I show the seller how my 800 Call Capture system gathers accurate contact data from our print and web advertising.

___10. During my expired listening consultation, I show sellers how I market my listings on over 40 different websites as well as how to make their listing stand out on the web with multiple pictures posted to multiple websites.

___11. I provide a single property website customized for each of my sellers that uses the property address as the URL (i.e., 333 ElmStreet.com).

___12. I show sellers how I market my listings through at least fifteen different video web channels including YouTube.

___13. I can easily handle any objection that the owner of an expired listing may have.

Knead the Dough Secret #48
The primary reason that listings expire is that the previous agent wasn't strong enough to persuade the seller to set a realistic price.

Seven Reasons Listings Expire

There are a number of reasons that listings expire. The most important reason is the price. No matter how good or how poor the property is the property won't sell if it's overpriced. In most cases when a listing expires, it's because the agent simply wasn't strong enough to persuade the seller to list it at a competitive price. In addition to overpricing, there are six other reasons why listings expire:

1. The property is in poor condition.

2. The property has an issue related to the financing.

3. The seller is not motivated.

4. Something about the location or the actual property is undesirable.

5. The marketplace is uncertain due to declining values, unemployment, recession, etc. This is most common when you're in a buyer's market.

6. The property was not marketed aggressively.

Common Complaints You May Hear from Owners of Expired Listings

Complaint 1: The agent promised more than they actually delivered.

Complaint 2: The agent didn't follow up.

Complaint 3: There weren't enough open houses, advertising, etc.

Complaint 4: When a listing expires, the sellers often have a number of real estate agents contacting them to see if they would like to list. This may make the seller angry, especially if there was little traffic during the time the property was an active listing. Be prepared to answer the following objection:

How come you never showed my home?

OR

How come you never saw my property while it was listed?

Overcome this objection by saying:

Mr. Seller, I actively work to find buyers for my listings. That's what you want if you were working with an agent isn't it—to have your agent stay focused on selling your home rather than selling someone else's home?

Remember to use charge neutral and wait for the seller's response before saying anything.

Knead the Dough Secret #49
In life, it's best to be the first-born, the second wife, and the third listing agent on a property.

The Positive Side of Working with Expired Listings

1. The sellers are often more realistic about their price than they were when they first listed their property.

2. The seller's need to sell has probably increased. This usually results in the seller being more aggressive about marketing their property.

3. When you do receive an offer, the seller will be much more likely to negotiate, and as a consequence, it's usually easier to place their property under contract.

4. Expired listings are one of the three best sources of right-now business.

Prospecting for Expired Listings

If you are going to prospect newly expired listings, it's best to call on the owner the morning the listing expires. The challenge is that you will be competing against everyone else who also prospects newly expired listings. If you are unable to visit the property in person, you can use a similar approach by phone. Here are two "tried and true" prospecting scripts for calling on owners of expired listings. The first script requires that you track the number of expired listings from other companies that have sold through your office. If this is your niche, you can use your personal numbers.

Expired Listing Script 1:

> **Agent:** *Good morning. This is Bernice Ross with ABC Real Estate. I specialize in assisting sellers who could not sell their homes with other companies. In the last six months, our office has sold the homes of 16 sellers who had been unable to sell their homes when they were listed with a different company. Is getting your property sold now a service you want?*

Expired Listing Script 2:

> **Agent:** *Good morning. My name is Bernice Ross with ABC Real Estate and I noticed that the listing on your home has expired. Are you still interviewing agents for the job of selling your home?*
>
> Prospect: Yes, we must sell soon and the agent who had the listing wasn't getting the job done.
>
> **Agent:** *Would you be offended if I looked at your home?*
>
> Prospect: No, I would not be offended.
>
> **Agent:** *Would tonight at 7:00 p.m. or tomorrow morning at 9:00 a.m. be better?*
>
> Prospect: Tomorrow morning at 9:00 would work.
>
> **Agent:** *Thank you for your time. If you need to reach me before tomorrow morning, my name again is Bernice Ross from ABC Real Estate and my phone number is 800-555-2222.*

If the prospect is unwilling to have you preview the property, use the following script.

> Prospect: I'm tired of dealing with you real estate people. I'm going to sell it myself.
>
> **Agent:** *Mr. Seller, I would like to give you a copy of* Get Your Property Sold Now! *If you do elect to list with an agent, it will help you determine which agents provide the best service. I have a copy with me. May I leave it with you?*
>
> Prospect: OK—thanks.

When you call on an expired listing in person, you must be prepared to do your listening consultation on the spot. It's a good idea to have a list of comparable sales as well as a complete listing package. It's also smart to prepare your supply and demand material. This is one of the most powerful tools to use with expired listings. Specifically, when you show the seller that only one out of ten houses is selling per month, you accomplish two things. First, you provide a rationale for why their property didn't sell. Second, you lay the groundwork for helping the seller understand how important it is for them to be realistic on their listing price. In addition to these tools, you will also need the following items when you knock on the seller's front door:

1. Materials for taking notes as you walk through the house. Your goal on the first contact is to ask questions and listen. Writing down what the seller says as well as what you observe sends a nonverbal signal to the seller that their house and their comments are important. If you're using a tablet computer, take it with you. It will make you stand out from the competition.

2. Your business card.

3. Your name badge where it is clearly visible when you knock on the seller's door.

4. A warm smile and a firm handshake.

Prospect Expired Listings Digitally

Younger owners who are active social networkers, may post that their property is for sale on public sites such as Zillow's "make-me-move" or on Facebook or MySpace. You can also track listings on sites such as Point2Homes or Trulia. When the listings disappear from these sites, there is a high probability that they have expired, especially if they haven't posted as being under contract or sold.

Prospecting Expired Listings by Mail

When the owners of an expired listing live outside the area, you may have to rely on prospecting via snail mail. This is only effective if the seller lives outside the area. Otherwise, it's best to have either direct face-to-face or telephone contact with the seller. If you have to use the mail, overnight your expired listing package to the seller. To differentiate yourself from the competition, scan a picture of the seller's property on the front of the envelope you use to send the seller your expired listing package.

The expired listing letter in Table 6 is extremely effective, especially when combined with the appropriate follow-up strategies. To fully utilize this technique, calculate the supply and demand data for the area where the seller's property is located and substitute those numbers for those found in the following example. If you use this letter, be sure that you provide all the services described. If you're sending this letter as part of a digital expired campaign, include links to videos of your properties, a sample single property website, a list of the 40 websites where you syndicate your listings, and where you syndicate your videos as well.

Table 6

Dear Mr. and Mrs. Seller,

Your property recently appeared on the Multiple Listing Service as having expired. If you are still interviewing agents for the job of selling your property, please take a few moments to review the materials in this package that can help you sell your home for the highest price possible in the shortest amount of time.

Supply and Demand Evaluation: This information tells how quickly the listing inventory is selling. In the market where your property is located, there is approximately 10 months of inventory on the market. What this means is that there is only a 10 percent chance that your property will sell in any given month and there is a 90 percent chance it won't sell. In fact, if no new listings were to come on the market, it would take 10 months to sell all of the current listings. This may be a key reason that your property did not sell during the time it was on the market.

Seller's Guarantee of Services. At ABC Realty, we believe that you deserve the highest level of professional, personalized service available. Consequently, we put our commitment of service in writing. As the listing agent, if I don't live up to the guarantee, you can have me replaced. All you have to do is to put the request in writing to my manager.

Ninety-Day Marketing Plan. To obtain the highest possible price for your property, the listing agent you choose must have a specific plan for marketing your property. I customize your marketing plan so your property has maximum exposure to the best qualified buyers. You'll find a sample plan in this package.

Aggressive Web Marketing Plan. If you list with our company, your property will be marketed on over 40 different websites, at least 15 different online video channels, as well as with a customized website that uses your property address as the URL (web address). To view what your customized website would look like, place the link below into the browser on your computer. (INCLUDE A LINK TO ONE OF YOUR CUSTOM WEB SITES.)

Thank you for taking the time to review this material. If your property is already listed with a broker, please disregard this letter.

Sincerely,

Additional Strategies for Locating Expired Listings

One of the best strategies for prospecting for expired listings is to join a service such as the one offered by TheRedX.com. They update you daily with the most recent expired listings, check the owners' names against the Do Not Call Registry, and provide a complete marketing program that makes this process much simpler.

Most agents go after the most recently expired listings. If you want to have little or no competition, consider prospecting listings that expired between four and twelve months ago and that have not changed ownership. Virtually no one prospects these old expireds. If you elect to prospect old expireds, check the public records to determine if there has been an ownership change since the property was first listed. Sometimes listing agents don't report the sale. In other scenarios, the lender has taken the property back through foreclosure. Remember, it's always smart to check whether the property has been conveyed.

If you elect to prospect old expireds by mail, simply delete the word "recently" from the first line of the letter in Table 6.

Prospecting Expired Lease Listings

The next technique is very effective if your Multiple Listing Service includes lease listings. Begin by identifying the properties that have been for lease. Determine whether the listing was leased or if the listing expired. If the property was leased, most property leases are for one year. Enter the property address into your tickler system to contact in nine months. You can prospect the owner for a listing as well as the tenant as a possible buyer.

In this case, drive by the property to determine whether or not it's vacant. If the property is vacant, the owner may consider listing the property for lease or for sale. Granted you may receive quite a few rental calls, but some of those renters may be buyers provided they have good credit. In fact, as long as interest rates stay relatively low, the cost of renting may be about the same as the cost of owning a home. To prospect this type of expired listing, you can knock on the owner's door, call them, or send them the expired listing letter in Table 6.

Previewing the Expired Listing

If the seller allows you to view the property, walk through and take detailed notes. Pay special attention to any concerns the sellers raise about how the property was marketed. Address these points in your listening consultation. It's equally important to allow sellers to vent any hostile feelings they may have about their previous agent or experience. NEVER criticize the other agent or company. Your only focus is to show the seller how you can assist them now.

As you walk through the property, you can ask the seller any of the following questions:

1. What is your motivation for moving?

2. What special features does your home have that may not be apparent to a buyer who is just walking through it for the first time?

3. What did you like about how your home was marketed in the past?

4. What didn't you like about how your home was marketed in the past?

5. When do you need to move?

6. What are the primary advantages of living in this neighborhood?

7. What do you think prevented your house from selling when it was listed before?

There's one other key point here: if the seller asks you about the price, it's better to do a full blown listening consultation than to quote a price without having laid the proper groundwork.

Differentiate Your Services on Expired Listening Consultations

What are some of the things you can include in your expired listing package that will make you stand out from the competition?

Strategy 1: Use a Seller's Guarantee of Services

Using a Seller's Guarantee of Services is an excellent way to relieve the seller's concerns that you will not get their house sold. Remember, if you don't live up to the guarantee, the seller can have another agent from your firm assigned to the listing.

Strategy 2: Premium Marketing Plan

An easy way to illustrate this is to give the sellers a copy of *Get Your Property Sold Now!* Check off the services that you provide and ask them to compare your services to those offered by competitors.

Strategy 3: Take multiple pictures of the property with your digital camera.

Use the photos to create a brochure that you include as the first page of your expired listing package. If you use an envelope to drop off your expired listing information, scan the photos on the outside of the envelope. You can also use the pictures on multiple websites.

Strategy 4: Use an 800 Call Capture System

Ask the sellers whether their previous agent had an 800 call capture system. Explain how 90 percent of the calls coming into most offices are lost since the person answering the call fails to obtain the caller's number. In contrast, call capture gathers up to 95 percent of the numbers. Lack of this system may be one explanation as to why the owner's property did not sell. Be sure to demonstrate the system.

Strategy 5: Prepare a single property website

These sites use the property address as the URL, such as 345ElmStreet.com. There are several excellent providers of this service. Usually it's smart to use the city and the zip code in addition to the name, since that's how most people search. The great news about the single property sites are that you can set up your seller's website ahead of time. If you do not get the listing, there is no charge for creating the site or registering the domain name.

Strategy 6: Provide a list of more than 40 different websites that you use to market your listings

Most agents do not provide extensive web marketing or even if they do, they don't adequately explain it to their sellers. Visit RealEstateCoach.com/handout for a downloadable graphic that illustrates this. Show the seller how you market your other listings and allow them to draw their own conclusions about why their house did not sell.

Strategy 7: Market on at least 15 different online video sites

Video syndication is one of the latest developments in marketing your listings. When you visit the owner of the expired listings, ask whether their property had been marketed adequately online, especially using video.

Overcoming Requests to Reduce Your Commission

Your local MLS may be one of your strongest allies when it comes to overcoming the request by the owner of an expired listing to discount your commission. In many markets, properties with discounted commissions expire more often than properties with full commissions. If this is the case in your local market, show the seller the expired listings. Use the following script when the seller asks you to discount your commission.

Expired Listing Commission Defense Script:

> Prospect: I'll list with you provided you take the listing at five percent like my last agent did.

Agent: *Listing with me will help you achieve three important results:*

1. You will get your property sold rather than having it expire.

2. You will obtain more money for your property.

3. Your sale will be more secure.

Hand the sellers the printout of all the recently expired listings.

Agent: *As you can see from this printout, most of the expired listings were listed with firms that discount. How much did those sellers save when their discount broker did not sell their house?*

Prospect: I guess they didn't save any money since their property didn't sell.

Agent: *You only pay the REALTOR® when you sell your house, right? There is no savings when there is no sale. When your house does not sell, the amount of commission is irrelevant.**

*Special thanks to Tim Burrell of RE/MAX Palos Verdes and Raleigh, North Carolina for sharing this script.

Chapter 25
Action Plan

Working with expired listings is one of the best ways to build your business, especially if you prospect old expireds or lease expireds where there is little competition. Practice your scripts until they sound natural and you can say them automatically. Mastery of your scripts will give you the confidence you need to convert expired listings into signed business.

Read the action steps and identify which actions you will take. Rewrite items that may not fit. Circle the number of each strategy that you plan to implement in your business and then record the date you complete the item in the space provided. Remember, small changes over time yield big results. Once you complete the items you have selected, move on to the next chapter.

Action Steps:

___ 1. Check off the days and times you will be prospecting. If you're prospecting expireds in person, the best time to reach them is in the morning. To firmly establish prospecting for expired listings as a habit, prospect on the same days each week for the next four weeks. Write down the times you will prospect next to the days on which you plan to prospect this week. Every 100 expired listing contacts will generate 10-20 viable leads.

Sunday _______ Monday ______ Tuesday ______ Wednesday ____

Thursday ______ Friday _______ Saturday _____

___ 2. List three things you will include in your expired listing package:

____

____

____

___ 3. I have prepared a generic version of an Expired Listing package that includes Supply and Demand data, a CMA, a Premium Marketing Plan, and a Seller Services Guarantee.

___ 4. In the future, I will refrain from criticizing the other agent, regardless of what the seller says.

___ 5. During my expired listing appointment, I will show the seller how my 800 Call Capture system captures accurate contact data from our print and web advertising.

___ 6. During my expired listing appointment, I will demonstrate how to make their listing stand out on the web with multiple pictures posted to multiple websites.

___ 7. I will contact the title company or check the public records for owners of expired listings who live outside the area.

___ 8. I plan to contact owners whose listings expired at least 90 days ago or that live outside the area.

Another primary source of right now business is For Sale by Owners (FSBOs). The next chapter explains how to convert them.

Chapter 26
For Sale By Owners: A Prime Source of Right-Now Business

What we obtain too cheap, we esteem too lightly.
Thomas Paine

Skills Check:
Put a checkmark (√) next to what you do now. Leave the remaining items blank. Review the action steps at the end of the chapter to determine the strategies that you will implement in your business.

___ 1. I regularly prospect For Sale By Owner (FSBO) listings.

___ 2. I locate FSBOs by checking the newspaper, taking a different route to the office each day, and by checking online.

___ 3. I work with a company that generates FSBO leads and cross checks them against the "Do Not Call List."

___ 4. I can easily handle the objection, "We're not listing our house with an agent!"

___ 5. I never tell sellers who are marketing their property themselves that I have a buyer for their listing.

___ 6. I avoid giving FSBOs pricing advice or other information that could create an agency relationship.

___ 7. I have a strategy that puts me in front of FSBOs at least twice per week.

___ 8. When I speak to FSBOs, I always tell them, "I will never ask you for the listing on your property." I always keep that promise.

___ 9. I use an 800 Call Capture system to assist me in prospecting FSBOs.

__ 10. I use *Get Your Property Sold Now!* as a prospecting tool to help sellers understand the complexity of marketing their property without the assistance of an agent.

Knead the Dough Secret #50
Maximum exposure to the market results in maximum price.

Bad News for FSBOs is Good News for You

In 2002, I wrote an article for *Inman News* predicting that the Internet would not be good news for people who were selling their home For Sale By Owner (FSBO). Angry readers responded saying that the web would make it easier for FSBOs to sell their property without the assistance of an agent.

According to a study conducted by the California Association of REALTORS®, the number of people who successfully sold their property themselves without the assistance of an agent in 2001 was 24 percent. In 2002, the number declined to 20 percent. In 2003, *The NAR Profile of Home Buyers and Sellers* reported that only 14 percent of home sellers actually sold their homes without the help of a real estate professional. In 2007, NAR reported that the number was 12 percent, a large proportion of which was composed of intra-family transfers.

Today, it is harder than ever for sellers to sell their property without an agent. It's virtually impossible for an individual seller to achieve a web presence. The result is that most FSBOs have to rely on a sign and an ad in the newspaper. Furthermore, even if sellers post their listings on one of the FSBO websites, most visitors there are hunting for bargains. Web statistics from Alexa.com show that traffic to FSBO listing sites has declined substantially over the last few years.

FSBOs can certainly post their listings on powerful sites such as Craigslist or Zillow. Some FSBO companies will post FSBO listings on multiple listing services. Nevertheless, these approaches pale in comparison to the 40+ sites that agents can post their listings on as well as the other strategies that they use to get their listings sold.

"Give to Get" FSBO Prospecting

Agents are often reluctant to prospect FSBOs because they fear rejection, yet FSBOs are one of the best sources for listings. The challenge is that few agents have a strategy to keep in contact with the FSBO long enough for the owner to give up on selling themselves and list with a broker. If and when they do list, most sellers list with the agent they have most recently seen face-to-face.

The first issue is where to locate FSBOs. Tried and true strategies include checking the newspaper, taking a different route to showings and the office, and searching on the web on sites such as Craigslist, Zillow under the "Make me move section," and social networking sites specific to your neighborhood. You can also check the For Sale By Owner websites or subscribe to one of the services that notifies agents of current FSBOs.

Once you have located a FSBO, the next step is to contact them to preview the property. Set up an appointment to preview the property in person. Use the following script:

For Sale by Owner Preview Script:

> **Agent:** *Good morning. This is Bernice Ross from ABC Real Estate. I noticed you were advertising your home for sale in the newspaper. Part of my job is to keep track of sales in my service area. Since I respect the fact that you are selling your home yourself, I promise that I will NEVER ask you for the listing on your home. Would you be offended by showing me your home?*
>
> FSBO: No, I wouldn't be offended.
>
> **Agent:** *Would this afternoon at 3:00 p.m. or tomorrow at 10:00 a.m. be better for you?*
>
> FSBO: Today at 3:00 is OK. What's your name again?
>
> **Agent:** *My name is Bernice Ross with ABC Real Estate. My phone number is 555-2222. I look forward to meeting you at 3:00 p.m. this afternoon.*

If the FSBO seems suspicious:

> FSBO: What do you really want?
>
> **Agent:** *I give you my word—I will not be asking you for the listing on your home.*

When you set the appointment, make sure you do it at a time when the seller will be there to chat with you. Do not get trapped into visiting their open house or viewing the property when they have a buyer viewing the property. Again, the goal is to form a connection with the seller that will allow you to come back repeatedly until they are ready to list their property.

The next issue is what to say when viewing the property. There are two effective ways to approach this issue.

Prospecting FSBOs:

Get Your Property Sold Now!

Get Your Property Sold Now! educates sellers on how to make the best decision possible in terms of selling their property. This simple guide walks the seller through 29 key decisions they will have to make if they decide to sell by owner. It also allows the seller to objectively compare the services different agents offer should they decide to list their property.

Knead the Dough Secret #51
"Get Your Property Sold Now!" not only helps you persuade the FSBO to list with you, it also knocks out competitors who don't provide as much service.

Avoid giving FSBOs pricing information or advice about contracts that could create an agency relationship even in the absence of a signed listing. Doing so can result in serious liability. Here's what to say when you view the property.

FSBO "Get Your Property Sold Now!" Script:

Agent: *Mrs. Seller, I'm Bernice Ross from ABC Real Estate. Thank you for taking the time to allow me to preview your home today. Would you mind pointing out the special features that might not be obvious as we walk through the property?*

As you walk through the property, ask about what you observe and take detailed notes on the property's features. Once you finish viewing the home:

Agent: *Mrs. Seller, thanks again for showing me your home and for helping me keep up on the activity in the market.*

At this point, the seller is waiting for you to say something about listing their home. Most sellers can't believe you would actually look at their property and then not ask them to list it. As you take a step out the door, stop halfway and say,

Agent: *Oh by the way, would you like a copy of a seller's guide called* Get Your Property Sold Now! *It shows you how to get the highest possible price*

for your property in the shortest amount of time. There's also a list of pitfalls to avoid. I could drop off a copy at 3:00 p.m. tomorrow or would Thursday morning at 10:00 a.m. be better?

FSBO: Tomorrow at 3:00 p.m. would work, but why are you being so helpful?

Agent: *As I mentioned to you on the phone, I will never ask you for the listing on your home. What I would like to do, however, is to earn the right to receive your referral business.*

FSBO: All right, I'll see you tomorrow at 3:00 p.m.

Agent: *Thank you. I think you will find the information in* Get Your Property Sold Now! *to be very helpful. I look forward to seeing you tomorrow afternoon at 3:00 p.m.*

Before you give *Get Your Property Sold Now!* to any seller, be sure that you have read it. The seller may ask you about the content or may use it to compare your services to those of a competitor. In case the seller decides that it is time to hire a broker, offering as many of the services outlined in the guide is the surest way to earn the right to list the property.

If the client is a Boomer or a Traditionalist, follow up immediately by dropping the FSBO a handwritten note thanking them for letting you preview their property. Include one of your business cards inside the note. If the FSBO is a Gen X or Gen Y, send a text message. You never know if the day they receive your note or your text message is the day that they will decide to list their property. Remember, if you use this approach, you must never ask for the listing and never tell the seller you have a buyer for the property, even if you do. The last thing they are going to do is to list the property with an agent when there's a chance they can sell it themselves.

Prospecting FSBOs Using 800 Call Capture

Another powerful approach relies on using an 800 Call Capture system. Since call capture systems generate a list of the people who call to hear your pre-recorded message, you can print this out and take it to the FSBO. Imagine how powerful it is to give FSBOs a list of people who are calling about their listing. Ideally, it's best to do this face-to-face since the sellers are most likely to list with the agent that they have seen face-to-face most recently.

Remember to demonstrate the system by having the FSBO call on one of your other listings and listening to your pre-recorded message. When the system calls you back, show the seller your caller I.D. that shows their number. Also, if they ask about the "Do Not Call List," explain that because the caller initiated the contact, you can call back without violating the law.

For Sale by Owner Call Capture Script:

Agent: *Mr. Seller to obtain the highest price possible for your property, you must capture every buyer lead that comes in from your sign and your advertising, wouldn't you agree?*

FSBO: That certainly makes sense.

Agent: *I provide a complimentary service to sellers who are marketing their property called 800 Call Capture. This system captures the correct phone numbers of anyone who calls from your advertising 95 percent of the time, even if their phone number is unlisted. Would you like to see how the system works?*

FSBO: All right

Have the seller call your 800 number and listen to a pre-recorded message about one of your other listings. Turn on your cell phone while the seller listens. When the system calls you back, hand the phone to the seller. Ask if the number looks familiar. In case the sellers have an unlisted number and are curious about how you generated their number, use the following script.

Agent: *Because you called my 800 number and I paid for the call, I am entitled to access your telephone number.*

FSBO: How does this help me?

Agent: *With your permission, I can set up my system to leave a detailed message about your property. I will drop off the numbers twice a week of people who call so you can call them back.*

FSBO: Why are you being so helpful?

Agent: *My goal is to earn the right to receive your referral business or represent you if you should elect to purchase a property where there will be a real estate* *commission paid to the buyer's agent. I promise to never ask you for the listing on your home.*

FSBO: I can still receive my own phone calls on my own number, right?

Agent: *Absolutely. This system only affects people who call on the 800 number to hear a message about your property.*

FSBO: There's no obligation or cost to me, right?

Agent: *That's correct. All I have to do is to provide you with the sign rider and you can begin marketing with it now.*

FSBO: OK, let's get started.

The best approach to listing FSBOs is to give the seller a reason to see you repeatedly by offering some sort of service. In addition to your 800 Call Capture system, you can also drop off useful information on how to stage properties, a moving checklist, a list of sites that accept FSBO listings, or other valuable information. This "give to get" approach is the most effective way to earn the sellers' trust.

Pitfalls to Avoid

An important point to note: do NOT give the FSBO any real estate advice because you could be creating an agency relationship. This includes pricing information, advice on disclosures, title information, etc. If the FSBO relies on your representations and something goes wrong, you can be liable for damages.

In addition, avoid using the old lie that "I have a client for your property." Even if you do, never show the property unless you have a one-party listing in place and have addressed the required agency issues. Besides, if the sellers think that your buyer may purchase their property, they will often wait to list until your buyer decides what to do.

Some agents attempt to convert FSBO listings by placing ads for FSBOs in places like Craigslist. Agents who do this have probably created an agency relationship. This is particularly troublesome when other agents are doing the same thing. When different agents reference different prices for the same FSBO property, someone is misrepresenting the seller. Furthermore, many states prohibit the running of "blind" ads. You must disclose that you are a broker or agent.

Working with For-Sale-by-Owners is a great way to locate right-now business. An important point to remember when prospecting FSBOs is that up to 88 percent of all FSBOs do ultimately list their homes with an agent. Your goal is to continue to provide the seller with service until they list their property, sell it, or take it off the market. Using the scripts and strategies in this chapter will help you dramatically increase your prospecting success rate. Specifically, regularly prospecting FSBOs usually yields a 10 to 20 percent return for a well trained agent.

A second key point is to stay focused on what is best for the seller, not on capturing their business. When you approach the business from this point, there's less resistance to listing with you as compared to agents who are too pushy. FSBOs have always been one of the best sources for right-now business. If you're not prospecting this valuable resource, now is a great time to begin.

Chapter 26
Action Plan

If you're ready to develop your business by prospecting more FSBOs, the steps below will help you meet your goal. As in previous chapters, identify the action steps that you would like to take. Rewrite items that may not fit. Circle the number of each strategy that you plan to implement in your business and then record the date you complete the item in the space provided. If you select more than one item, place the items in priority order and work on implementing one item at a time. Once you complete the items you have selected, move on to the next chapter.

Action Steps:

___ 1. Check off what days you will be prospecting for FSBOs and what times. If you're prospecting FSBOs in person, the best time to see them is generally during the week when they don't have as much traffic. Calling on FSBOs when there is a prospect previewing the property is generally a bad idea. Your goal is to catch the FSBO when they are relaxed and have time to have a conversation with you. To firmly establish the FSBO prospecting habit, plan prospecting for FSBOs on the days you check below for at least four weeks.

Sunday ______ Monday______ Tuesday _____ Wednesday ____

Thursday _____ Friday _______ Saturday _____

For the next 30 days, prospect at these times. Do NOT schedule listing appointments or buyer appointments in these time slots. The only reason to cancel your prospecting time is to handle a transaction problem or a personal emergency great enough that you would have canceled a listening consultation under the same circumstances. Your goal is to create a habit that will sustain you throughout the year, much as attending your weekly office meeting does. If you do miss a prospecting appointment, reschedule it as soon as possible. Every 100 FSBO contacts normally generate 10-20 viable leads.

___ 2. Put a check mark by the strategies you will use to locate FSBOs:

___ a. Drive a different route to the office each day looking for FSBO signs.

___ b. Search the newspapers for FSBOs.

___ c. Check the Internet for FSBO leads (use Google and type in your area and the words "For Sale By Owner" Real Estate).

___ d. I will work with a company that generates FSBO leads and cross checks them against the Do Not Call List.

___ e. Check Craigslist, Zillow, and social networking sites.

___ 3. I have mastered a FSBO telephone prospecting script.

___ 4. In the future, I will always promise FSBOs that I will not ask them for the listing on their property.

___ 5. If FSBOs ask why I am being so helpful, I will tell them that my goal is to earn their referral business.

___ 6. I will use my 800 Call Capture system to assist me in prospecting FSBOs.

___ 7. I mastered at least three questions I can ask FSBOs as I preview their property.

___ 8. In the future, I will prospect FSBOs by using *Get Your Property Sold Now!*

Working with FSBOs and expired listings can be challenging. In the next Recipe for Success, Barb Van Stensel shares what works for her in converting FSBOs and expireds into signed business.

Recipes for Success
Don't Allow Your Property to Get Lost in the Marketplace
Barb Van Stensel
Keller Williams, Chicago

Barb Van Stensel is one of the most amazing agents I have ever met. When we first started working together, she had lost her hearing and had to read people's lips when she worked with them. About two years ago, new hearing aids restored part of her hearing. I remember her excitement when she said she had heard the sounds of the bus, running water, and the birds singing for the first time in many years. Here, Barb shares her Recipe for Success for working with For Sale By Owners (FSBOs) and expired listings.

I regularly work with FSBOs and expired listings. Why? These are the people who need a highly skilled REALTOR® who communicates well and can get their property sold and closed in today's complex market. These sellers are knowledgeable and use the Internet as their information highway to understanding. Yet most REALTORS® fail to give sellers credit for understanding. Furthermore, many agents lack the ability to help sellers correctly position their property in today's marketplace. Others lack a business plan that they can follow to successfully close transactions. Where does this leave the seller? Expired or FSBO. That's when the rash of "obituaries" starts to arrive at the seller's door. You know the letter:

> *Dear Mr. and Mrs. Expired,*
>
> *Your home has expired and is no longer on the MLS. Your REALTOR®, the real estate company, or your pricing may be the cause. I have a sure fired way to get your home sold in the least amount of time with the most amount of money. My plan will guarantee your success.*

Who are you kidding? Not the seller.

I prospect expired listings by mail. I send a letter with short sentences and paragraphs. Here's what I do:

1. First, I explain the reasons for my letter: Your home expired on the MLS. I attach a copy of the listing sheet with this letter.

2. Announce their feelings: In today's market, many sellers are panicking, wondering if their homes will ever sell.

3. Give them the Good News: Today's homes are still selling, but only when:

    - They are priced right and competitively, from the start. Was yours?

    - They are marketing using Internet technology. Was yours?

    - There is a National Listing Service and more than one Multiple Listing Service. Was your listing on all of these?

    - They are properly staged, free of clutter, and decorated to appeal to the masses. Was yours?

FACT: There is too much competition; don't allow your property to get lost in the marketplace.

FACT: Just because it's a Buyer's Market, doesn't mean that you can't sell your home!

4. Ask them if they "Googled" their last agent. If they can't find their agent, how can the buyer find their home? I always include a Google and Yahoo printout of the search results for my name. I challenge the sellers to do the same for any other agents they are interviewing.

5. I also include my website activity and hits graph, the listing activity for my listings on the MLS, and the tracking statistics from Point2Agent.com. I fold each piece separately and place it in a #10 quality envelope that is hand addressed with a first-class postage stamp. The envelope is so thick that the seller will open up your mail. Unlike the other agents, I'm not sending them the obituary on the failure of the sale of their home.

When I first meet with the owners, I qualify them to determine if they are able to sell and to assess their motivation. I do not reminisce about why they did not sell, the feelings that they experienced, or the anger they harbor.

My clients tell me that I'm unusual because I show them "The Facts." My technique is pretty simple. I begin by telling them what's going on in the market, why there is such a huge amount of inventory, why there are 12 short sales in their backyard, how that affects them, as well as the reasons that the median price drops down every month. And we're not talking pennies—we're talking a serious chunk of change!

I'm forging ahead with the goal of becoming the "leading lady in my farm." I know there's stiff competition from other agents. But see, my competition is actually with myself and not with anybody else. I know what I can do and how to do it! I know my competitor's strengths and weaknesses. I have my ammo. I don't put down other agents or companies. Instead, I emphasize my strengths that will help the owners get their property sold and closed.

What do I look for in a client? I want them to be loyal to me. It isn't about satisfying that client, because there is no loyalty in satisfaction. I let my clients know that I am loyal to them!

Oh, and by the way, they aren't hiring my hearing. They are hiring my brains, knowledge, skill, experience, ability to stay in constant communication, and to close their transaction.

Advanced Real Estate Dough™ Recipes

Recipes for Success
A Crisis of Conscience

We need to throw out those rule books, lose the words
"short sale" from our real estate lexicon,
and KEEP these people in their homes!
Frances Flynn Thorsen

Frances Flynn Thorsen, in an article entitled "Short Sales Are Not the Route to Financial Redemption for Homeowners," (RealTown Blog, March 3, 2008) raised an issue that almost no one in the real estate industry has addressed. In our rush to become foreclosure experts and to close more short sales, we have neglected the most important role that we could play in resolving the heartbreaking tragedy of this situation—assisting homeowners in restoring their hope and providing them with a path to staying in their homes. Below, she makes an impassioned plea to put our energy first in helping people stay in their homes rather than helping to boot them out. For additional resources to assist homeowners facing foreclosure or short sales, see her article at:

http://realtown.com/articles/view/let-s-learn-how-to-help-americans-keep-their-homes

I know what it's like to go through foreclosure. I was the victim of a predatory lending scheme, like many other homeowners in this country. When a family loses their home, children are often removed from the school they are attending, friendships are destroyed, and shame results. The family's credit is ruined, which can result in even more serious problems if a family member becomes ill or faces any other type of drain on their finances.

The challenge is that trainers and get-rich-quick types are hawking the opportunities to be had by taking advantage of the foreclosure market. One trainer wanted to enlist 30,000 agents to do short sales in 2008. If each agent conducted 3.3 short sale transactions that would mean 100,000 families would be displaced from their homes including over 150,000 children.

As an industry, we have an obligation to help clean up this mess. REALTORS® are among the most generous people on the planet. We band together to build houses for Habitat, we assist disaster victims, and we give back to our communities on a regular basis.

What we can do now is to get the word out that there is help for troubled homeowners. AcornHousing.gov is a non-profit organization that assists troubled homeowners in staying in their homes. Their success rate is 60 percent.

HopeNow.com, a consortium of lending institutions that are assisting troubled borrowers before they lose their property, reports a 67 percent success rate.

On March 6, 2008, the White House announced a new USA Freedom Corps Financial Literacy Initiative that seeks volunteers to counsel those who are facing issues connected with the subprime crisis. This new resource helps to connect individuals with expertise in financial and housing services with volunteer opportunities designed to assist homeowners avoid foreclosure and remain in their homes.

If the lender is not being cooperative, homeowners have several other options. First, the homeowner needs to bypass the collections department. These people lack the authority to make modifications to loans. Instead, have them call the main number for the lender and ask for the workout department.

With big lenders, it's often hard to get to the right person. Many local banks are stepping in and assisting borrowers in their communities with new financing.

Another option is to work with a consumer advocate attorney. According to Brian Mildenberg, a Philadelphia attorney specializing in predatory lending,

> *Any homeowner who has a loan value that exceeds the sale of a property should discuss the matter and review his paperwork with an attorney who specializes in consumer protection law and foreclosure. Competent attorneys routinely find errors and discrepancies in loan documents and disclosures and they negotiate lower interest rates, reduced balances, and favorable terms for their clients. Sometimes loan brokers have made inconsistent loan representations regarding the benefits of the loan. Some states and federal consumer protection laws require the lender to pay attorney fees when they lose a case.*

In other words, don't rely on a regular real estate attorney for this job. Often there are errors in the loan documents that will give the borrower much-needed leverage in negotiating a workout. You can locate a consumer advocate attorney at http://NACA.net. They offer multiple initiatives to assist consumers who believe that they are victims of predatory lending practices.

Here's the bottom line. We need to stop asking whether or not homeowners QUALIFY for a workout or a refinance! Attorneys who specialize in consumer protection law say, "If a homeowner has a loan amount that EXCEEDS the value of a home, (s)he may have a cause of action in court!" That says to me that ANY HOMEOWNER who is upside down is best served by speaking with a consumer protection specialist who can review loan paperwork and supporting documents and hear the consumer's recitation of events. The first consultation is often free. Homeowners ALWAYS have options!

Chapter 27
Foreclosures, Short Sales, and REOs: No Easy Recipe

Borrow money from a pessimist—they don't expect it back.
Source Unknown

Skills Check:
Put a checkmark (√) next to what you do now. Leave the remaining items blank. Review the action steps at the end of the chapter to determine the strategies that you will implement in your business.

___ 1. Before taking any listing, I always check the loan balances on the property, not only by asking the seller about them, but also by checking with the title company or other independent source.

___ 2. I know how to show lenders who refuse a short sale or workout with my clients the benefits of accepting an offer now rather than waiting to complete the foreclosure process.

___ 3. I always have the sellers review their loan documents to see if they have a prepayment penalty prior to listing their property.

___ 4. When clients have trouble working out a short sale, prepayment penalty, or other difficulty with the lender, I refer them to a consumer attorney who can help them with the process.

___ 5. I advise foreclosure and short sale clients to contact the lender's workout department or a loss mitigation company.

___ 6. I always check the public records to determine if there are any state, local, or IRS tax liens.

___ 7. I advise sellers in short sale situations to consider taking out a personal loan from their lender to cover at least part of the cost of the short sale in exchange for the lender agreeing not to provide a negative rating on their mortgage.

___ 8. I advise sellers to talk with their tax professional or attorney regarding whether they should stop making payments in a short sale situation.

___ 9. I always advise sellers to check with their tax professional to determine the consequences of entering into a short sale agreement or giving a deed in lieu of foreclosure.

___10. I know how to persuade banks who own REOs (real estate taken by the bank in foreclosure) to accept realistic offers from qualified buyers.

> **Knead the Dough Secret #52**
> Helping homeowners stay in their homes is more important than earning a commission.

Not for the Faint of Heart

Without a doubt, assisting clients who are facing foreclosure, a short sale, or bankruptcy is one of the most gut wrenching and frustrating experiences that any agent can face. Whether you represent the buyers or the sellers, once a property becomes "distressed," the odds of getting it successfully closed go down dramatically.

Distressed properties include properties where there has been a delinquency and the lender has begun the foreclosure process. The term "REO" refers to "real estate owned," i.e., property that has gone through the foreclosure process and is now owned by the bank.

The term "short sale" refers to a situation where the seller lacks sufficient equity to close a transaction unless the lender takes a reduction in their loan payoff. Short sale properties may or may not be in some stage of foreclosure. When this occurs, the seller must contribute additional funds or ask the lender to reduce their loan amount in order to close the sale. Short sales normally occur in flat or declining markets. It's also common when large numbers of buyers have purchased with no money down. Part of the subprime mess resulted from the fact that so many buyers purchased property with nothing down or obtained a refinance that left them with no equity when the market shifted.

For example, on a $300,000 sale where the seller has no equity, the sellers would need to come up with approximately $24,000 in closing costs if they paid a six percent commission. If owners can't keep up their payments, there is a high probability that they will be unable to come up with enough money to pay these costs. Consequently, one of the following scenarios normally results:

1. To save money, the owner may try to sell the property without representation. In markets where there is a glut of inventory, chances are slight that the seller will be successful.

2. The owner allows the property to go into foreclosure. Depending on the state, the seller may pick up six to nine months of "free" rent by not paying their existing mortgage. Once the lender completes the foreclosure proceedings, they still may have to evict the delinquent seller from the property. This may take an additional 30 to 60 days. In the meantime, the seller's credit is ruined for the next 7 to 10 years.

3. The owners/agents approach the lender about lowering the balance due on the loan so that the property can be sold at current prices.

4. The seller gives the keys back to the lender, sometimes known as a "deed in lieu" of foreclosure.

5. The seller declares bankruptcy and attempts to delay foreclosure while the bankruptcy proceeds.

What many sellers don't realize is that there are additional options. Among these are:

1. Staying in the property and keeping up the payments. In most areas, the normal real estate cycle is ten years. Thus, even if the market is doing poorly, it should be in an upswing in 24 to 48 months. If feasible, sometimes it's best to stay put and preserve your credit.

2. Go to the lender and ask for reduction in the interest rate or a change in the payment program.

3. Rent the home and move to a less expensive property until the market improves.

4. Seek assistance from a consumer attorney, not a real estate attorney. There are often errors in the loan documents that give the borrower considerable leverage with the lender.

5. Hire a loss mitigation firm to negotiate a workout or short sale.

Persuading lenders that they should reduce their loan balance to close the transaction, pay the closing costs, and pay a full commission is no simple task. Instead, the most common response in this scenario is, "We'll just foreclose on the property." The following script illustrates how to motivate reluctant lenders into being more flexible.

Short Sale Offer Script:

> *If you foreclose on the property, you will achieve the highest possible price in the shortest amount of time by listing with a top agent. This means that you will pay the commission anyway. Given that sales/prices are declining and market time is increasing, it may take a number of months to sell the property after foreclosure. This means that you will have the commission costs, months of holding costs, and a possible loss in value because of the substantial amount of competing inventory. Selling now may actually net you more money than waiting. Would you prefer to lock in a sale today or would you prefer to wait and net less for the property?*

Any time you speak with a lender, it's critical that you have hard statistical data to show them. Your data should include how much inventory is on the market, how much the inventory has increased or decreased in the last six months, as well as whether prices are increasing, decreasing, or staying flat.

A Simple Guide to Working with Distressed Properties

Use the following tips when working with distressed properties.

1. **Before taking any listing, check the existing loan balances**
   When you take a listing, failure to check for all liens on a property is one of the most dangerous mistakes you can make. Never rely on what the seller says that they owe. They may show you the balance on their first and forget to mention that they have delinquent property taxes as well as a home equity line of credit. Consequently, it's critical to check all liens on the subject property. Depending upon the laws in your area, you may be able to obtain this information from the title company. You can also pay a fee to companies such as Zabasearch.com or Intellius.com to do a complete background check that includes bankruptcies, liens, and other information you may need to complete the sale. This is well worth the money because people who are in trouble sometimes do not pay their income or property taxes.

2. **Check the seller's loan documents for prepayment penalties**
   One of the most difficult situations in closing any sale occurs when the seller has a pre-payment penalty in their loan documents. Most borrowers are unaware of these. The typical prepayment penalty is six months of interest and sometimes even more. Lenders are more likely to enforce these when interest rates are going down. Another way a short sale may result is when the lender demands that the prepayment be included as part of their payoff. This is particularly troublesome

when no one is aware of the prepayment penalty until the transaction is ready to close. The usual outcome is that the agent attempts to piece together additional funds from the sellers and buyers.

This can place the brokers in an awkward position, especially if the lender demands that the brokers take a cut in their commission. To overcome this situation, show the lender the cost of completing the foreclosure, fixing the property up, as well as their holding costs. If prices in your area are declining, be sure to include the cost of the decline in your holding costs calculation. For example, on a $300,000 property where the market is declining at four percent per year, the additional loss would be $12,000 on an annualized basis. Thus, if it takes the lender five months to foreclose, a month to get the property ready for sale, and another four months to sell and close, the lender will make the equivalent of 10 months of payments plus losing $10,000 in depreciation. Using these numbers is the best way to get the lender to be flexible.

If the lender is uncooperative, a different approach is to hire a consumer attorney to review the loan documents. There may be an error that will give you considerable negotiation power with the lender. Do not rely on a real estate attorney. This is a specialized area of consumer law. Involving an attorney may garner the attention you need to close the transaction.

3. **Who is the decision maker?**

Most lenders sell the loans they originate on the secondary market. In fact, it's common for a single mortgage to be resold several times. When you have a short sale, one of the greatest challenges is locating the person who has the power to approve the short sale. If you are aware that your sellers are going to lack sufficient funds to close their transaction, don't put the property on the market until you have confirmed that the lender will work with you to close the short sale. If you cannot obtain this confirmation, don't waste your time or money marketing a property that you will not be able to close.

One of the best ways to help your sellers navigate through this process is to make sure that they're speaking to the right people at their lender. Owners who are facing a short sale or foreclosure typically contact the customer service department or the department that handles delinquencies. These people generally lack the authority to negotiate a workout for the clients. Consequently, a better approach is to contact the lender's main telephone number and ask for the workout department. You are much more likely to achieve a successful outcome.

Another alternative is to contact a loss mitigation company. These people already have the contacts the owner will need to resolve the problem. Typically, there is little, if any cost to the owner. The loss mitigation company receives part of the commission. While it may be tempting to take on this process on your own, the time and effort it will take would be better spent developing other sources of business.

4. **Tax liens are the kiss of death**

   Sellers sometimes have delinquent property taxes or IRS tax liens that do not show up on the title report. In general, you can usually resolve most state and local tax issues. On the other hand, the one area where there is almost no flexibility is the IRS. Even if you persuade a lender to take a reduction in their loan, the IRS literally takes months to release a tax lien. If the seller has an IRS tax lien, the probability is high that you will be unable to close the sale. Consequently, it's extremely important that you check for tax liens prior to listing a property and spending your hard-earned money on marketing it.

5. **Numbers are your friend**

   When the lender comes back at you with their appraiser's list of comparable sales, the burden is on you to show whether those sales are accurate. It's also important to show the lender whether the market is increasing or decreasing. An excellent way to do this is with a square footage CMA (comparable market analysis). Based upon the prices for the last six months, show the lender the average price per square foot for the specific subdivision in which the subject property is located. Next, go back to the preceding six months and find the average price per square foot. Calculate the difference to show the lender whether the prices are going up, staying flat, or declining. In the case where there is a decline, the lender will probably get even less for the property by waiting as opposed to doing a short sale with your buyer.

6. **Have the sellers review the tax consequences prior to entering into a short sale agreement or giving a deed in lieu of foreclosure**

   Be adamant that your client seek the advice of their CPA or tax attorney before proceeding with a short sale transaction or allowing their property to go through foreclosure. In most cases, the amount the lender reduces the sellers' payoff is considered to be forgiveness of debt. This amount can be taxable. If the seller has little or no income, there may not be any additional tax liability. Only a tax professional can make this determination. On the other hand, failure to report the forgiveness of debt as income may result in charges of fraud and/or tax evasion. If the IRS discovers this, they can file an IRS tax lien on any of the sellers' assets. The IRS has the power to deduct money from the sellers' bank accounts without the sellers' consent. Furthermore, IRS tax liens are difficult to expunge from the sellers' credit report and can take months to resolve. Again, do not enter into a transaction until the sellers have examined all the legal and financial ramifications of taking a reduction in their loan balance.

7. **Should the seller stop making payments?**
It seems counter-intuitive that many lenders will turn down your request for a short sale if the seller is currently making the payments. The only time some lenders will consider a short sale is if the seller is delinquent. This presents a particularly difficult dilemma. Sellers who keep their payments current are protecting their credit rating. On the other hand, if they cannot do a short sale, they cannot move. Avoid advising them what to do because ultimately it's their decision. An excellent way to address this challenge is to work with a loss mitigation company. Often they will be able to negotiate a short sale even if the seller is not delinquent. If the seller does not want to work with a loss mitigation company, refer them to a tax attorney or CPA who can advise them of their options as well as what they can do to minimize the negative impact on their credit.

8. **Negotiate a personal loan to close the gap**
If the lender refuses to negotiate a short sale, one option that can protect the seller's credit as well as helping you to close the transaction is to ask the lender to make the seller a personal loan to cover the amount of the short sale. Most lenders are willing to make the seller a personal loan to avoid declaring a loss when the transaction closes. While the sellers may resist this idea at first, it can actually result in a considerable savings when they apply for future loans or credit cards. If the seller has a delinquency on their home loan, they will pay higher interest rate on future purchases. For example, assume that a borrower with excellent credit pays six percent for their fixed rate loan. The borrower with a foreclosure or delinquent payments may be required to pay 10 percent. On a $200,000 loan, the difference in interest payments would be $8,000 in the first year, or $24,000 in three years. Clearly, in most cases, it's better to pay off the difference rather than having a default.

9. **Distressed properties—good deal or money pit?**
Many buyers don't understand the complexity of purchasing a property that is in foreclosure. Buying the property at the foreclosure auction usually means that you are buying the property without any disclosures, inspections, or loan contingencies. If you are representing clients on the purchase of a distressed property, have them do their due diligence prior to making a bid on the property. Obtain copies of the title report, check for tax liens, and check the seller's

background to see if they have IRS tax liens that may prevent them from delivering clear title. Obtain thorough inspections and make sure that the lender will be able to make a loan on the property.

Some people think that foreclosed property is a good buy. In most cases, if it were such a good buy, it would have sold prior to the foreclosure sale. While this is not always the case, many times the owners trash the property and there's nothing the lender can do until the foreclosure is complete. Once the lender does obtain title, many lenders don't maintain the property. In fact, the problem is so severe that some cities are choosing to bulldoze empty houses rather than having these neighborhoods transformed into havens for crack houses and other criminal activity.

Distressed properties can also be a money pit for the agent. Agents who list these properties often have to dig into their own pockets to maintain them. Unfortunately, many times these expenses are not reimbursed. Furthermore, you can work for months on closing a distressed property and then have the transaction fall apart at the last minute.

10. Agent BEWARE!

Lenders are now actively trying to make the real estate industry take responsibility for any post-sale liability that results from a foreclosure or short sale. Many agents agree to handle property management services for the lender, often out of their own pocket. This presents two very serious problems. First, since the agent was responsible for the property management, the lender can claim they were not responsible for the condition of the property. This shifts the liability to the agents and their brokers. Furthermore, many agents do not have coverage on their errors and omissions insurance for property management activities. If you are representing distressed properties, have your attorney review all documentation very thoroughly. Furthermore, you must absolutely insist that buyers have the property inspected and you must make a detailed disclosure of the property condition as required by your state. In addition, check your errors and omissions insurance. If your policy does not cover this scenario, do not take the listing!

Short sales are only for those agents who have excellent negotiation skills and who can skillfully illustrate to the lender the costs of waiting to sell. Mastering these few simple steps can help to avoid a great deal of grief. Furthermore, it will prevent you from wasting your hard-earned marketing dollars on a listing that cannot close.

Chapter 27
Action Plan

It takes patience and skill to close short sales. You must also track how many months of inventory are on the market. If your local area drops below six months, short sales will begin to disappear as the inventory shrinks. As in previous chapters, identify the steps that you would like to take. Remember, implement only one or two changes at a time to avoid being overwhelmed.

Action Steps:

___ 1. Before taking any listing, I will always check the loan balances on the property, not only by asking the seller about them, but also by checking with the title company or other independent source.

___ 2. I can easily explain to lenders who refuse a short sale or workout for my clients the benefits of accepting an offer now rather than waiting to complete the foreclosure process.

___ 3. In the future, I will always have the sellers review their loan documents to see if they have a prepayment penalty prior to listing their property.

___ 4. When clients have trouble working out a short sale, prepayment penalty, or other difficulty with the lender, I will refer them to a consumer attorney who can help them with the process.

___ 5. I will explain to my short sales seller the importance of contacting their lender's workout department or using a loss mitigation company.

___ 6. I will always check the public record to determine if there are any state, local, or IRS tax liens.

___ 7. In the future, I will advise sellers to check with their tax professional to determine the consequences of entering into a short sale agreement.

___ 8. I advise my sellers to talk with their tax professional or attorney about whether they should stop making payments in a short sale situation.

___ 9. In order to protect the seller's credit in a short sale, I will advise them to take a personal loan to mitigate part of the lender's loss.

The next Recipe for Success is the ultimate "escrow from hell."

Recipes for Success
"The Ultimate Escrow from Hell"

Bernice Ross
RealEstateCoach.com

Normally I reserve "Recipes for Success" for interviews with other agents and industry experts. After 30 years in the business, I have yet to find another agent who has had a transaction as bizarre as the one described below. This transaction is Murphy's Law epitomized—if it could go wrong, it did!

In 1993, a good friend was facing foreclosure on a property in Malibu. His tenant had not paid the rent for nine months. I took the listing knowing that we were facing a short sale as well as foreclosure on both the first and second mortgages.

There were numerous other problems. The land in the area was so unstable that the city had condemned the property. Nevertheless, every house in the area was still occupied. Making matters worse, the water and gas lines were above ground in case there were more landslides.

One day a buyer who was interested in the property called to write an offer. She was absolutely livid at her buyer's agent and demanded that I represent her on the sale. After a considerable amount of negotiation, our company worked out a 33 percent referral fee to her original agent.

The buyer's offer required a short sale. The seller was so desperate that any offer was fine with him. The buyer had to sell her house in a neighboring area before she could close on the Malibu house. I took the listing on the buyer's house and wrote the offer as a contingent sale. Her house sold quickly. Nevertheless, her sale was contingent upon closing the Malibu property.

The seller filed an eviction proceeding and finally persuaded the tenant to move out. The day the tenant was supposed to move, the Malibu fire erupted. Believing that the property would burn in the fire, the tenant ripped out as many fixtures as possible. That same day, the first mortgage holder turned down the short sale request.

I sat with my seller and watched the fire whip through Malibu. He had a beautiful red coral tree in his backyard. The news crew reported that the fire was on his street. We watched with horror as a red coral tree in what appeared to be his backyard burned along with the house in front of it.

Four days later, we were able to access the area. We drove past over a hundred burned houses. Imagine the relief when we turned on to the seller's street and discovered that his house was one of only six on the street that had survived the fire.

I contacted the buyer and outlined the options, ending the conversation by saying, "It's your choice, what would you like to do?" Her answer was that she still wanted the house, despite the fire and the damage caused by the tenant. She correctly believed that the insurance company would repair the damage or issue a check to handle the repairs. Since she planned to remodel, this worked well with her plans.

The next issue was the lender's unwillingness to accept the short sale because "the comparable sales data said that the property was worth more." I asked for a supervisor who also argued with me about the data. I drove out to Malibu and took pictures of all the comparable sales. Every single comparable sale had burned down. The lender still refused the short sale. At that point, the second lien holder declared bankruptcy. The bankruptcy proceeding prevented the first mortgage holder from proceeding with their foreclosure. The first trust deed holder decided to work with the short sale.

In the meantime, the City of Los Angeles instituted a judicial foreclosure for non-payment of property taxes. The second trust deed holder's bankruptcy did not delay the City's foreclosure action. In addition to a state income tax lien of $20,000, there was a $5,600 judgment from a different lender for non-payment on a different property. There was also another $48,000 special assessment to pay for the repairs to the utility and sewer lines serving the area.

The action proceeded. A huge rainstorm caused additional movement throughout the area. The physical inspection revealed a crack running through the entire length of slab. The city inspector indicated that there would probably be another special assessment of $10,000 to pay for the additional movement in the area. Since our company had three sides on this transaction, we agreed to pay the special assessment if the transaction closed.

Once again, I outlined the buyer's options and gave her the choice to cancel. She still wanted the property; however, she asked the lender to make a partial payment on the back property taxes. Our reasoning was that if she cancelled the transaction, the first trust deed holder would have to pay the taxes anyway.

The City was continuing with their foreclosure proceeding. The sale was set for March. On January 17, the Northridge earthquake struck. There were new cracks in the foundation.

The second lien holder requested an under-the-table payoff to exempt the property from bankruptcy. We refused and he released the seller anyway.

As we approached the closing date, the buyers were approved, but with 10 conditions. The buyer finally lost her temper and threatened to sue everyone if both houses didn't close.

To make matters even worse, Federal Express lost the loan documents. The title company agreed to fund off a fax copy. The day before close, another $3,700 in "escaped" taxes appeared on the title report. None of the attorneys and no one at the title company had ever heard of "escaped taxes" before.

We did ultimately close and I did get most of my commission. The buyer moved in and made the property into a showplace. She later sold it for $700,000 more than she paid.

The most important lesson I learned from this whole fiasco was this: When I asked my client why she continued to stay in the transaction with one disaster after another, this is what she said.

> *Each time that something went wrong, you outlined what my options were and then you let me make my own decision. You always emphasized that it was my choice and that I was in control. If you had pressured me in any way whatsoever, I would have cancelled in a heartbeat. It was clear to me how hard you were working on my behalf and that you only had my best interests at heart.*

Chapter 28
Hot New Recipes:
A Look at the Future

All we have to do is to stay six months ahead of
the competition and we will dominate the market.
Jon Douglas

Skills Check:
Put a checkmark (√) next to what you do now. Leave the remaining items blank. Review the action steps at the end of the chapter to determine the strategies that you will implement in your business.

___ 1. I monitor innovations in the real estate business in order to stay ahead of my competitors.

___ 2. During the last year, I have added at least one new component to my business that differentiates me from my competitors.

___ 3. I feel comfortable experimenting with innovation. If one approach doesn't work, I can always try something else.

Words of Wisdom

Back in the early 1990s, I spent nearly a year creating a comprehensive new agent training program for the Jon Douglas Company. Much to my dismay, my entire program ended up at a competitor in a few short months. I was devastated. Jon Douglas's advice has guided my business since then. "All we have to do is to stay six months ahead of the competition and we will dominate the market." He was right. We consistently had 50 to 70 percent market share in Bel Air, Beverly Hills, Brentwood, Pacific Palisades, and Santa Monica because of the company's focus on innovation.

Although the pace of change can be overwhelming, to dominate your market you must be proactive about innovating. Fortunately, today's innovations continue to simplify how we conduct business. Try two or three new strategies each year. If they work, integrate them into your business. If not, try something else. The rest of this chapter provides a glimpse of real estate in the future as well as potential opportunities. Remember, you only have to be six months ahead of the competition to dominate your market.

(Due to the rapid changes in technology, some of the companies discussed below may no longer be in business, will have changed their names, or have merged with other companies. The goal here is not to promote a specific site or strategy, but merely to illustrate the direction of current innovations.)

Demographic Trends that Will Influence Home Ownership

Based on the current birth and immigration rates in the United States, the buyers and sellers of the future will be more evenly distributed between age groups and gender. America will continue to grow older as well. The U.S. Census Bureau projects that by 2050, 20 percent of the population will be over the age of 65.

In a report released on August 13, 2008, the U.S. Census Bureau also projected that minorities will be the majority by 2042. By 2050, minorities will represent 54 percent of the total population of 439 million. The number of Hispanics will nearly triple, from 46.7 million in 2008 to approximately 133 million in 2050 (15.6 to 30.2 percent). The black population will rise from 41.1 million to 65.7 million (14 to 15 percent) and the Asian population will increase from 15.5 million to 40.6 million (5.1 to 9.2 percent). In contrast, the non-Hispanic white population will stay relatively stable, growing from 200 million today to 203.3 million by 2050. Immigration will also continue to increase.

Hot New Recipe:

Translate your listings (and the main pages of your website) into multiple languages to meet the diversity needs of tomorrow's clients. If you speak another language, advertise in that language. If your company has an international presence, attend your company's conferences and meet as many international agents as possible. Do the same thing when you attend national, state, or other major conventions. Use social networking to keep in contact.

Consolidation

As new applications arrive at a dizzying pace, vendors are consolidating services in order to create one-stop shopping for both consumers and real estate professionals. Until recently, you had to hire different companies to create your website, automate your newsletter, provide video, create brochures, and track transactions. "Mashups" (different functions combined on one site, such as an on-line price evaluation tool, a geo-specific mapping application, and rich neighborhood information) help agents create the interactivity and the one-stop shopping that today's consumers crave. For example, current mashups include single sites that offer blogging platforms, agent-to-agent social networking, tools for creating both web and print ads, polling tools, and online real estate games that allow web visitors to help set prices on active listings.

Hot New Recipe:
Mashup your website by using any of the following:

1. EveryBlock.com displays business reviews, permits, crimes, liquor licenses, real estate listings from Trulia and Redfin, restaurant inspections, zoning agenda items, as well as maps pinpointing relevant locations for the cities that they serve.

2. Gasbuddy.com helps your visitors locate cheap gas with real time information from consumers.

3. Eventful.com claims to be the "world's leading events website" and has a comprehensive list of events occurring near your local address.

4. RottenNeighbor.com reports on noise, odor, and other neighborhood nuisances. People can "rat out" bad neighbors and nasty landlords, as well as reporting those who are terrific.

5. Introin.com provides information about the availability of rentals as well as an evaluation of the buildings and their landlords.

6. Walkscore.com provides a "walkability" score from 1-100 based upon the convenience of various businesses to the residents, income mix, parks and public space, nearby schools, bike paths, accessibility for the disabled, and convenience of mass transit.

For those who don't want to blog, using mashups can be a winning solution. Many of these applications are free and can keep web visitors returning day after day. Granted, your web visitors could find this information on their own, but why bother when you have everything so conveniently located in one place? Best of all, you will have this marvelous website packed with fresh local content and you didn't have to research or create it—someone else did it for you!

The Paperless Revolution

Whether it's marketing, uploading information to the Multiple Listing Service (MLS), managing your contact database, or using a transaction tracking platform to keep everyone in the transaction informed, you can do it all on a tablet PC. Thousands of agents have already discovered the power of going paperless. Tablet PCs simplify communication and reduce the work required to close transactions. Because tablet PCs create a digital paper trail, they are also a powerful risk management tool. Together with digital signatures and digital storage, tablet PCs are making paper obsolete. Not only will your business be more "green," all those files and pieces of paper on your desk will be a distant memory.

Hot New Recipe:
Get the competitive edge by going paperless with a tablet PC. When you carry your tablet with you on an appointment, you send a nonverbal message that you are tech savvy. Clients sign offers, listing agreements, and all other documents directly on your tablet. During listing appointments, show clients the video virtual tours of your other listings. Take notes on your tablet during inspections and your handwritten notes are automatically converted into a Word document. This feature alone can result in a time savings of up to 60 percent.

Most of the forms and documents you will need to go digital are already available online. To simplify the transition, look for a scanner that creates PDF files of your documents. Some of the latest models can convert words contained within images into text. Scan your paper files into the scanner and you now have a digital record.

MLS 5.0

There's no question that real estate services will continue to consolidate. Statewide Multiple Listing Services are already in the works and a National Multiple Listing Service may not be far behind. Saul Klein, in a white paper dated August 7, 2008, shared his vision of what the next generation of the MLS will be. Key points include:

1. Real estate professionals must be at the "center of the conversation" rather than the center of the transaction. MLS 5.0 will be open, collaborative, self-organizing, and self-policed.

2. MLS 5.0 will include public areas that will include online communities, social networking, and a "property wiki" for both REALTORS® and consumers. In order to maintain confidentiality about access to properties and other issues, there will be private aspects of the site as well.

3. MLS 5.0 will address generational differences and expectations while also being multi-lingual.

4. There will be an agent rating system.

5. MLS 5.0 will be parcel based, rather than listing based. This means that buyers can make offers on both listed and unlisted properties.

6. There will be a "single point of entry" for listing data. Brokers and agents will specify where they want their listings distributed—newspapers, radio, television, or other web portals.

Hot New Recipe:
Klein's vision of MLS 5.0 reinforces the importance of the collaborative model discussed in this book. Become the "center of the conversation" by becoming the expert in your area. Consider setting up your own social network on sites like Ning.com. Another strategy is to actively engage in the conversation on other social networks with those who live in your area. Again, it's not about you. It's about being meeting the needs of others.

Welcome to My Cloud

We are already beginning to see the first wave of cloud computing. Cloud computing will revolutionize how you experience the web in two important ways. First, today's Internet is a complicated web of wires and routing centers. We are currently in the process of shifting to fiber optics and more sophisticated linking centers known as the "grid." Instead of taking three hours to download a feature length movie, you will be able to complete the download in seconds.

As the grid spreads, you will be able to transmit three dimensional, holographic images. Imagine contacting your buyers and taking them on a three dimensional tour of all of your listings from the holographic imaging center in your home or office. Consumers will walk through the neighborhood in a three dimensional space. The gas-guzzling days of chauffeuring people around for hours will be a distant memory.

Cloud computing will also change the way you use the web. You will no longer need a box computer tethered to a cable or dial-up connection. Software and maintenance updates will disappear. Instead, you will use a device similar to the iPhone to access the Internet. "The cloud" will store all of your data using universal wireless. You will be able to connect any time and anywhere.

Hot New Recipe:
As bandwidth increases, look for explosive growth in applications that rely on cloud computing technology. If you're not accustomed to working with the "cloud," (i.e., working from your mobile or tablet PC), take steps now to free yourself from your box computer. Experiment with the new technologies that intrigue you. Most importantly, have fun playing. If you are technologically challenged, have any of the Gen Y's you know show you how to use these exciting new tools.

The Next Generation of Search

As cloud computing spreads, online search will continue to improve. In mid-2008, two new search engines, Cuil and SearchMe.com, launched with new platforms for conducting web search. While the Cuil technology was poorly received by the high tech world, SearchMe may be the tool of choice in the future. SearchMe speeds up your search by allowing you to preview sites prior to clicking through. SearchMe also includes a brief description of the site's content. Rather than having to guess whether a site is a good fit, SearchMe gives you instantaneous feedback.

Look for vertical search engines such as Trulia, Oodle, and Zillow to continue to innovate for the real estate space. For example, Zillow has implemented an online game that allows users to select their favorite kitchen from a number of photos. They can then compare their selection with the results from all the other users who made selections.

Hot New Recipe:

SearchMe eliminates the pay-per-click ads that appear on other search engines as well as annoying pop-ups. The result is that you save tremendous amounts of time since you no longer have to scroll back and forth between the search engine and the pages you are searching. Furthermore, you can upload your photos and videos as well. Best of all, if SearchMe doesn't catalogue your site, you can submit it for inclusion.

To take advantage of vertical search, consider setting up a profile on Zillow and Trulia. Visit these sites once or twice per week and answer questions. The more questions you answer, the more you enhance your online credibility.

You may also want to consider using CPM advertising (cost per 1,000 impressions) as an alternative to print. For example, Zillow offers a CPM tool that allows you to display your ad in a specific zip code. Zillow charges based upon how often your ad appears rather than the number of users who click through to your site. Instead of a three-line print that can cost $50.00 or more, you can obtain 5,000 impressions specific to your zip code by working with Zillow's tool.

Not Just Another Digital Alarm Clock

Chumby.com is another outstanding example of consolidation. A "Chumby" can function as a dashboard for your computer or you can purchase a "Chumby clock." The clock is a little larger than a coffee cup and connects to your wireless network. Once you download the applications you want, you can personalize your selections. Wake up to your favorite music, podcasts, or television shows. Chumby provides you with the weather forecast, a live video feed of traffic in many areas, sports scores in real time, up-to-the minute news reports, as well as favorite radio and television shows. It also allows you to view your pictures, manage your MySpace account, track auctions on eBay, search classified sites such as Craigslist, play games, and send e-cards.

Hot New Recipe:
If you're still tethered to your desk for computing functions, a Chumby can help you break away for a minimal cost. Use your Chumby to experience web-based functions when and how you want them. Chumby can play an important role in making your environment as supportive as possible. It would also make a great closing gift for a special client.

Have Social Graph Will Travel

A "social graph" is your online sphere of influence. It includes your "friends" and other web connections. As social networking continues to evolve, cloud computing strategies will allow you to take your social graph wherever you go. One aspect of this trend is known as "presence services." This technology tells you when your friends are online as well as whether their mobile device can receive a picture message or a video call. Today's "passive" address books will soon give way to "active" address books that tell you when people are available to share a blog post, begin an IM (instant messaging) session, or receive a text message.

Hot New Recipe:
If you plan to be in business five years from now, becoming part of the online real estate conversation is critical. Regardless of where you choose to participate, take advantage of Yoono.com that aggregates various social media sites in a single place. Yoono allows you to easily manage all of your passwords, RSS feeds, "tweets," and other digital communications.

Social Media Weds Word of Mouth Marketing

Referrals always result from word of mouth marketing. Today, people are increasingly turning to the web to investigate agents and brokerages before they hire them. Sites such as Yelp.com allow users to sound off about what makes them unhappy. Other real estate based sites encourage consumers to rate their agent and their listing or purchase experience.

In addition to these sites, consumers will continue to check the web for your online reputation. They will look for recommendations on sites such as LinkedIn as well as visiting Facebook and MySpace to determine what you may have posted in the past.

Hot New Recipe:
If possible, obtain a video endorsement from each of your clients. Make it easy for consumers to find this by posting both your written and video testimonials on a single page of your website or blog. Link your testimonial page to other social networking sites as well as to your agent profile on Zillow and Trulia.

"Crackberries" and "iPodification"

Phil Knight, Chairman and Founder of Nike, uses the term "iPodification" to refer to how the iPhone and other smart phone devices are changing virtually every aspect of our lives. Using Bluetooth technology, Nike shoes will be able to track how far you have run, calories expended, and much more. Some consumers take iPodification so seriously that it even influences the type of car they will buy. In fact, there is a whole new type of addiction to "crackberries" (a new word that combines BlackBerry with "crack" cocaine). This trend will intensify as smart phone applications continue to proliferate.

In the future, smart phones will be your organizer, television, theater, TV remote, laptop, house key, credit card, debit card, money, and passport. They will track your taxes and medical records and keep them secure using your unique genetic identity. You will use your phone to locate empty parking spaces, check the weather, and to read books. Mapping programs will show you whether someone that you would like to see is nearby or if the new restaurant down the street is any good. In fact, in the Netherlands, you can already purchase a house using your cell phone.

Your phone will be able to do even more. Nokia is developing a new phone called the "Morph." Based upon nanotechnology, Morph may be able to detect if your food is spoiled, the presence of allergens, as well as the flu virus and other airborne diseases. It will be solar powered and have a "hydrophobic" surface that allows it to repel spills including water. "Morph" will be able to change forms from a phone to a bracelet or keyboard. One concept includes the ability to wrap Morph around your wrist like a watch and customize the "skin" to match whatever you are wearing that day.

Hot New Recipe:

The 3G version of the iPhone provides just a fraction of what will be available in the future. While the iPhone doesn't work with most MLS lock boxes, BlackBerry and Palm devices do. If you don't already own a smart phone, it's time to join the mobile revolution. The latest smart phones allow you to do virtually everything that you can do with your regular computer plus also serving as a GPS, restaurant guide, camera, and much more.

More Transparency, Less Privacy

While the term "transparency" has multiple meanings, in terms of the real estate industry, it often implies openness, communication, and accountability. The current trend is for all aspects of the real estate transaction to move online. Sales prices, identities of buyers and sellers, as well as your personal data will become increasingly easy to access.

Amazon currently uses "predictive marketing" to make book recommendations based upon your previous search and purchase patterns. Point2 also has a predictive marketing tool that monitors user viewing habits and then displays the houses that best fit those patterns. While these applications are designed to create a better customer experience, others are not as benign.

An important new trend is "deep packet inspection" (DPI). DPI goes beyond transparency and may be a major invasion of your privacy. DPI can protect your computer from viruses, but it can also send your data to law enforcement for analysis. It provides your ISP (Internet Service Provider) with the ability to block, shape, monitor, and prioritize the data you send and receive. In other words, it is capable of assembling a record of your email, web browsing habits, Voice-Over-Internet Protocol (VoIP), and passwords. It's safe to assume that anything you text, email, or post on a website is public. If you don't feel comfortable making a statement in front of an attorney during a deposition, then don't say it, especially digitally.

Hot New Recipe:
Managing your online reputation is critical. A number of new sites allow consumers to rate agents on their performance. A devastating review can ruin your online reputation and seriously damage your career, even if the comment is not true. One of the ways to protect yourself is to place a "Google alert" on your name. Google will notify you whenever an item appears about you online as well as giving you a link to the site where the item is posted. It's equally important to protect your clients' data as well.

Point2Agent's predictive marketing tool provides consumers with a more satisfying web viewing experience since it matches the houses that best fit their previous search patterns. Look for predictive marketing to eventually replace drip email and other types of "canned" campaigns.

The Online Masquerade Party

Because of security and privacy issues, people are becoming increasingly unwilling to provide information about themselves online. "Avatars" (i.e., an imaginary character that portrays you online) provide people with a means to maintain their privacy and/or to create a fantasy online identity. SecondLife and Google's "Lively" allow you to create an avatar that represents you in their virtual worlds. Future buyers and sellers will learn about real estate, not necessarily from real life, but from an online virtual experience such as that provided by SecondLife. While this trend is common in gaming, some experts suggest that over half of the online purchases by 2015 will occur using an avatar.

Hot New Recipe:
If you are unfamiliar with avatars and online virtual realities, visit SecondLife or Lively to become familiar with how to work with an avatar. If you are a Gen X or Gen Y agent, consider setting up your own virtual real estate practice in one of these virtual worlds. You never know when it will lead to a real world client.

3-D Video Tours

With the increased capacity that will come with the grid, video applications will become the preferred vehicle for web marketing. Texting will soon give way to video messaging. Virtual tours will give way to HDTV tours.

Beyond that, we will be able to have buyers experience walking through a house while standing in front of a big screen television. A PlayStation 3 game called "Creature Feature," allows you to hook up your PSEye video cam and then it projects everything in the eye of the camera into the game. The goal is to take these funny little creatures called "Blurbs" to safety. The Blurbs on screen follow your movements. Wherever you move, they follow. Watching people play Creature Feature is hilarious as they jump and twist around to avoid obstacles and get the Blurbs to safety on the screen.

What does this mean for the future of real estate? Virtual tours will eventually be able to put the buyers in the house, all from the convenience of any room equipped with a video camera and big screen television.

Since we already have 3-D holographic technology, look for 3-D virtual tours sometime in the next decade. Instead of using your car to show property, your walk-through may be with a set of 3-D goggles.

Hot New Recipe:
Today's web visitors want interactivity. If you're not using video already, start experimenting with these tools today to be prepared for tomorrow.

You can also take advantage of people's interest in decorating online by adding Obeo's powerful space designer feature to your listings. In houses where they produce a virtual tour and create a floor plan, Obeo's system allows your web visitors to change wall colors, the type of wood in cabinets, counter tops, flooring, as well as exterior and interior wall colors. More importantly, it tells you how many unique visitors are coming from the web vs. how many are coming from the brokerage community. When you have 50 or more views from brokers and no showings, you have a powerful tool for persuading sellers to be more realistic about their price.

Houses of the Future

Houses of the future will be intelligent. "Sustainable design " integrates all systems in the house to work together holistically rather than independently. Look for home networking systems to combine your data lines, radio, video, camera security, and other smart systems in one place. Smart houses will "come to life" when you are home and turn off when you leave.

Mixed-use communities will continue to grow in popularity as an increasing number of people choose places where they can walk rather than having to drive. As more people also elect to telecommute to work, having two home offices will become highly desirable. Aging Boomers will want smaller, more upscale, one-story houses, especially if they have "snoring" rooms that allow everyone to get a good night's sleep.

In the United Kingdom, they have begun building houses out of recycled trash (*Trend Hunter*, 2007). Look for more emphasis on "green" solutions from the past, such as Santa Fe-style homes that are made from bales of hay and have sealed "dirt" floors. The thick walls reduce both heating and cooling bills.

At the other end of the spectrum, nanotechnology research has created nano polymer particles that turn into a liquid when squeezed under pressure, flow into the cracks, and then harden to form a solid material. When added to gypsum, they will actually help houses to "heal" themselves from earthquake damage. (*Science Daily,* April 3, 2007.)

Natural forms of energy will continue to grow in importance. Vivian Alberts of the University of Johannesburg is credited with inventing a unique metal alloy that converts light into energy for a fraction of the cost of today's solar cells. The thickness is five microns (a human hair is 20 microns.) The typical household would need about a 30 square feet or the size of a typical living room to supply all its electrical needs. For the first time, solar will become less expensive than coal.

Hot New Recipe:

Become a specialist in how to create the perfect home work environment, how to make your home more "green," or more energy efficient. Provide a wealth of resources on your website or blog and engage in the online conversation regarding these important topics.

You don't have to apply all of these innovations in your business to dominate your market. Instead, stay a few steps ahead of your competitors. If you do, you will have plenty of *Real Estate Dough*™ for years to come.

Chapter 28
Action Plan

This is the final action plan of this book. Look over the various "Hot New Recipes" and decide on one innovation that you are willing to implement now. Write that item in the space provided below and record the date when you complete the item. Remember, small steps taken over time produce big results. Experiment with two or three innovations per year and you will dominate your market.

Action Steps:

___ 1. In the future, I will monitor innovations in the real estate business in order to stay ahead of my competitors.

___ 2. The one innovation from this chapter that I would like to add to my business in the next 30 days is: ________________________________

___ 3. If something I try doesn't work, I feel comfortable eliminating that activity and experimenting with something new.

Epilogue
Which Recipe Will You Choose?

Success is not the key to happiness. Happiness is the key to success. If you love what you are doing, you will be successful.
Herman Cain

The Ultimate Success Recipe

The "Ultimate" Success Recipe is simple. It's whatever you love to do that allows you to generate and convert leads. Are you willing to experiment with the "recipes" from this book or will you put it aside and never do anything with it?

If you're ready to make more *Real Estate Dough*™, review the Action Plans as well as the "Hot New Recipes" in the preceding chapter. Identify the items that make you feel excited and energized. Put these on your list of "preferred recipes." Ignore everything else.

Once you have completed your preferred recipe list, review what you selected. Identify your top five favorites. What sounds the most appealing? What was motivating enough that you were excited about trying it? Rank order the top five and then begin to work on implementing them.

If you discover that you need help or would enjoy connecting with others about the topics in this book, consider the following options.

Create an Environment of Success

Remember Buckminster Fuller's advice: "Environment is stronger than will." After *Waging War on Real Estate's Discounters* was released, our readers wanted help creating an environment that would support their success. As a result, many brokers and trainers wrote their own programs around the book. Some companies had book clubs where they went through a chapter per week.

As a result, we have created a rich variety of training programs to supplement this book. Here's what to look for on our sites at RealEstateCoach.com and RealEstateDough.com

1. **You read about how to negotiate—now do something about it!**
   If you are you ready to make your profits soar in your business, order *Real Estate Dough*™ *the Negotiation Game!* This lively, fun new card game is the most powerful method ever created to give you the face-to-face experience doing the number one money money-making skill you need—negotiating. Your negotiation skills will make or break your sales career. *Real Estate Dough*™ *the Negotiation Game*

hones your negotiation skills by showing you how to master the art of win-win negotiations, communicate effectively with people from different age groups, implement tactics and strategies that translate into real dough for your business, and leverage your negotiation skills to maximize your return in any negotiation situation. *Real Estate Dough*™ *the Negotiation Game* is the perfect way to learn negotiation skills in a fun and safe environment. If you want to unlock the secrets of having a more profitable real estate or sales career, start playing today to earn more *Real Estate Dough*™ tomorrow!

2. **New and experienced agent training programs**
   Our clients wanted more training on how to put the concepts in *Real Estate Dough*™ to work in their businesses. In response to the demand, we are pleased to offer a robust training program designed specifically for individual agents. This program is available on CD with a supporting workbook. It guides you through the activities and exercises that you need today to make plenty of dough for years to come.

3. **Real Estate Dough™ Training Programs for Managers, Broker/Owners, and Trainers**
   This program provides everything you need to train new or experienced agents on the powerful concepts in this book. Included in the package are copies of the book, a separate workbook for each agent, PowerPoint slides to use during live training sessions, plus trainer notes and exercises—everything you need to help your new and experienced agents to start making more "dough" now.

4. **Keep your competitive edge with ListenAndLearnRealEstate.com**
   If you want to stay ahead of the competition, sign up for our Listen and Learn Real Estate audio podcast program. With over 100 new titles in 2008 alone, this is the simplest way to stay light years ahead of your competitors. Each month, there are eight new podcasts. For example, if you enjoyed the Recipes for Success from Jennifer Cummings or Michael Russer, you can listen to their one-hour interviews there. Listen and Learn also keeps you up-to-date on technology innovation, contains the latest cool new tech tools, proven top producer strategies, plus how to cope with market shifts. You can opt to hear two selected sessions per month for a minimal fee or enjoy the entire library for less than a $1.00 per day.

5. **The Real Estate Dough Book Club!**
   Join us for a lively discussion on core concepts from the book. Topics and times will be published in our free newsletter, RealClues. All you need is your phone to participate. Visit RealEstateCoach.com to learn more.

6. **The Ultimate Dough Making Secret—Coaching**
   You will succeed faster and more easily with the help of an individual or group coaching program. Having a personal coach can help you create the life and the business you have always wanted. Visit RealEstateCoach.com to see if individual or group coaching is the right solution for you.

7. **Free Newsletter and Free Luxury Real Estate Blog**
   Visit our luxury blog at www.LuxuryClues.com to keep plenty of Luxury Real Estate Dough™ flowing into your pockets or subscribe to our free, weekly newsletter at RealEstateCoach.com.

Are You Ready to Take Action Now?

Then don't wait—get to work on implementing the top item on your list. This is the first step on your journey to personal excellence. Remember, you only have to be the expert in one small market segment and implement one or two innovations per year to dominate the competition.

When you choose to raise the bar in terms of your professionalism, consumer service, and excellence, you also help to raise the bar for our entire industry. The more agents who commit to providing buyers and sellers with tremendous value, the harder it will be for those who lack these standards to compete. I encourage you to join me on this road to excellence.

On a final note, I am extremely grateful to you for being one of our readers. If you enjoyed this book, share it with a friend. Brainstorm ideas on what you can do to be more effective. If you have a strategy that you would like to share, please email me personally at Bernice@RealEstateCoach.com. Thank you again for being one of our valued customers. Now go out and make lots of *Real Estate Dough*™!

Acknowledgements

I am extremely grateful to our wonderful clients, readers, and the thousands of agents who have attended my seminars and educational sessions. Without your continued support of our products and services, this book would never have become a reality. In addition, I would like to express my sincere appreciation to each of the following people who contributed to the creation of this book.

Shane Bowlin, a valued friend, a brilliant business partner, and so much more. Shane is the guiding force who takes my ideas and makes them into a reality. She has guided this entire effort from start to finish including laying out the final manuscript, proofing, locating our graphics artist, overseeing the work with our publisher, coordinating the website design, marketing, and a host of other tasks too numerous to list. Without her wisdom and expertise, this project would never have come into being.

J.I. Kleinberg is a long-time friend and an extraordinarily talented editor and copy writer. She is the co-author of *Fat, Stupid, Ugly: One Woman's Courage to Survive.* Judy's editorial comments were a major factor in the success of my first book, *Waging War on Real Estate's Discounters.* Her editorial wisdom and guidance have been equally important in this project.

Mary Weaver of Training4Learning.com is a gifted trainer and course writer. Mary made numerous contributions to our new game *Real Estate Dough*™ *Negotiation* including creating the Rules Booklet, the PowerPoints, play mats, plus helping us through all aspects of development. Mary is also the creative force behind most of the ancillary training materials for this book.

Brad Inman, founder of *Inman News* and real estate visionary, graciously agreed to write the foreword for this book. I am honored to be one of Brad's weekly columnists and am grateful to the entire team at *Inman News.* Special thanks to Don Berlanger, Elaine Baker, Glenn Roberts, and Dave Alessandro for their support of my writing as well as our work at RealEstateCoach.com.

I am also grateful to the two other editors I was privileged to work with at *Inman News:* Jessica Sweesey and Marcie Geffner. Both helped me to grow as a writer.

Cheryl Klinginsmith of Klinginsmith & Company did a brilliant job in designing the cover for this book. This is the fourth book cover Cheryl has designed for us. She also designed the latest version of our website. Each time we work with Cheryl, her work far exceeds our expectations.

To my friends and colleagues from the former Jon Douglas Company, thanks for a 17-year run of being "the best in the business." Special thanks to Jon Douglas for his leadership in setting the bar of professionalism so high, his commitment to always doing the right thing for the customer, and for the honor of being the Executive Director of Training for his company for five years. I hope this book conveys the standard of excellence Jon Douglas sought to create.

A note of thanks to Lou Piatt, Diana Brookes, Fran Flanagan, Randy Forbes, Betty Graham, Jon Greenleaf, Lori Hawkins, Peter Hernandez, Laura Lee Anthony, Tom Dunlap, and to all the other members of the former JDCO management team. I am also grateful to all the talented trainers I have worked with in the past, including Cathy Brown, Wanda Bolint, Carol Ellis, Cynthia Freeman, Karen Greensweig, Stan (Stock) Jonekos, Nancy Plotkin, Gaye Rainey, Nancy Sanborn, Larry Scott Young, and the late Ray Haddad. Each of them helped me grow as both a businessperson and a trainer. Their shared wisdom appears throughout this book.

A heartfelt thanks to Gary Keller, Dave Jenks, and Jay Papasan, best-selling authors of *The Millionaire Real Estate Agent, The Millionaire Real Estate Investor, Flip,* and *Shift.* The agent interviews are a direct result of Gary's recommendation that sharing stories from agents "makes the material come alive." Gary's and Dave's support for *Waging War on Real Estate's Discounters* was the foundation for that book's success. Their books continue to help thousands of agents have both a better business and a better life.

Teresa Boardman, blogger extraordinaire and fellow *Inman* columnist, generously shared her secrets for blogging success. Teresa's humor shines in whatever she writes. Furthermore, Teresa's simple approach of capturing your local lifestyle in pictures has helped hundreds of other agents launch successful blogs as well.

To "Go-Givers" Bob Burg and John David Mann, their book *The Go-Giver* provided me with the missing piece for our personal business success—being willing to receive as well as to give. Burg's other book, *Endless Referrals,* is a superb resource on how to build your business working with the referral model.

Joel Burslem does a tremendous job in his blog, The Future of Real Estate Marketing and at *Inman News.* Joel's advice was critical in shaping the chapters on how to best work with Gen X and Gen Y in today's rapidly changing technology environment.

Jennifer Cummings, author, speaker, and real estate marketing guru—her life and work is an inspiration to those who face life's most difficult challenges. She constantly models the "give to get" philosophy and is a gift to those who have the opportunity to work with her. Jennifer shows us all how to "walk the talk."

Huge thanks to Marc Davison of 1000 Watt Consulting. When I grow up, I would like to write as well as Marc writes. His work is brilliant and his insights have been a consistent guiding light for our business and for my own personal development. I am especially grateful to Marc for recommending me as a columnist for *Inman News.*

Gary Elwood and Rick Owens of Proquest Technologies are largely responsible for the strategies on how to incorporate call capture into listing presentations. They also shared their company's research on how call capture technology increases lead generation and lead conversion rates.

"You-nique" thanks to Butch Grimes, speaker, trainer, radio show host, and podcast expert, for graciously sharing his innovative strategies including how to put both the fun and the service into your real estate business.

Steve Kantor of BestAgentBusiness.com for sharing the results of his in-depth consumer studies, for the wisdom gathered from his "Billion Dollar Agents," as well as for his work in expanding the virtual assistant model to assist agents in building successful teams.

Thanks to Malcolm Kaufman for his friendship and for sharing his "Pulse of the Market" newsletter, that provides a detailed snapshot of the San Francisco market each month. His work is a superb example of how agents can provide value to the specific niche they serve.

Mike Kelly, a pioneer in real estate radio broadcasting, for illustrating the pitfalls in working with distressed property, the importance of mastering market statistics, and most importantly, for helping both agents and consumers gain a better understanding of the business.

Saul Klein, CEO of Internet Crusade and Point2Agent.com, one of the great visionaries in the real estate industry who is making his vision a reality. Saul's leadership continues to benefit real estate professionals and consumers everywhere.

Heartfelt thanks to Roz Kriener of NAR for all the work she does to make the NAR conventions successful, for her suggestions for "1031 Exchanges" for our game, *Real Estate Dough™ Negotiation,* as well as for the tremendous insight and support she has provided for my speaking career.

Special thanks to Donna Lee Laue of UniqueGlobalEstates.com (a listing portal that indexes $1 million-plus properties in 41 different countries) for her support of our business as well as her leadership in serving luxury agents and sellers worldwide.

Roger Noujeim and all the other great people at Point2Agent.com, thank you for the tremendous support and for the amazing tools that you provide for our industry. Roger has generously shared Point2's internal research. He also helps me stay on top of the latest technology innovations as well as providing guidance on how agents can best integrate these innovations in their business.

Mike Parker of Blackwater Consulting did a terrific job of educating me on the finer points of SEO and why it's a poor idea to take this project on yourself.

Jack Peckham of RECyber.com is a font of wisdom on the subject of real estate technology. Jack's monthly interviews and RECyber's annual on-line convention have been a wonderful source for information on how to incorporate new technology effectively into an agent's business.

Anne Randolph, founder of *LORE* Magazine and co-author of the annual *Real Trends Report,* graciously shared her research about the opportunities available to real estate professionals working in the investment side of the business. Thanks for setting the standard for both research and leadership in this industry.

Jerry Rossi, of RossiSpeaks.com, speaker, trainer, bon vivant, and author of *Dog Eat Dog* and *Vice Versa* and *Stop It,* sincere thanks for all that he has done to help me grow my speaking skills, for his never ending encouragement and optimism, and for his contributions in helping thousands of agents to improve their businesses.

"Mr. Internet," aka Michael Russer, for generously sharing the strategies from his On-Line Dominance course as well as a wealth of tips on how to market successfully on the web.

Special thanks to Alexandra and Ron Seigel of Napa Consultants for their coaching on how to create a "break away" brand and for their leadership in assisting luxury agents everywhere. They were also the inspiration for our luxury real estate blog, LuxuryClues.com.

Ira Serkes, the happiest agent in Berkeley, for sharing his formula for success that illustrates that bigger is not necessarily the route to happier.

Special thanks to Karen and Steve Sopko of Creative Bandwidth for the creative spark that resulted in our exciting new game, *Real Estate Dough™ Negotiation.* Their contributions will help thousands of agents improve their negotiation skills while having plenty of fun in the process.

Frances Flynn Thorsen, agent, editor, blogger, and "Really Awesome Woman" in real estate, whose passion for helping people stay in their homes rather than going through foreclosure has touched the lives of many in the most meaningful way possible. Fran's courageous stand is an important reminder that our first responsibility is to help people stay in their homes, rather than hastening the foreclosure process.

Jeff Turner, CEO of RealEstateShows.com, for his insights on video marketing, how to work effectively using Twitter, and his emphasis on the human side of technology.

Barb Van Stensel, who has built a successful real estate business despite being deaf, has made innovating in her real estate business a way of life. Barb's dedication to constantly growing her business expertise and to providing stellar service to her clients makes her a rising star on the Chicago real estate scene.

Erica West, WeSellFountainHillsLifestyles.com, for sharing a treasure trove of creative marketing ideas, including the notion of marketing using an "Equity Checkup" rather than a CMA.

Verl Workman, speaker, trainer, and someone who puts what he preaches from the podium to work in an active real estate practice, special thanks for the guidance and support. At long last, all those conversations about doing a joint project may finally come to fruition.

RealEstateCoach.com would not exist without our talented team of real estate coaches who have provided real estate coaching services to our clients since 1999. Roy Argall, David Brown, Christine D'Amico Johnson, Joeann Fossland, Ginger Jenks, Patti Kouri, Judy Lowry, Alvah Parker, Sharon Teitlbaum, Jeff Thompson, Jim Vuoculo, and Gary Wood, each of you is a gift not only to the clients you serve, but to entire real estate industry.

RealEstateCoach.com also relies on a number of other companies who make it possible to deliver our products to our clients. Special thanks to Darlene Lyons, Nita Lyons, and Ginger Sorosky of Broker Agent Speaker's Bureau who handle my speaking engagements; Dick Maney of Maney Telefilm (audio CD recording and production); Marty Crouch of Web Valence (web hosting, newsletter publication, and spam slayer); James Komozinsky of Practice Pay Solutions; National Media (audio CD production); and to our publisher, Rossdale Press.

A heartfelt thanks to the very special coaches/mentors who have helped me on my personal journey, including Marilyn Naylor, Meryl Moritz, Karen Whitworth, and the late Thomas Leonard.

And last, but not least, Byron Van Arsdale, my husband, partner, coach, best friend, and now a new title—Chief Dough Maker! Thank you for keeping me laughing, writing, and for the joyous journey that we are blessed to travel together.

Bibliography

Ariely, D. (2008). *Predictably Irrational.* New York: Harper Collins.

Barnes, L. (July 27, 2007). What's up with the housing market this week? www.inman.com/buyers-sellers/columnists/loubarnes/whats-housing-this-week

Burg, B. (2006). *Endless Referrals.* New York: McGraw Hill.

Burg, B. & Mann, D. (2008) *The Go Giver.* New York: Penguin.

California Association of REALTORS®. (2003). *Internet Study of Buyers and Sellers.*

California Association of REALTORS®. (2007). *Internet Study of Buyers and Sellers.*

Canfield, J. (2008). How to Accelerate Your Success with a Mastermind Group. www.EvanCarmichael.com/Entrepreneur-Advice/565/How-to-Accelerate-Your-Success-with-a-Mastermind-Group.html

Hicks, E. & Hicks, J. (2006). *The Law of Attraction.* Hayhouse Inc. HayHouse.com

Kantor, S. (2007). *Billion Dollar Agent—Lessons Learned.* www.LifeBushido.com

Kantor, S. (2008). Unpublished study of real estate buyer and seller marketing preferences. www.LifeBushido.com

Kantor, S. (2008). *Real Estate in 2008.* www.LifeBushido.com

Klein, S. (August 7, 2008). What is MLS 5.0? http://www.realtown.com/about/resources/FutureofMLS

McKinney, F. (2006). Unpublished speech, Miami, Florida: Inman Luxury Connect Conference.

Morgan, J. (Feb. 10, 2005). Who are the Gen Y Students? *Inside California State University, Chico* 35 (5).

National Association of REALTORS® (2007). *Member Profile.*

National Association of REALTORS® (2003). *Profile of Home Buyers and Sellers 2003.*

National Association of REALTORS® (2007). *Profile of Home Buyers and Sellers 2007.*

Point2Agent.com (2008). Rich Listings; Rich Agents. Point2 Agent Photo Effectiveness Study.

Randolph, A. (2008). Room for Improvement: Perspectives of Real Estate Consumers and the Professionals Who Serve Them: A Comprehensive Study of Consumer Attitudes, Behaviors and Preferences in the Residential Real Estate Transaction.

Rapaille, C. (July 8, 2005). Cracking open your wallet, A Psychologist Demonstrates a Feel for the Market. www.cbsnews.com/stories/2005/07/05/60II/main706417.shtml

Rapaille, C. (2007). *The Culture Code.* New York: Broadway Books.

Rapaille, C. (2001). *7 Secrets of Marketing in a Multi-Cultural World.* Provo, Utah: Executive Excellence Publishing.

Revoir, P. (August 23, 2007). Silver Surfers Beat the Young as Web Wizards. MailOnLine.
http://www.dailymail.co.uk/sciencetech/article-477140/Silver-surfers-beat-young-Web-wizards.html

Reis & Trout, (1986). *Marketing Warfare.* New York: McGraw Hill.

Rosenthal, R. (September 1973). The Pygmalion Effect Lives. *Psychology Today,* 56-63.

Ross, B. (2005). *Waging War on Real Estate's Discounters.* Austin, Texas: Rossdale Press.

Schmitt, B. (2003). *Customer Experience Management.* Hoboken, NJ: John Wiley & Sons.

Science Daily. (April 3, 2007). "Self-healing" House: Building-in Earthquake Resistance? http://www.sciencedaily.com/releases/2007/04/070402153349.htm

Streitfeld, D. (January 22, 2008). Feeling Misled on Home Price Buyers Sue Agent. *New York Times.* http://www.nytimes.com/2008/01/22/business/22agent.html?_r=1&pagewanted=1&th&emc&oref=slogin

Thomas, J. & Thomas, T. (2007). *The Power of Opposite Strengths.* http://www.oppositestrengths.com

Thorsen, F. (March 3, 2008). Let's help Americans keep their homes. RealTownBlog.com. http://www.realtown.com/articles/view/let-s-learn-how-to-help-americans-keep-their-homes

Trend Hunter Magazine. (April 4, 2007). http://www.trendhunter.com/trends/homes-of-the-future-self-healing-earthquake-proof-homes-built-from-trash

Turner, J. (2008). Unpublished interview.

Twenge, J. (2006). *Generation Me: Why Today's Young Americans Are More Confident, Assertive, Entitled — and More Miserable than Ever Before.* New York: Free Press.

Winslow, O. (August 13, 2008). Census Report See Minorities Becoming Majority by 2042. Newsday.com. http://www.newsday.com/news/local/longisland/ny-licens0814,0,1551401,print.story

Yun, L. (2007). "Marketing to Gen Next" slide 47. National Association of REALTORS®.